Azure DevOps Explained

Get started with Azure DevOps and develop your DevOps practices

Sjoukje Zaal

Stefano Demiliani

Amit Malik

BIRMINGHAM—MUMBAI

Azure DevOps Explained

Copyright © 2020 Packt Publishing

Commissioning Editor: Vijin Boricha
Senior Editor: Shazeen Iqbal
Content Development Editor: Ronn Kurien
Technical Editor: Sarvesh Jaywant
Copy Editor: Safis Editing
Project Coordinator: Neil Dmello
Proofreader: Safis Editing
Indexer: Pratik Shirodkar
Production Designer: Joshua Misquitta

First published: December 2020
Production reference: 1101120

Published by Packt Publishing Ltd.
Livery Place
35 Livery Street
Birmingham
B3 2PB, UK.

ISBN 978-1-80056-351-3

www.packt.com

Packt.com

Subscribe to our online digital library for full access to over 7,000 books and videos, as well as industry leading tools to help you plan your personal development and advance your career. For more information, please visit our website.

Why subscribe?

- Spend less time learning and more time coding with practical eBooks and Videos from over 4,000 industry professionals

- Improve your learning with Skill Plans built especially for you

- Get a free eBook or video every month

- Fully searchable for easy access to vital information

- Copy and paste, print, and bookmark content

Did you know that Packt offers eBook versions of every book published, with PDF and ePub files available? You can upgrade to the eBook version at packt.com and as a print book customer, you are entitled to a discount on the eBook copy. Get in touch with us at customercare@packtpub.com for more details.

At www.packt.com, you can also read a collection of free technical articles, sign up for a range of free newsletters, and receive exclusive discounts and offers on Packt books and eBooks.

Contributors

About the authors

Sjoukje Zaal is a CTO, Microsoft Regional Director, and Microsoft Azure MVP with over 20 years of experience in architecture-, development-, consultancy-, and design-related roles. She works at Capgemini, a global leader in consultancy, technology services, and digital transformation.

She loves to share her knowledge and is active in the Microsoft community as a co-founder of the user groups Tech Daily Chronicle, Global XR Community, and the Mixed Reality User Group. She is also a board member of Azure Thursdays and Global Azure. Sjoukje is an international speaker and is involved in organizing many events. She has written several books and writes blogs.

Stefano Demiliani is a Microsoft MVP in business applications, an MCT, a Microsoft Certified DevOps Engineer and Azure Architect, and a long-time expert on Microsoft technologies. He works as a CTO for EID NAVLAB and his main activities are architecting solutions with Azure and Dynamics 365 ERPs. He's the author of many IT books for Packt and a speaker at international conferences about Azure and Dynamics 365. You can reach him on Twitter or on LinkedIn or via his personal website.

I dedicate this book to my little daughter, Sara. In the past few months, I have spent so much time away from you; I hope you can now appreciate the work done and understand me.

Amit Malik is an IT enthusiast and technology evangelist focused on the cloud and emerging technologies. He is currently employed by Spektra Systems as the director of technology, where he helps Microsoft partners grow their cloud businesses by using effective tools and strategies. He specializes in the cloud, DevOps, software-defined infrastructure, application modernization, data platforms, and emerging technologies around AI. Amit holds various industry-admired certifications from all major OEMs in the cloud and data space, including Azure Solutions Architect Expert. He is also a **Microsoft Certified Trainer (MCT)**. Amit is an active community member of various technology groups and is a regular speaker at industry conferences and events.

About the reviewers

Vassili Altynikov is the founder and a principal DevOps architect at Blend Master Software.

With nearly two decades of software development, application architecture, and technical consulting experience, he is helping organizations establish and improve their DevOps practices to deliver better-quality software faster.

Abhishek Jaiswal is an Azure DevOps engineer with 6 years of experience in the IT industry and professional certifications in Azure and AWS. He started his career as an application support engineer and later moved to cloud technologies. Abhishek has domain knowledge in the telecom and banking/finance sectors. Abhishek is passionate about learning new technologies and upgrading his skills.

I would like to thank my parents and brothers for their support and motivation.

Packt is searching for authors like you

If you're interested in becoming an author for Packt, please visit `authors.packtpub.com` and apply today. We have worked with thousands of developers and tech professionals, just like you, to help them share their insight with the global tech community. You can make a general application, apply for a specific hot topic that we are recruiting an author for, or submit your own idea.

Table of Contents

2
Managing Projects with Azure DevOps Boards

Section 2: Source Code and Builds

3
Source Control Management with Azure DevOps

4
Understanding Azure DevOps Pipelines

5

Running Quality Tests in a Build Pipeline

6

Hosting Your Own Azure Pipeline Agent

Section 3: Artifacts and Deployments

7

Using Artifacts with Azure DevOps

8

Deploying Applications with Azure DevOps

Section 4: Advanced Features of Azure DevOps

9

Integrating Azure DevOps with GitHub

10

Using Test Plans with Azure DevOps

11

Real-World CI/CD Scenarios with Azure DevOps

Other Books You May Enjoy

Index

Preface

DevOps has become a real buzzword in recent years. DevOps is a combination of cultural philosophies, practices, and tools that increases an organization's ability to deliver applications and services at high speed and with high quality. Azure DevOps is a **Software as a Service (SaaS)** platform from Microsoft that provides an end-to-end set of tools for developing and deploying software by applying DevOps techniques. This book starts with an overview of the Azure DevOps platform before diving into various tools and features, such as boards for project management, repos for source control management, build and release pipelines, test plans, artifacts, and more.

After reading this book, you will have a complete and clear vision of what Azure DevOps can offer you to improve your development life cycle.

Who this book is for

This book is for solution developers/architects and project managers who want to apply DevOps techniques to their projects and use Azure DevOps to manage the entire process of developing applications of quality.

What this book covers

Chapter 1, Azure DevOps Overview, gives you a full overview of the Azure DevOps features and toolsets, such as boards, repos, pipelines, test plans, and artifacts.

Chapter 2, Managing Projects with Azure DevOps Boards, explains the project management features of Azure DevOps in detail and shows you how to use boards and work items, how to create sprints, and how to manage backlogs and track all your activities.

Chapter 3, Source Code Management with Azure DevOps, explains how you can handle source control with the Azure DevOps Repos feature and Git. It shows you how to create repositories, how to handle commits, pushes, and pulls, how to handle branches, and more.

Chapter 4, Understanding Azure DevOps Pipelines, shows you how to create a build pipeline for your code with Azure Pipelines and how best to handle continuous integration.

Chapter 5, Running Quality Tests in a Build Pipeline, explains how to create and execute quality tests for your code in a build pipeline.

Chapter 6, Hosting Your Own Azure Pipeline Agent, shows you how to create your own build agents and use them in a build pipeline.

Chapter 7, Using Artifacts with Azure DevOps, explains how to use artifacts (package feeds) to create and share packages and add fully integrated package management to your continuous integration/continuous delivery pipelines.

Chapter 8, Deploying Applications with Azure DevOps, explains how to use release pipelines to handle the continuous deployment of your code and how to use stages and approvals before releasing code into a production environment.

Chapter 9, Integrating Azure DevOps with GitHub, shows you how to integrate Azure DevOps tools with GitHub and use both applications for your continuous integration/ continuous delivery processes.

Chapter 10, Using Test Plans with Azure DevOps, shows you how to manage your project's testing life cycle with test plans in Azure DevOps.

Chapter 11, Real-World CI/CD Scenarios with Azure DevOps, shows you some real-world scenarios of continuous integration/continuous delivery processes being handled with Azure DevOps.

To get the most out of this book

To follow the topics described in this book, you need to have a valid subscription with Azure DevOps. You can activate a free account by going to the following link:

`https://azure.microsoft.com/en-us/services/devops/`

Software/hardware covered in the book	OS Requirements
Azure DevOps	Any

If you are using the digital version of this book, we advise you to type the code yourself or access the code via the GitHub repository (link available in the next section). Doing so will help you to avoid any potential errors related to the copying and pasting of code.

Download the example code files

You can download the example code files for this book from GitHub at `https://github.com/PacktPublishing/Learning-Azure-DevOps---B16392`. In case there's an update to the code, it will be updated on the existing GitHub repository.

We also have other code bundles from our rich catalog of books and videos available at `https://github.com/PacktPublishing/`. Check them out!

Download the color images

We also provide a PDF file that has color images of the screenshots/diagrams used in this book. You can download it here: `http://www.packtpub.com/sites/default/files/downloads/9781800563513_ColorImages.pdf`.

Conventions used

There are a number of text conventions used throughout this book.

`Code in text`: Indicates code words in text, database table names, folder names, filenames, file extensions, pathnames, dummy URLs, user input, and Twitter handles. Here is an example: 'You can download the file named `node-v6.12.3-x64.msi` and install it using the interactive installer.'

A block of code is set as follows:

```
using System;
using PartsUnlimited.Models;


namespace AzureArtifacts
{
    class Program
    {
        static void Main(string[] args)
        {
            Console.WriteLine('Hello World!');

            CartItem caritem = new CartItem()
```

When we wish to draw your attention to a particular part of a code block, the relevant lines or items are set in bold:

```
[Net.ServicePointManager]::SecurityProtocol = [Net.
SecurityProtocolType]::Tls12
Install-Module AzureRM -AllowClobber
```

Any command-line input or output is written as follows:

```
docker run \
  -e VSTS_ACCOUNT=<name> \
  -e VSTS_TOKEN=<pat> \
  -it mcr.microsoft.com/azure-pipelines/vsts-agent
```

Bold: Indicates a new term, an important word, or words that you see onscreen. For example, words in menus or dialog boxes appear in the text like this. Here is an example: 'Log in with your Microsoft account and in the left menu, select **Artifacts**.'

> Tips or important notes
> Appear like this.

Get in touch

Feedback from our readers is always welcome.

General feedback: If you have questions about any aspect of this book, mention the book title in the subject of your message and email us at customercare@packtpub.com.

Errata: Although we have taken every care to ensure the accuracy of our content, mistakes do happen. If you have found a mistake in this book, we would be grateful if you would report this to us. Please visit www.packtpub.com/support/errata, selecting your book, clicking on the Errata Submission Form link, and entering the details.

Piracy: If you come across any illegal copies of our works in any form on the Internet, we would be grateful if you would provide us with the location address or website name. Please contact us at copyright@packt.com with a link to the material.

If you are interested in becoming an author: If there is a topic that you have expertise in and you are interested in either writing or contributing to a book, please visit authors.packtpub.com.

Reviews

Please leave a review. Once you have read and used this book, why not leave a review on the site that you purchased it from? Potential readers can then see and use your unbiased opinion to make purchase decisions, we at Packt can understand what you think about our products, and our authors can see your feedback on their book. Thank you!

For more information about Packt, please visit `packt.com`.

Section 1: DevOps Principles and Azure DevOps Project Management

In this section, DevOps principles, Azure DevOps key concepts, and project management will be covered.

This section contains the following chapters:

- *Chapter 1, Azure DevOps Overview*
- *Chapter 2, Managing Projects with Azure DevOps Boards*

1

Azure DevOps Overview

This chapter introduces the first topics of this book: **DevOps** principles and **Azure DevOps** project management. In this chapter, we are going start by introducing DevOps and provide an overview of the different DevOps principles. Then, we are going to cover the key concepts of Azure DevOps and the different services that Azure DevOps offers. Finally, we are going to introduce the scenario that we will be using throughout this book.

The following topics will be covered in this chapter:

- Introducing DevOps
- Understanding DevOps principles
- Introducing Azure DevOps key concepts
- Discovering Azure DevOps services
- Introducing the scenarios

Let's get started!

Introducing DevOps

For a long time, development and operations had been divided into isolated modules with both separate concerns and responsibilities. Developers wrote the code and made sure that it worked on their development systems, while the system administrators were responsible for the actual deployment and integration in the organization's IT infrastructure.

As there was limited communication between these two isolated modules, both teams worked mostly separated on their projects. However, they heavily depended on each other because there was no cross-platform knowledge across the different teams.

This fitted in nicely with the Waterfall Methodology that was used for most projects. The Waterfall Methodology is based on the **Software Development Life Cycle (SDLC)**, which has clearly defined processes for creating software. The Waterfall Methodology is a breakdown of project deliverables into linear sequential phases, where each phase depends on the deliverables of the previous phase. This sequence of events may look as follows:

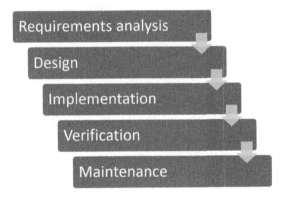

Figure 1.1 – Waterfall Methodology

The Waterfall Methodology is well suited for projects in the following circumstances:

- Early in the development life cycle, customers and developers agree on what will be delivered, with minimal to no changes during the development of the project.

- For integration with external systems, it is common for multiple components of the software to be designed in parallel. In these cases, it is desirable to have the design document complete at an early stage in the development life cycle.

- Various team members are involved in other projects simultaneously as well. For example, business analysts can gather the requirements and create the design while developers are working on another project.

- Where it is not possible to break down the requirements phase, customers are not fully engaged in smaller deliverables.

However, customers may not exactly know what their requirements are before they see working software. This can result in changing the requirements, thus leading to redesign, reimplementation, and reverification. This can dramatically increase the costs of the project.

Due to this, Agile and DevOps were introduced in 2009 and have slowly taken over the world of software development. They replaced the Waterfall Methodology for most projects that are out there. DevOps is a natural extension of Agile and continuous delivery approaches, and it stands for development and operations. It is a practice that merges development, IT operations, and quality assurance into one single, continuous set of processes.

The following diagram illustrates the different parts that DevOps consists of:

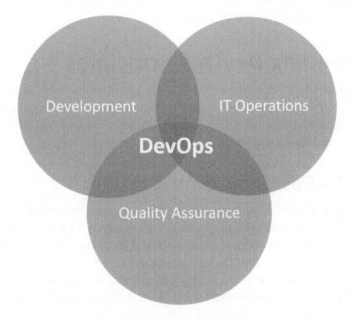

Figure 1.2 – DevOps methodology

It is a team-based and iterative approach to development where all stakeholders, such as developers, administrators, testers, and a representative of the customer, are part of the same team. Applications are delivered in functional components, and rather than creating schedules and tasks at the start of the project, the project is divided into smaller phases, called sprints. The duration of each sprint is defined up front and has a list of deliverables that are planned at the start of each sprint. All those deliverables are defined together with the customer and prioritized by business value by the customer. At the end of each sprint, when work is completed, it is reviewed and evaluated by the team through daily builds and end-of-sprint demos.

This results in the following advantages:

- By working directly with the project team throughout the whole project, the customer will experience a stronger sense of ownership.

- The customer has opportunities to see the work being delivered in an early stage of the project and can make appropriate decisions and changes to it.

- Development is more business and value focused. This is a result of working closer with the customer and having a better understanding of their needs.

- An Agile way of working enables us to quickly create a base version of the product, which can be built upon in the next iterations.

Now that we have covered a very brief introduction to DevOps, we are going to look at the different DevOps principles.

Understanding DevOps principles

There are a lot of different definitions when it comes to DevOps. Most of them are good at explaining the different aspects of finding the right flow in delivering software and IT projects. In the upcoming sections, we will highlight six DevOps principles that we think are essential when adopting a DevOps way of working.

Principle 1 – Customer-centric action

Nowadays, it is important that software development projects have short cycles and feedback loops, with end users and real customers integrated into the team. To fully meet the customers' requirements, all activity around building software and products must involve these clients. DevOps teams and organizations must continuously invest in products and services that will allow clients to receive the maximum outcome, while also being as lean as possible to continuously innovate and change the chosen strategy when it is no longer working.

Principle 2 – Create with the end in mind

Organizations need to act more like product companies. They should focus more on building working products that are sold to real customers. This engineering mindset needs to be shared by all employees. This is required to realize those products. This means that they should let go of the approach where each unit focuses on a particular role with their own scoped responsibility.

Principle 3 – End-to-end responsibility

In most traditional software development projects, the software and services that are developed are handed over to operations, where they then deploy and maintain those solutions after the initial development process. By adopting a DevOps way of working, the DevOps teams become fully responsible and accountable for the project they deliver. This means that once the product has been delivered by the team and it needs to be maintained, it still remains under the responsibility of the team. The team will also provide support for the product until it reaches its end of life. This greatly increases the level of responsibility of the team and the quality of the products that are developed.

Principle 4 – Cross-functional autonomous teams

Organizations that work with vertical and fully responsible teams will need to let these teams work completely independently throughout the whole life cycle. To enable these teams to work completely independently, a broad and balanced set of skills are required. Team members need to have T-shaped profiles instead of old-school IT specialists who are only skilled in their own role. Examples of skills that every team member should have include development, requirement analysis, testing, and administration skills.

Principle 5 – Continuous improvement

Another part of end-to-end responsibility is that, for organizations, it is important to adapt changes continuously. There can be a number of changing circumstances, such as new technology that has been released, changing customer requirements, and so on. Continuous improvement is a strong focus in DevOps when it comes to optimizing for speed and costs, minimizing waste, easy of delivery, and to continuously improve the software and services that are being built and released. An important activity to embed inside these cycles is experimentation. This will allow teams to develop a way of learning from their failures, which is essential to continuous improvement.

Principle 6 – Automate everything

To fully adopt and embed a continuous improvement culture inside an organization, most organizations have a lot of waste and tech depth to eliminate. To work with high cycle rates and to process the instant feedback from customers and end users as soon as possible, it is imperative to automate everything. This means that not only the software development process should be automated using continuous delivery (which includes continuous development and integration), but also the whole infrastructure landscape needs to be automated. The infrastructure also needs to be ready for new ways of working. In this sense, automation is synonymous with the drive to renew the way in which the team delivers their services to their customers.

In this section, we have covered the six principles that are very important when adopting or migrating to a DevOps way of working. In the next few sections, we are going to look at what Azure DevOps has to offer as a tool that supports teams so that they can work in a DevOps oriented manner.

Introducing Azure DevOps key concepts

Azure DevOps provides a wide variety of services for DevOps teams so that they can plan, work, collaborate on code development, and build and deploy software and services. Most DevOps teams rely on several tools and build custom toolchains for each phase in the application life cycle.

The following diagram shows the phases that are defined in the application life cycle:

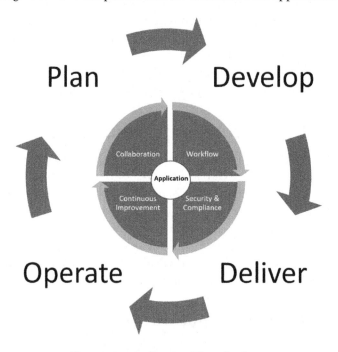

Figure 1.3 – Application life cycle phases

In the following sections, we'll explain these phases and the corresponding Microsoft tooling and products in more detail.

Plan

During the planning phase, teams can use Kanban boards and backlogs to define, track, and lay out the work that needs to be done in Azure Boards. They can also use GitHub for this. In GitHub, an issue can be created by suggesting a new idea or stating that a bug should be tracked. These issues can be organized and assigned to teams.

Develop

The development phase is supported by Visual Studio Code and Visual Studio. Visual Studio Code is a cross-platform editor, while Visual Studio is a Windows- and Mac-only IDE. You can use Azure DevOps for automated testing and use Azure Pipelines to create automatic builds for building the source code. Code can be shared across teams with Azure DevOps or GitHub.

Deliver

The deliver phase is about deploying your applications and services to target environments. You can use Azure Pipelines to deploy code automatically to any Azure service or on-premises environments. You can use Azure Resource Manager templates or Terraform to spin up environments for your applications or infrastructure components. You can also integrate Jenkins and Spinnaker inside your Azure DevOps Pipelines.

Operate

In this phase, you implement full-stack monitoring for monitoring your applications and services. You can also manage your cloud environment with different automation tools, such as Azure Automation, Chef, and more. Keeping your applications and services secure is also part of this phase. Therefore, you can use features and services such as Azure Policy and Azure Security Center.

To support the full life cycle of analyzing, designing, building, deploying, and maintaining software and infrastructure products and services, Azure DevOps provides integrated features that can be accessed through any web browser.

Azure DevOps offers a combination of solutions and tooling that can be used to create unique and custom workflows throughout each of the application life cycle phases. These solutions will be described in the upcoming sections.

Continuous integration and continuous delivery (CI/CD)

You can automate each DevOps process with CI/CD (and continuous deployment) in Azure DevOps. CI is used in the development phase of a project and refers to building and testing code in a fully automated way. Every time you commit changes to the master branch, the changes will be validated and then packaged into a build artifact automatically. With CD, the delivery phase is automated. Every time a build artifact is available, the artifact is automatically deployed to the desired environment. When continuous integration and continuous deployment are both used by development teams, the code remains ready for production at any time. The only thing that teams must do to deploy a working application into production is trigger the transition from development to deploy. This will make the automated build artifact available for deployment. This triggering can be as simple as pressing a button.

With Azure DevOps, you also implement continuous deployment. Adding this to your development life cycle means that you can automate the entire process, from code commit to production. The trigger between the development and delivery phase is completely automatic. So, when code changes are validated and pass all the tests that are performed during the development phase, the changes will be published to production automatically as well. This means that customers will receive the new version, along with the improvements for it, as soon as they are available.

Agile development support

Azure DevOps supports teams that adopt Agile development methods with planning, tracking, and reporting capabilities. This will result in shorter release cycles and full visibility in the software development process. You can use Azure Boards, which will be covered in more detail in the next section of this chapter, to manage backlogs and define, assign, and track work items. You can also use advanced analytics and reporting and create custom dashboards to track progress.

Version control

A version control system, also known as a source control system, is an essential tool for multi-developer projects. It allows developers to collaborate on the code and track changes. The history of all the code files is also maintained in the version control system. This makes it easy to go back to a different version of the code files in case of errors or bugs.

Azure DevOps supports two different types of source control: Git (distributed) and **Team Foundation Version Control (TFVS)**. With Git, each developer has a copy of the source repository on their development machine. All branch and history information is included inside the source repository. Each developer works directly with their copy of the repository and all the changes are shared between the local and source repositories as a separate step. Changes can be committed on the local filesystem, and version control operations can be executed without a network connection. Branches can be created easily on the dev machine and later, they can be merged, published, or disposed by the developer separately. With TFVC, developers have only one version of each file on their local dev machines. All the others, as well as the historical data, are maintained only on the server. The branches are created on the server as well.

Infrastructure as Code

Teams can also manage the infrastructure in Azure DevOps. Infrastructure components that are used in a project, such as networks, virtual machines, and load balancers, can be managed using the same versioning features and capabilities that are used for the source code.

Used together with continuous delivery, an **Infrastructure as Code (IaC)** model generates the same environment every time it is deployed. Without IaC, teams need to configure and maintain the settings of all the individual deployment environments manually, which is a time-consuming and error-prone task. The most plausible outcome is that, over time, each environment becomes a *snowflake*, which is a unique configuration that cannot be reproduced automatically anymore. This inconsistency across environments will lead to issues during the deployment phase.

Configuration Management

Configuration Management refers to all the items and artifacts that are relevant to the project and the relationship between them. Those items are stored, retrieved, and uniquely identified and modified. This includes items such as source code, files, and binaries. The configuration management system is the one true source of configuration items.

Using Azure DevOps, resource configuration across the entire system can be managed by teams to roll out configuration updates, enforce desired states, and automatically resolve unexpected changes and issues. Azure offers multiple DevOps tools and capabilities for configuration management, such as Chef, Puppet, Ansible, and Azure Automation.

Monitoring

You can use Azure Monitor to practice full-stack continuous monitoring. The health of your infrastructure and applications can be integrated into existing dashboards in Grafana, Kibana, and the Azure portal with Azure Monitor. You can also monitor the availability, performance, and usage of your applications, whether they are hosted on-premises or in Azure. Most popular languages and frameworks are supported by Azure Monitor, such as NET, Java, and Node.js, and they are integrated with DevOps processes and tools in Azure DevOps.

Discovering Azure DevOps services

In this section, we are going to introduce the different services that are offered by Azure DevOps. These services can be used to support teams throughout the whole life cycle of realizing business value for customers.

Azure Boards

Azure Boards can be used to plan, track, and discuss work across teams using the Agile planning tools that are available. Using Azure Boards, teams can manage their software projects. It also offers a unique set of capabilities, including native support for Scrum and Kanban. You can also create customizable dashboards, and it offers integrated reporting and integration with Microsoft Teams and Slack.

You can create and track user stories, backlog items, tasks, features, and bugs that are associated with the project using Azure Boards.

The following screenshot shows an example of an Azure Board:

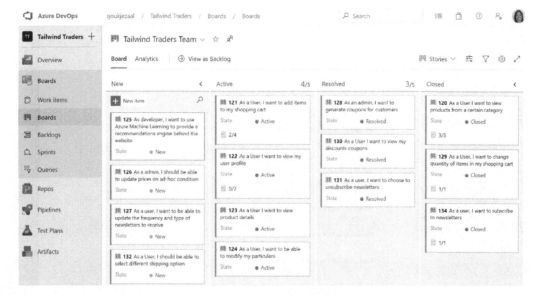

Figure 1.4 – Azure Boards

Azure Repos

Azure Repos provides support for private Git repository hosting and for **Team Foundation Server Control** (**TFSC**). It offers a set of version control tools that can be used to manage the source code of every development project, large or small. When you edit the code, you ask the source control system to create a snapshot of the files. This snapshot is saved permanently so that it can be recalled later if needed.

Today, Git is the most used version control system among developers. Azure Repos offers standard Git so that developers can use the tools and clients of their choice, such as Git for Windows, Mac, third-party Git services, and tools such as Visual Studio and Visual Studio Code.

The following screenshot shows an example of the commits you can push to a repo in Azure:

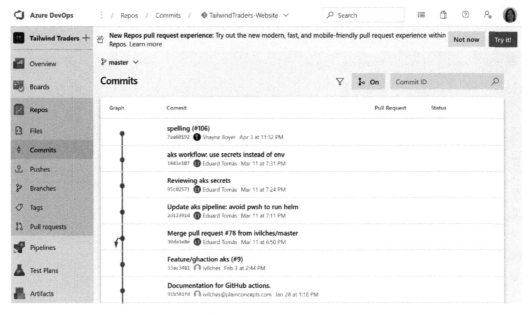

Figure 1.5 – Azure Repos

Azure Pipelines

You can use Azure Pipelines to automatically build, test, and deploy code to make it available to other users and deploy it to different targets, such as a **development, test, acceptance, and production (DTAP)** environment. It combines CI/CD to automatically build and deploy your code.

Before you can use Azure Pipelines, you should put your code in a version control system, such as Azure Repos. Azure Pipelines can integrate with a number of version control systems, such as Azure Repos, Git, TFVS, GitHub, GitHub Enterprise, Subversion, and Bitbucket Cloud. You can also use Pipelines with most application types, such as Java, JavaScript, Node.js, Python, .NET, C++, Go, PHP, and XCode. Applications can be deployed to multiple target environments, including container registries, virtual machines, Azure services, or any on-premises or cloud target.

The following screenshot shows an example of a run for an Azure Pipeline:

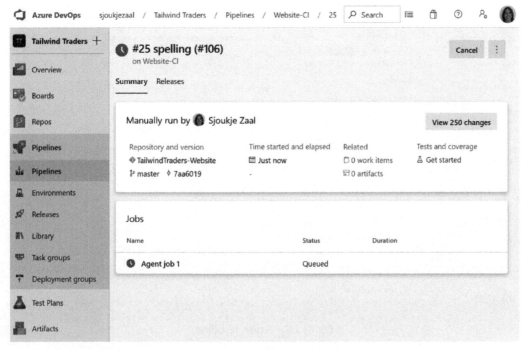

Figure 1.6 – Azure Pipelines

Azure Test Plans

With Azure Test Plans, teams can improve their code quality using planned and exploratory services in Azure DevOps. Azure Test Plans offer features for planned manual testing, exploratory testing, user acceptance testing, and for gathering feedback from stakeholders. With manual testing, tests are organized into test plans and test suites by testers and test leads. Teams can begin testing from their Kanban boards or from the Work Hub directly. With user acceptance testing, the value that's delivered to meet customer requirements is verified. This is usually done by designated testers. Exploratory testing includes tests that are executed by the whole development team, including developers, product owners, and testers. The software is tested by exploring the software systems, without the use of test plans or test suites. Stakeholder feedback gathering is done outside the development team by marketing or sales teams. Developers can request feedback on their user stories and features from Azure DevOps. Stakeholders can then respond directly to the feedback item.

The following screenshot shows an example of an Azure Test Plan:

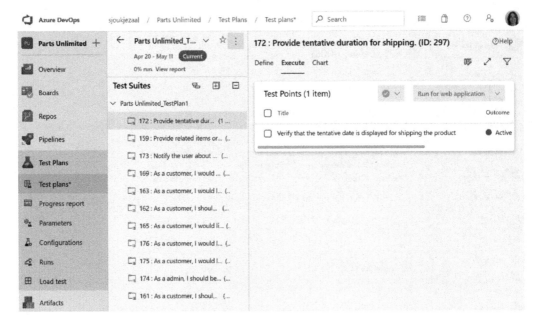

Figure 1.7 – Azure Test Plan

Azure Artifacts

With Azure Artifacts, you can create and share NuGet, npm, Python, and Maven packages from private and public sources with teams in Azure DevOps. These packages can be used in source code and can be made available to the CI/CD pipelines. With Azure Artifacts, you can create multiple feeds that you can use to organize and control access to the packages.

The following screenshot shows an example of a feed in Azure Artifacts:

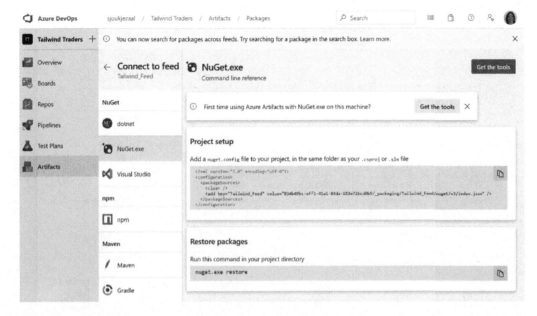

Figure 1.8 – Azure Artifacts

Extension Marketplace

You can download extensions for Azure DevOps from the Visual Studio Marketplace. These extensions are simple add-ons that can be used to customize and extend your team's experience with Azure DevOps. They can help by extending the planning and tracking of work items, code testing and tracking, pipeline build and release flows, and collaboration among team members. The extensions are created by Microsoft and the community.

The following screenshot shows some of the extensions that can be downloaded from the marketplace:

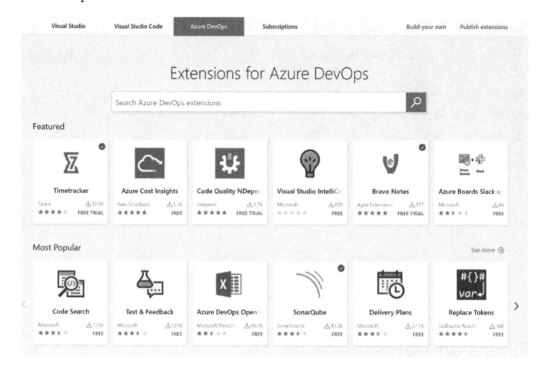

Figure 1.9 – Extension Marketplace

The services that we introduced in the previous sections will be explained more thoroughly in the upcoming chapters of this book. In the next section, we will introduce the scenarios that will be used throughout this book.

Introducing the scenarios

Throughout this book, we will use two different scenarios for our demos. We are going to use sample projects that can be generated and installed in your Azure DevOps environment by using the DevOps generator. For this book, we are going to install Tailwind Traders and Parts Unlimited. Tailwind Traders is an example retail company that showcases the future of intelligent application experiences, while Parts Unlimited is an example e-commerce website.

Creating the starter project

To create the scenario project, we are going to use the Azure DevOps demo generator, which will generate the sample project for us. These projects are free to use. Before you generate the project, you need to install two different Azure DevOps extensions from the marketplace, both of which are used by the Tailwind Traders project. These extensions are as follows:

- **ARM Outputs**: This extension reads the output values of ARM deployments and sets them as Azure Pipelines variables. You can download and install the extension from `https://marketplace.visualstudio.com/items?itemName=keesschollaart.arm-outputs`.

- **Team Project Health**: This extension enables users to visualize the overall health of builds, thereby delivering a visual cue similar to Codify Build Light. You can download the extension from `https://marketplace.visualstudio.com/items?itemName=ms-devlabs.TeamProjectHealth`.

Once the extensions have been installed inside your Azure DevOps organization, you can generate the sample project:

1. First, navigate to the following site: `https://azuredevopsdemogenerator.azurewebsites.net/`.

2. Click the **Sign in** button. If you don't have an Azure account yet, you can sign up for a trial account by clicking the **Get started for free** button:

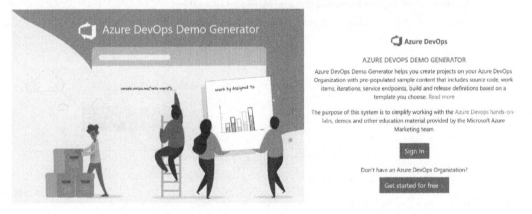

Figure 1.10 – Azure DevOps demo generator

3. Name the project `Tailwind Traders`, select an organization, and select a template by clicking the **Choose template** button. Select **Tailwind Traders** from the list and click **Select Template**.

4. After filling in these details, the page should look as follows:

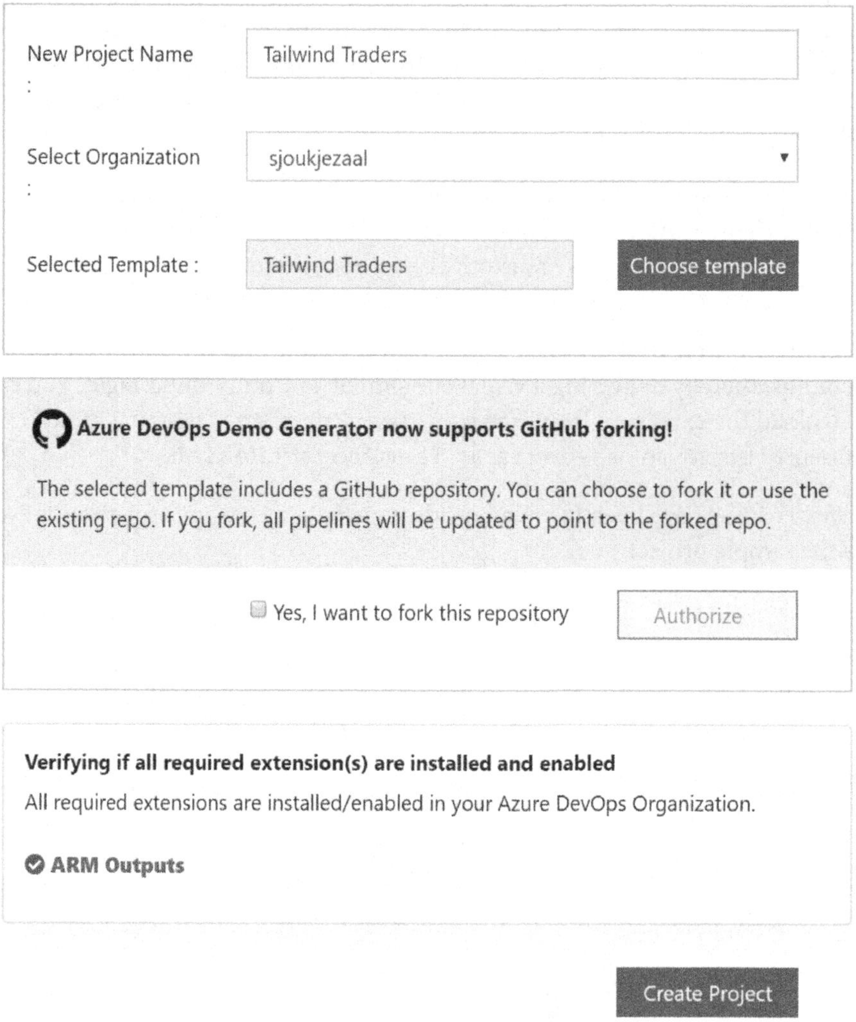

New Project Name :	Tailwind Traders	
Select Organization :	sjoukjezaal ▾	
Selected Template :	Tailwind Traders	Choose template

Azure DevOps Demo Generator now supports GitHub forking!

The selected template includes a GitHub repository. You can choose to fork it or use the existing repo. If you fork, all pipelines will be updated to point to the forked repo.

☐ Yes, I want to fork this repository   Authorize

Verifying if all required extension(s) are installed and enabled

All required extensions are installed/enabled in your Azure DevOps Organization.

✔ **ARM Outputs**

Create Project

Figure 1.11 – Creating a new project

5. Click the **Create Project** button.

6. With the project created, navigate to `https://dev.azure.com/`.

7. Log in with your credentials and select the organization where you created the project. Select the **Tailwind Traders** project to see if anything has been generated.

8. Repeat these steps to create the **Parts Unlimited** project in your DevOps environment.

> **Tip**
> For more information about the Tailwind Traders sample project, refer
> to the following site: `https://github.com/Microsoft/`
> `TailwindTraders`. For more information about the Parts
> Unlimited example, refer to `https://microsoft.github.io/`
> `PartsUnlimited/`.

Summary

In this chapter, we covered some of the basics of DevOps and covered the six different DevOps principles. Then, we covered the key concepts of Azure DevOps and the different solutions that Azure DevOps has to offer to support teams throughout each of the application life cycle phases. After that, we looked at the different features that Azure DevOps has to offer, and we introduced and created the two scenarios that we will use in the upcoming chapters of this book.

In the next chapter, we are going to cover how to manage projects with Azure Boards.

Further reading

Check out the following links for more information about the topics that were covered in this chapter:

- Extension Marketplace: `https://marketplace.visualstudio.com/azuredevops`

- Azure Automation documentation: `https://docs.microsoft.com/en-us/azure/automation/`

- Azure DevOps demo generator: `https://docs.microsoft.com/en-us/azure/devops/demo-gen/use-demo-generator-v2?view=azure-devops&viewFallbackFrom=vsts`

- An overview of the Tailwind Traders reference apps for Azure: `https://www.youtube.com/watch?v=EP-PME-1tq0`

2
Managing Projects with Azure DevOps Boards

In the previous chapter, we introduced DevOps and covered the six principles. We also briefly covered the key concepts and the different services of Azure DevOps. Finally, we introduced the scenarios that we will be using throughout this book.

In this chapter, we are going to cover **Azure Boards** in more detail. We will start with the different processes and process templates that are available in Azure DevOps. Then, we will create a new organization in Azure DevOps. We imported a sample project and organization called Tailwind Traders in the previous chapter. We will use this example for the rest of this chapter. We will use this Tailwind Traders project to create a new project and learn how to create and manage the different project activities using Azure Boards.

The following topics will be covered in this chapter:

- Understanding processes and process templates
- Creating an organization
- Creating a project
- Creating and managing project activities

Technical requirements

To follow this chapter, you need to have an active Azure DevOps organization. The organization that we'll be using in this chapter was created in *Chapter 1, Azure DevOps Overview*.

Understanding processes and process templates

With Azure Boards, you can manage the work of your software projects. Teams need tools to support them that can grow and that are flexible. This includes native support for Scrum and Kanban, as well as customizable dashboards and integrated reporting capabilities and tools.

At the start of the project, teams must decide which process and process templates need to be used to support the project model that is being used. The process and the templates define the building blocks of the Work Item tracking system that is used in Azure Boards.

Azure DevOps supports the following processes:

- **Basic**: This is the simplest model that teams can choose. It uses **Epics**, **Issues**, and **Tasks** to track the work. These artifacts are created when you create a new basic project, as follows:

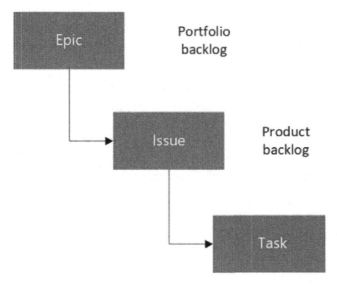

Figure 2.1 – Basic process

- **Agile**: Choose Agile when your team uses the Agile planning process. You can track different types of work, such as **Features**, **User Stories**, and **Tasks**. These artifacts are created when you create a new project using the Agile process. Development and test activities are tracked separately here, and Agile uses the Kanban board to track User Stories and bugs. You can also track them on the task board:

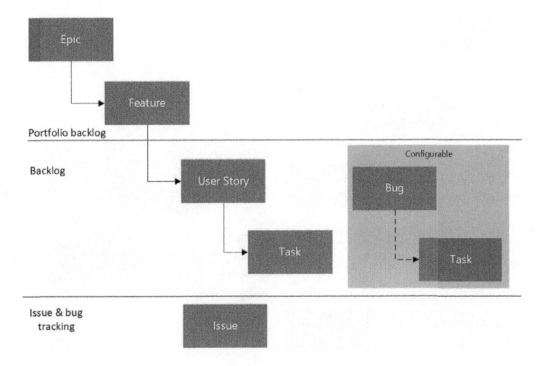

Figure 2.2 – Agile process

- **Scrum**: When your team is practicing the Scrum methodology, choose the Scrum process. This will create **Product backlog items (PBIs)**, **Tasks**, **Bugs**, and more artifacts for the team. You can track artifacts using the Kanban board, or break PBIs and bugs down into tasks on the task board. The Scrum process is shown in the following diagram:

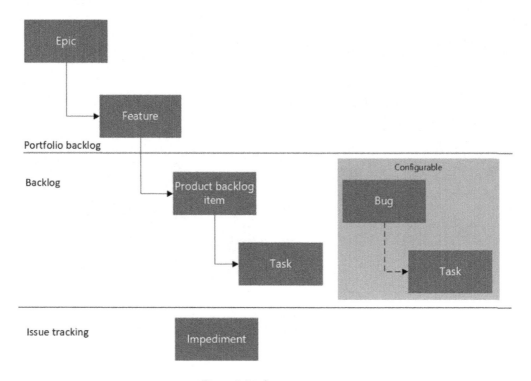

Figure 2.3 – Scrum process

- **CMMI**: When your team follows a more formal project method that requires a framework for process improvement and an auditable record of decisions, the **Capability Maturity Model Integration (CMMI)** process is more suitable. With this process template, you can track requirements and change requests, risks, and reviews:

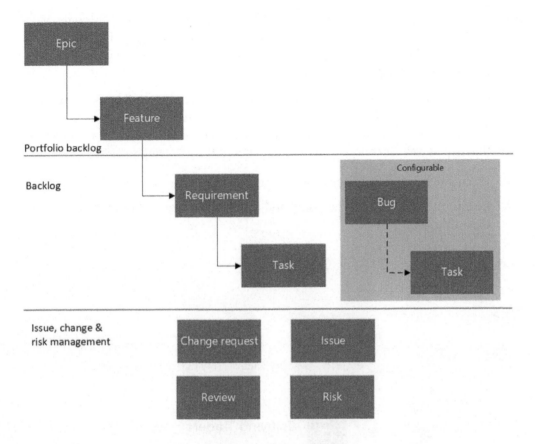

Figure 2.4 – CMMI process

Now we have covered some basic information about the different processes and process templates that are available in Azure DevOps, we will cover how to create a new organization.

Creating an organization

An organization in Azure DevOps is used to connect groups of related projects. You can plan and track your work here and collaborate with others when developing applications. From the organization level, you can also integrate with other services, set permissions accordingly, and set up continuous integration and deployment.

In the previous chapter, we introduced the scenarios that we will be using throughout this book. Tailwind Traders is an example retail company that is showcasing the future of intelligent application experiences. By generating a project using the DevOps generator, the organization and the project were automatically created.

However, there are cases where you might need to create an organization manually, such as when you first start to use Azure DevOps in an organization, or when it is a logical fit to create a separate organization based on permission requirements. So, we are going to cover this step as well. Therefore, you need to perform the following steps:

1. Open a web browser and navigate to `https://dev.azure.com/`.

2. Log in with your Microsoft account and from the left menu, click on **New organization**:

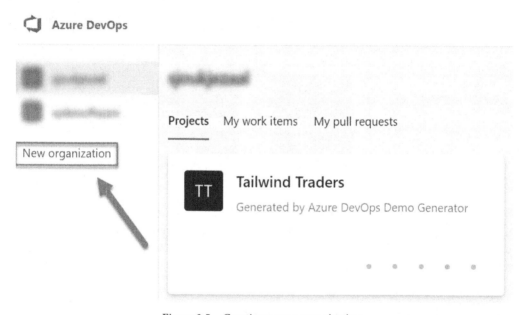

Figure 2.5 – Creating a new organization

3. In the wizard, give the organization a name, such as `PacktLearnDevOps`, and choose the location where you want to host the project:

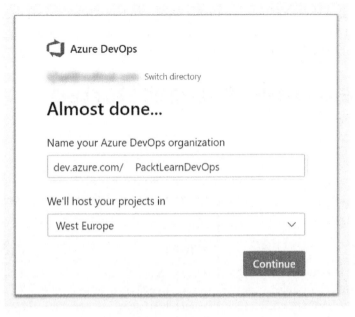

Figure 2.6 – Naming the project

4. Click **Continue**.

With that, the organization has been created. In the next section, we are going to learn how to add a new project to this organization.

Creating a project

After creating a new organization, Azure DevOps automatically gives you the ability to create a new project. Perform the following steps:

1. The wizard for creating a project is automatically displayed once you've created a new organization. There, you can specify the project's name. In my case, I named it LearnDevOps.

2. You can also choose if you want your project to be **Public**, so that everyone on the internet can view it, or **Private**. If you choose the latter, you need to give access to users manually. We will choose **Private** for this demo:

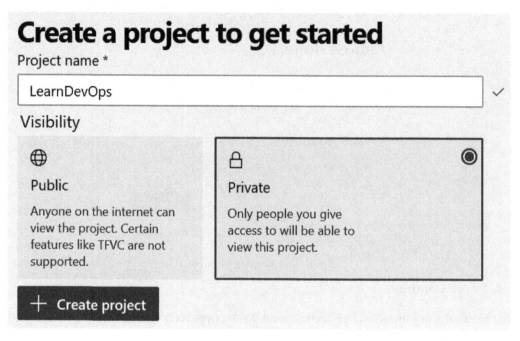

Figure 2.7 – Creating a new project

3. Click + **Create project** to create the new project. It will be added to the organization that we created in the previous step.

4. There is another way to create a new project. You can do this separately from creating an organization as well. There will be a lot of cases where you'll want to add a new project to an existing organization. For that, click on the organization's name in the left menu. You will be redirected to the overview page of the organization. There, in the top-right corner, click on + **New project**:

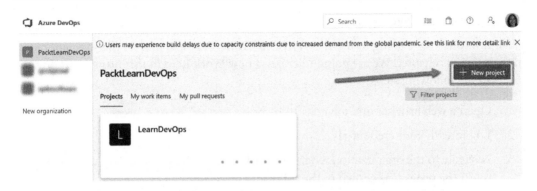

Figure 2.8 – Adding a new project to an existing organization

5.   From there, the same wizard for creating a new project will be displayed.

We have now covered how to create a new organization and add a project to it. For the remaining sections of this chapter, we are going to leave this organization and project as-is, and we are going to use the Tailwind Traders project that we imported in *Chapter 1, Azure DevOps Overview*.

In the next section, we will cover how to create and manage different project activities.

Creating and managing project activities

Azure DevOps offers different project features that can be used by teams to manage their software development project, such as Work Items, backlogs, sprints, boards, and queries. These will be covered in the following sections.

Work Items

Teams use artifact Work Items to track all the work for a team. Here, you will describe what is needed for the software development project. You can track the features and the requirements, the code defects or bugs, and all other items. The Work Items that are available to you are based on the process that was chosen when the project was created.

Work Items have three different states: **new**, **active**, and **closed**. During the development process, the team can update the items accordingly so that everyone has a complete picture of the work related to the project.

Now, let's create a new Work Item.

Creating a new Work Item

From now on, we are going to use the **Tailwind Traders** sample project that we generated in the previous chapter. We are going to create a new Work Item in this project. To do this, perform the following steps:

1. Open a web browser and navigate to `https://dev.azure.com/`.

2. Log in with your credentials.

3. Navigate to the organization where the **Tailwind Traders** project was created and select the project, as shown in the following screenshot:

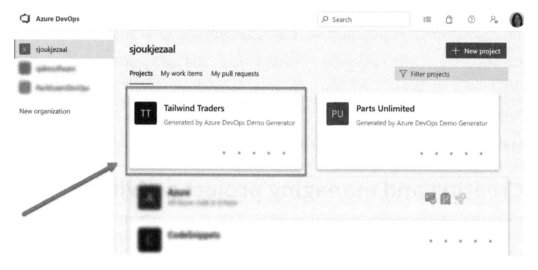

Figure 2.9 – Selecting the Tailwind Traders project in Azure DevOps

4. Next, from the left menu, select **Boards** and then **Work items**:

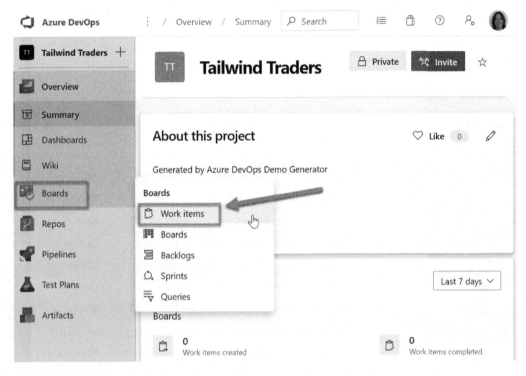

Figure 2.10 – Navigating to the Work Items

5. On the next screen, you will see an overview of all the Work Items that were generated automatically when we created the Tailwind Traders project:

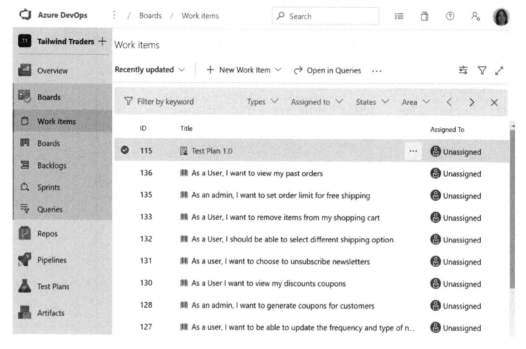

Figure 2.11 – Overview of all the sample Work Items

6. To create a new Work Item, click on **+ New Work Item** from the top menu. There, you will see the different types of Work Items that you can create according to the project type that was selected during creation. In the case of Tailwind Traders, the Agile type is used (see the *Understanding processes and process templates* section at the beginning of this chapter for more details):

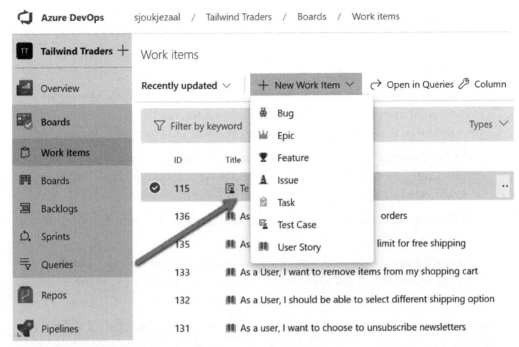

Figure 2.12 – Work Item types

Now, let's create a new User Story. To do so, click on **User Story** from the list. Now, follow these steps:

1. A new window will open where you can specify the values for the User Story. Add the following:

    a) **Title**: As a user, I want to edit my user profile.

    b) **Assigned**: Here, you can assign the Work Item to a specific person.

    c) **Add tag**: You can also add tags to this Work Item. These tags can be used for searching later. I've added a tag called **Profile Improvements**.

    d) **State**: Because this is a newly created item, the state is automatically set to **New**.

    e) **Iteration**: Here, you can specify which sprint you want to add this User Story to. You can also do this later from the backlog. I've added it to iteration **2**.

    f) **Description**: As a user, I want to edit my user profile. This is a rich text editor where you can also format the description to your needs.

g) **Discussion**: Here, you can add additional comments related to this Work Item. You can link it to another Work Item using *"#"* followed by "the name of the Work Item", link a particular pull request using *"!"* followed by the "name of the pull request", or mention a person using *"@"* followed by the "name of the person".

h) **Priority**: You can prioritize your User Story here. The priority here is just a number to indicate the importance of the Work Item, not the priority of it. The priority can be decided from the board by dragging the User Story up and down.

i) **Classification**: You can also classify this item. The generator created two different categories for the **Tailwind Traders** project. Here, you can select **Business** or **Architecture**. In this case, the item is more business-related.

j) **Development**: Here, you can link the item to a specific branch, build, pull request, and so on.

k) **Story points**: Using story points, you can estimate the amount of work required to complete a User Story using any numeric unit of measurement. The value in this field is based on the velocity of the team:

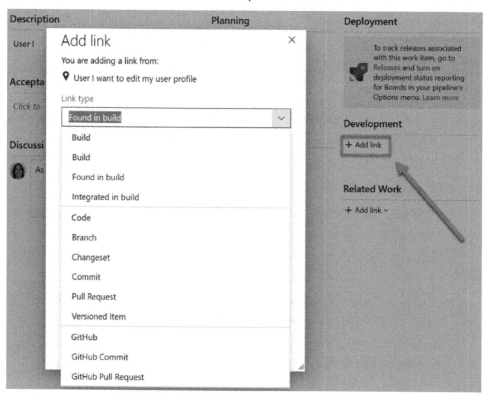

Figure 2.13 – Linking the item to a specific development process

2. **Related Work**: You can also link the item to other items or GitHub issues, such as parent-child relationships, **Tested By**, **Duplicate Of**, and so on:

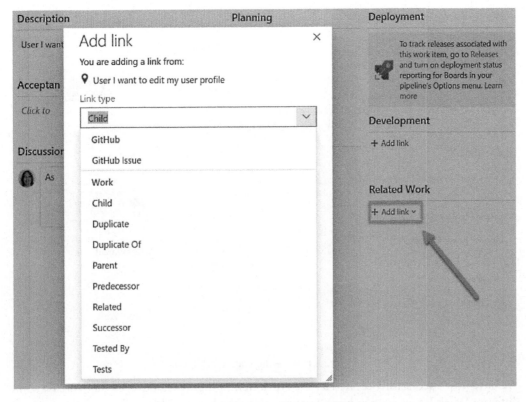

Figure 2.14 – Linking the item to related work

3. After filling in these fields, click the **Save** button at the top-right-hand side of the screen:

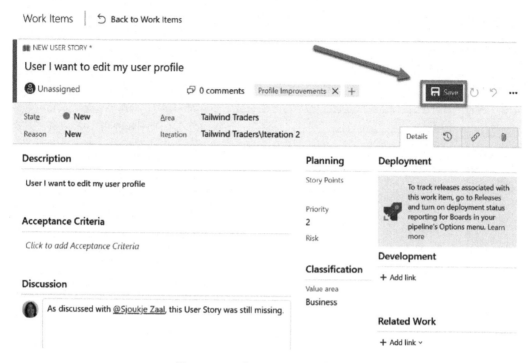

Figure 2.15 – Saving your Work Item

We have now successfully created a new Work Item. I highly encourage you to create some different Work Items, such as bugs, features, tasks, and so on. This way, you will become familiar with the different types of forms that come with each.

> **Important Note**
>
> For more information on how to create the different Work Items, refer to the following website: `https://docs.microsoft.com/en-us/azure/devops/boards/work-items/about-work-items?view=azure-devops&tabs=agile-process`.
>
> For more information about the different fields that are used in the Work Item forms, refer to this website: `https://docs.microsoft.com/en-us/azure/devops/boards/work-items/guidance/work-item-field?view=azure-devops`.

In the next section, we are going to look at backlogs and sprints in more detail.

Backlogs

The product backlog is a roadmap for what teams are planning to deliver. By adding User Stories, requirements, or backlog items to it, you can get an overview of all the functionality that needs to be developed for the project.

From the backlog, Work Items can be easily reordered, prioritized, and added to sprints.

Let's take a look at how backlog works:

1. In Azure DevOps, open the **Tailwind Traders** project again.

2. Next, from the left menu, select **Boards** and then **Back log**. Then, select **Tailwind Traders Team backlogs**:

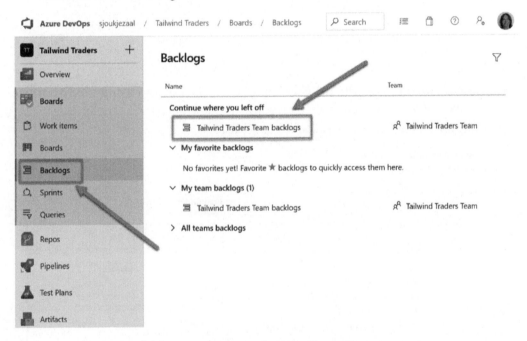

Figure 2.16 – Navigating to the backlog of the project

3. Here, you will see all the different User Stories for the project, including the one that we created in the previous demo. From the top-right, you can select the different types of Work Items that come with the project template:

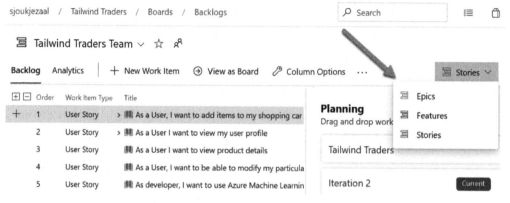

Figure 2.17 – Different types of Work Items

4. For now, we will stick with the User Stories view. You can also reorder and prioritize the Work Items from here. Let's reprioritize our newly created User Stories by dragging it between numbers 2 and 3 in the list:

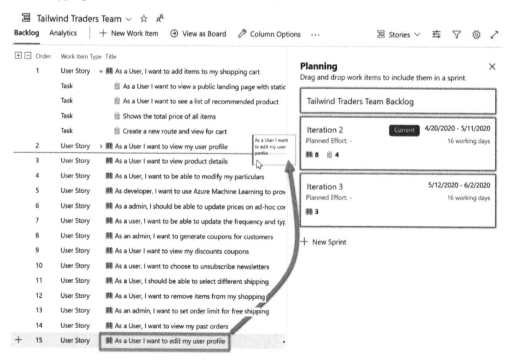

5.   From the backlog, you can also add Work Items to the different sprints. During creation of the Work Item, we added this User Story to Sprint 2. From here, we can drag this item to a different sprint if we want to:

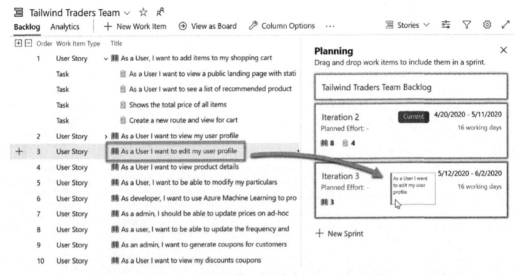

Figure 2.19 – Dragging the User Story to another sprint

6. You can also change the view to see more Work Items that are related to these User Stories. By clicking on the view options shown on the left-hand side of screen, you can enable different views. Enable **Parent**, which displays epics and features:

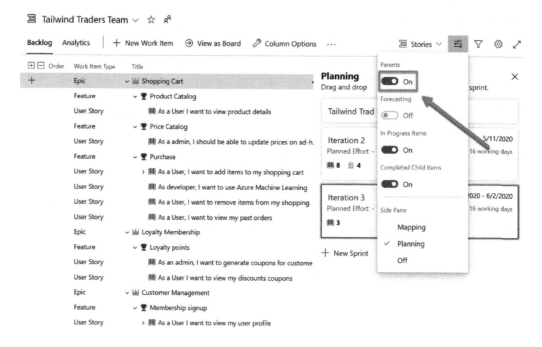

Figure 2.20 – Displaying the parent items

7. By dragging the different types of Work Items, you can also easily create different types of parent-child relationships. For instance, you can drag our newly created User Story to the **Membership signup** feature and create a relationship between them:

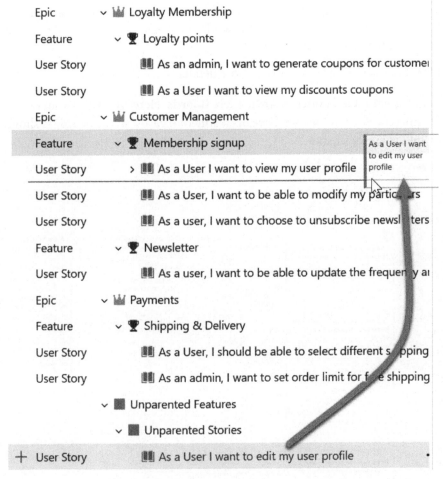

Figure 2.21 – Creating a parent-child relationship

In this section, we covered the backlog and how to prioritize User Stories, as well as how to add them to sprints. You can also create a view with a parent-child relationship based on the different Work Items you have.

In the next section, we are going to look at Boards in more detail.

Boards

Another way to look at the different Work Items you have is by using boards. Each project comes with a preconfigured Kanban board that can be used to manage and visualize the flow of the work.

This board comes with different columns that represent different work stages. Here, you can get a comprehensive overview of all the work that needs to be done and what the current status of the Work Items is.

Let's look at Boards in Azure DevOps in more detail:

1. From the left menu, under **Boards**, select **Boards**. Here, you will see an overview of the different Work Items that have been added to cards on the board, as shown in the following screenshot:

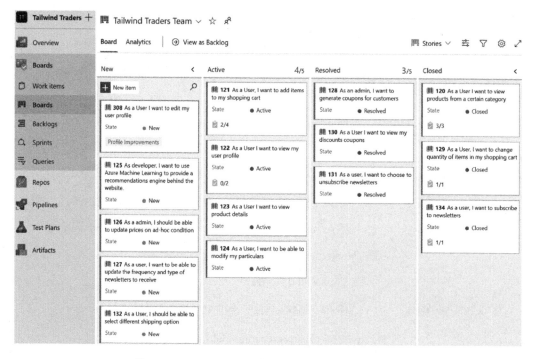

Figure 2.22 – Overview of the Tailwind Traders board

The Work Items are displayed according to the status of the items. In the **New** column, the items that the team has not committed to yet are displayed. Then, there's items that are currently being picked up by the team. These are displayed in the **Active** column.

There are also Work Items that are being **Resolved**, which means the development part has finished but they still need to be tested. Items that have passed these tests and meet the *Definition of done* are moved to the **Closed** column.

2. From here, you can also drag items to different columns, view the items in the backlog, and make changes to them by clicking on the three (...) at the top-right of the item, as follows:

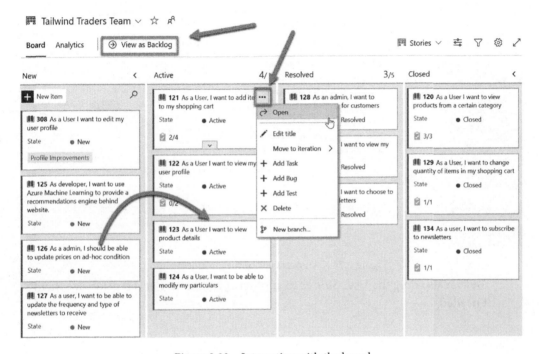

Figure 2.23 – Interacting with the board

With that, we have provided an overview of what boards have to offer. In the next section, we are going to look at sprints in more detail.

Sprints

According to the project template that is chosen, sprints can have a different name. In our Tailwind Traders project, the Agile project template is being used. This changes the name to **Iterations**. However, Azure DevOps treats these the same as **Sprints**.

Iterations or **Sprints** are used to divide the work into a specific number of (mostly) weeks. This is based on the velocity that a team can handle; that is, the rate at which the team is burning the User Stories.

Let's look at the Sprint View in Azure DevOps in more detail:

1. From the left menu, under **Boards**, select **Sprints**. By default, the backlog view will be displayed. Here, you will see an overview of the **User Stories** again, except this time for the current sprint, as shown in the following screenshot:

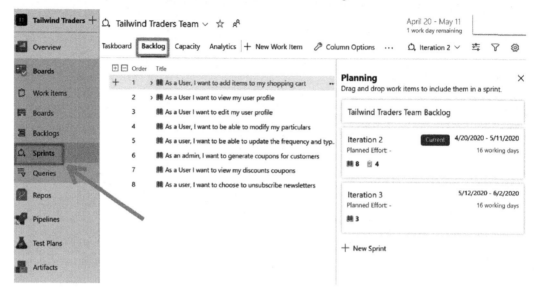

Figure 2.24 – An overview of the current sprint

You can also drag the User Stories to another sprint in here and reprioritize them if needed.

2. By clicking on **Taskboard** from the top menu, you will see a different view of the Work Items in the sprint, similar to what happens in Boards. This time, the items that are in the current sprint are displayed at the backlog task level:

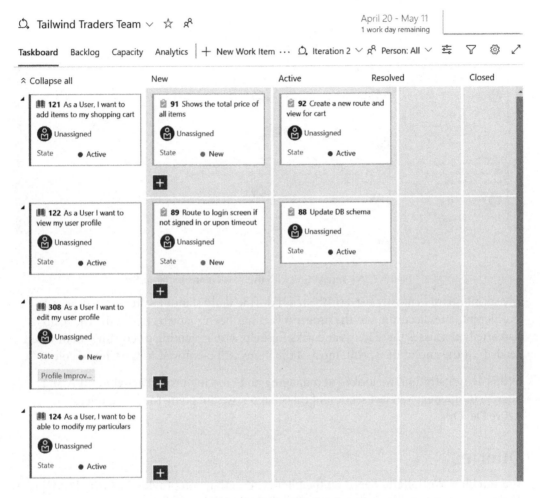

Figure 2.25 – Sprint in a Kanban board

3. From here, you can drag items to different columns, create new Work Items if needed, and filter through the different sprints:

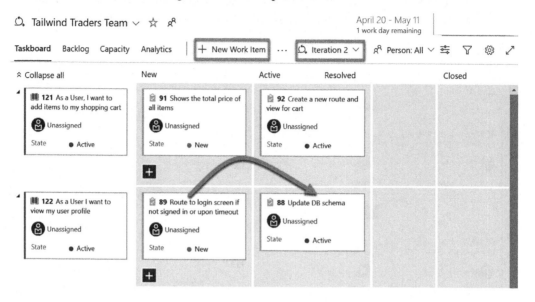

Figure 2.26 – Interacting with the Work Items in the sprint

The sprint board is mostly used by the team during daily standups. Items are dragged to different lanes according to the progress that has been made by the team. The team also briefly discusses these items and asks for help with executing or creating them when needed. At the end of the sprint, most of the items will be moved to the **Closed** column.

In this demonstration, we looked at managing and creating project activities in Azure Boards. In the next and last section of this chapter, we are going to look at queries in Azure DevOps.

Queries

You can filter Work Items based on the filter criteria that you provide in Azure DevOps. This way, you can easily get an overview of all the Work Items that are in a particular type, state, or have a particular label. This can be done within a project, but also across different projects.

To create different queries and search for Work Items, perform the following steps:

1. From the left menu, under **Boards**, select **Queries**. Then, from the top menu, select **+ New query**:

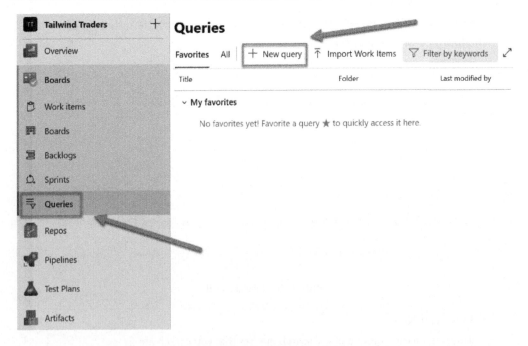

Figure 2.27 – Creating a new query

2. Next, let's create a query that will be searching for a User Story with the tag **Profile Improvements**. On the query screen, select the option shown in the following screenshot:

Figure 2.28 – Creating a query

3. Then, click on **Run query**. The result will display the Work Item that we created in the first step of this section:

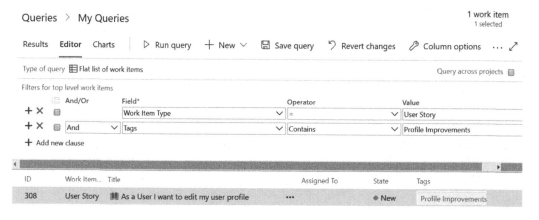

Figure 2.29 – Search result

> **Important Note**
> This was a basic example of the search queries that you can create.
> For more in-depth information, you can refer to `https://docs.microsoft.com/en-us/azure/devops/project/search/overview?view=azure-devops`.

With that, we have covered the basics of how to run a query to filter Work Items. This concludes this chapter.

Summary

In this chapter, we covered Azure Boards in more depth. We started by looking at the different project templates that you can choose from based on the methodology that your organization embraces. Based on that project template, different Work Items are created that can be used for planning the project. These Work Items can be added to backlogs and relationships can be created for a logical view of the project items. They can also be added to sprints.

In the next chapter, we are going to focus on source code management in Azure DevOps.

Further reading

Check out the following links for more information about the topics that were covered in this chapter:

- What is Azure Boards?: `https://docs.microsoft.com/en-us/azure/devops/boards/get-started/what-is-azure-boards?view=azure-devops&tabs=agile-process`

- Choosing a process: `https://docs.microsoft.com/en-us/azure/devops/boards/work-items/guidance/choose-process`

- Tracking work with User Stories, Issues, Bugs, Features, and Epics: `https://docs.microsoft.com/en-us/azure/devops/boards/work-items/about-work-items?view=azure-devops&tabs=agile-process`

- Creating your Product Backlog: `https://docs.microsoft.com/en-us/azure/devops/boards/backlogs/create-your-backlog?view=azure-devops&tabs=agile-process`

- How workflow states and state categories are used in Backlogs and Boards: `https://docs.microsoft.com/en-us/azure/devops/boards/work-items/workflow-and-state-categories?view=azure-devops&tabs=agile-process`

Section 2: Source Code and Builds

In this section, Azure builds are covered as well as how to manage your source code in Azure DevOps.

This section contains the following chapters:

3
Source Control Management with Azure DevOps

Source control management (SCM) is a vital part of every company that develops software professionally, but also for every developer that wants to have a safe way to store and manage their code.

When working in teams, it's absolutely necessary to have a safe central repository where all your code is stored. It's also necessary to have a system that guarantees that the code is safely shared between developers and that every modification is inspected and merged without raising conflicts.

In this chapter, we'll learn how Azure DevOps can help with managing source code professionally and securely. In this chapter, we'll cover the following topics:

- Understanding source control management
- Branching strategies overview
- Handling source control with Azure DevOps and Repos
- How to work with commits, pushes, and branches

- Working with pull requests
- Handling a pull request
- How to tag a particular code release

By the end of this chapter, you will have learned about all the concepts you can use to apply SCM techniques to your team using Azure DevOps.

Technical requirements

To follow this chapter, you need to have an active Azure DevOps organization and Visual Studio or Visual Studio Code installed on your development machine.

Understanding SCM

Source control (or version control) is a software practice used to track and manage changes in source code. This is an extremely important practice because it permits to maintain a single source of code across different developers and helps with collaborating on a single software project (where different developers works on the same code base).

SCM is an essential practice in any DevOps process. To adopt a source control policy, you should do the following:

- Select a source control management system to adopt (for example, install Git on a server or use a cloud-based SCM such as Azure DevOps Repos or GitHub)
- Store your code base in a repository managed by your source control management system
- Clone the repository locally for development by taking the latest code version (pull) stored in the central repository
- Commit and push your released code to the central repository
- Use different copies of the repository for developing in a parallel way (branches)

An SCM flow can be seen in the following diagram:

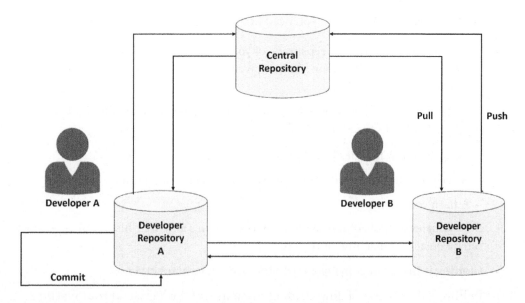

Figure 3.1 – Source control management flow

Git is absolutely one of the most popular SCM systems on the market. Git was created in 2005 by Linus Torvalds to aid in Linux kernel development. Git is free, open source, and entirely file-based, so no additional software is required to handle SCM except the Git engine itself.

Git has a workflow that can be summarized as follows (and that can be represented using the previous diagram):

1. You create a repository for your project on your Git hosting system.
2. You copy (or clone) the repository to your local development machine.
3. You create a new file in your local repository and then you save the changes locally (stage and commit).
4. You push the changes to the remote repository (push).
5. You pull the changes from the remote repository to the local one (to align your code with the remote repository if other developers have made modifications).
6. You merge the changes with your local repository.

When using Git as an SCM system, you need to memorize some key concepts:

- **Snapshots** are the way Git keeps track of your code history. A snapshot essentially records what all your files look like at a given point in time. You decide when to take a snapshot and of what files.

- **Commit** is the act of creating a snapshot. In a project, you create different commits. A commit contains three sets of information:

  -- Details on how the files has changed from the previous version

  -- A reference to the parent commit (previously occurred commit)

  -- A hash code name

- **Repositories** are collections of all the necessary files and their history. A repository can be on a local machine or on a remote server.

- **Cloning** is the act of copying a repository from a remote server.

- **Pulling** is the process of downloading commits that don't exist on your machine from a remote repository.

- **Pushing** is the process of adding your local changes to a remote repository.

- **Branches** are "versions" of your code base. All commits in Git live in a branch and you can have different branches. The main branch in a project is known as the `master`.

A Git flow is composed of the following actions:

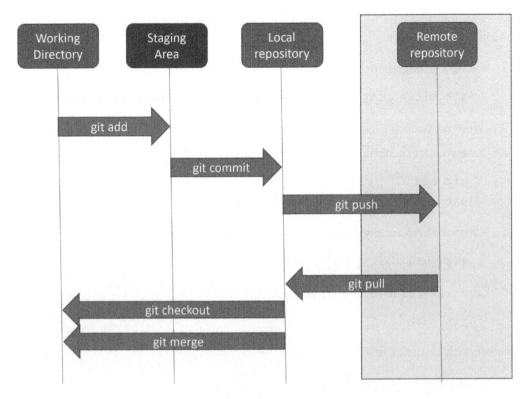

Figure 3.2 – Git flow

Let's look at how a commit flow occurs with Git. To create a commit on Git, you make some changes to your files and then you use the `git add` command to put these files into the staging environment. After that, you use the `git commit` command to create a new commit. This flow can be represented as follows:

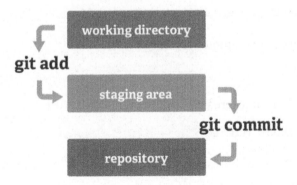

Figure 3.3 – Git commit

As an example, these are some Git commands you can use to activate the previously described SCM process:

1. Clone a remote repository locally:

```
git clone https://github.com/user/yourRemoteRepo.git
```

2. Work on your project.

3. Save your work locally:

```
git add .
git commit -m "my commit message"
```

4. Check if there are any updates from the remote server:

```
git pull
```

5. Save your work to the remote server:

```
git push
```

To work with branches, follow these steps:

1. Create a new branch and switch to it:

```
git checkout -b "branch1"
```

2. Work on the new features.

3. Save your work locally:

```
git add .
git commit -m "update from branch1"
```

4. Save your work to the remote server:

```
git push
```

5. Switch to the branch where you want to merge your work:

```
git checkout master
```

6. Merge branch1 into the master branch and save it to the remote server:

```
git merge branch1
git push
```

Once you've mastered these commands, you'll be ready to start using Git. In the next section, we'll provides an overview of branches and the possible branching strategies you can use.

Exploring branching strategies

A branch is a version of your code stored in an SCM system. When using SCM with Git, choosing the best branching strategy to adopt for your team is crucial because it helps you have a reliable code base and fast delivery.

With SCM, if you're not using branching, you always have a single version of your code (`master` branch) and you always commit to this branch:

Figure 3.4 – One flow

This "one flow" way of work is not recommended because it cannot guarantee that the `master` branch is stable, especially if you have more than one developer working on the same code.

There are different branching workflows (strategies) that you can adopt for your team, and the recommendation that normally I suggest is to start simple. With Git, there are three main branching strategies that you can adopt:

- GitHub Flow
- GitLab Flow
- Git Flow

In the following sections, we'll explore each of these strategies.

GitHub Flow

GitHub Flow is one of the most widely used branching strategies and is quite simple to adopt.

According to this workflow, you start from a `master` branch (which always contains the deployable code). When you start developing a new feature, you create a new branch and you commit regularly to this new branch. When the development work has been completed, you create a pull request to merge the secondary branch with the `master` branch:

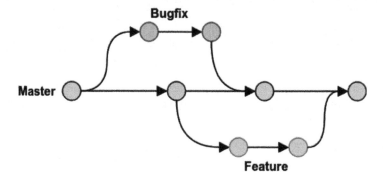

Figure 3.5 – GitHub Flow

This workflow is simple to adopt and good if you need to maintain a single version of your code in production. The only disadvantages are that you need to carefully check what you commit to the `master` branch. This is not recommended if you need to have multiple versions of your application in production.

GitLab Flow

GitLab Flow is another popular branching strategy that's widely used, especially when you need to support multiple environments (such as production, staging, development, and so on) in your SCM process. The following diagram represents this flow:

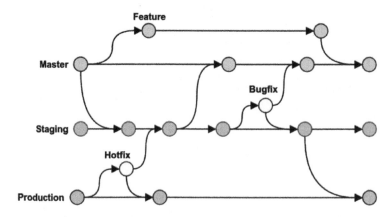

Figure 3.6 – GitLab Flow

According to this workflow, you should have at least three branches:

- **Master**: This is everyone's local version of the code.

- **Staging**: This is the branch where the *master* branch is branched into for testing purposes.

- **Production**: This is the released production code (where *staging* is merged).

This is useful if you want to maintain a stable production release, work separately on new features that can be moved to a testing environment (in order to be tested), and then merge that environment into the production release when testing has been completed.

Git Flow

Git Flow is a workflow that's used when you have a scheduled release cycle. The following diagram represents this flow:

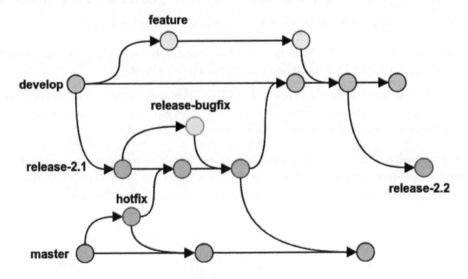

Figure 3.7 – Git Flow

According to this workflow, you have a **master** branch and a **develop** branch that are always live, and then some other branches that are not always live (can be deleted). The **master** branch contains the released code, while the **develop** branch contains the code that you're working on.

Every time you add a new feature to your code base, you create a **feature** branch, starting from the **develop** branch, and then you merge the **feature** branch into **develop** when the implementation is finished. Here, you never merge into the **master** branch.

When you need to release a set of features, you create a release branch, starting from the **develop** branch. Code in the **release** branch must be tested (maybe with bug fixes merged in) and then when you're ready to release the code, you merge the **release** branch into the **master** branch and then into the **develop** branch.

If a serious bug occurs in production, this flow says that you can create a **fix** branch from the **master**, fix the bug, and then merge this branch into **master** again directly. You can also merge it into the **release** branch if it's present, or into **develop** otherwise. If you have merged the code into the **release** branch, the **develop** branch will have the fix when you merge the **release** branch.

Handling source control with Azure DevOps

Azure DevOps supports the following source control management types:

- **Git**: This is a distributed version control system and is the default version control provider in Azure DevOps when you create a new project.

- **Team Foundation Version Control (TFVC)**: This is a centralized version control system where developers have only one version of a file locally, data is stored on a server, and branches are created on the server (path-based).

The first step when working with Azure DevOps is to create a new project inside your organization. When you create a new project with Azure DevOps, you're prompted to choose the version control system you want to use (shown in the red box in the following screenshot):

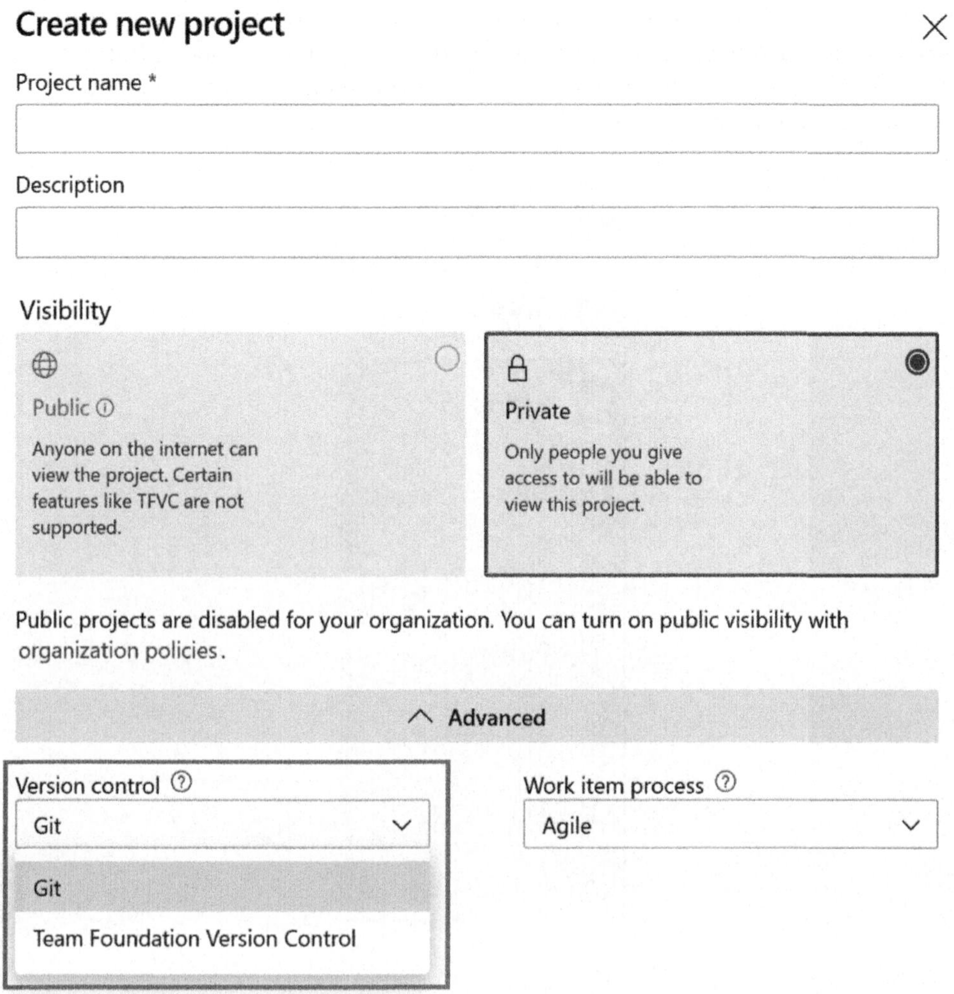

Create new project   ✕

Project name *

Description

Visibility

⊕   ○   🔒   ⦿

Public ⓘ   Private

Anyone on the internet can   Only people you give
view the project. Certain   access to will be able to
features like TFVC are not   view this project.
supported.

Public projects are disabled for your organization. You can turn on public visibility with
organization policies.

⌃ Advanced

Version control ⑦   Work item process ⑦

Git   ⌄   Agile   ⌄

Git

Team Foundation Version Control

Figure 3.8 – Create new project

By clicking the **OK** button, the new project will be created in your Azure DevOps
organization.

Once the project has been provisioned, you can manage your repositories by going to the **Repos** hub on the left bar in Azure DevOps (see the following screenshot). This is where your files will be stored and where you can start creating repositories and managing branches, pull requests, and so on:

Figure 3.9 – Repos

Starting from **Repos**, every developer can clone a repository locally and work directly from Visual Studio or Visual Studio Code while being connected to Azure DevOps in order to push code modifications, pull and create branches, make commits, and start pull requests.

When you start a new project from scratch, Azure DevOps creates an empty repository for you. You can load your code into this repository manually (via upload) or you can clone from a remote repository (for example, GitHub) to Azure DevOps.

In a single project, you can create different repositories and each can have its own set of permissions, branches, and commits. To create a new repository, just select the **Repos** hub and click on **New repository**, as shown in the following screenshot:

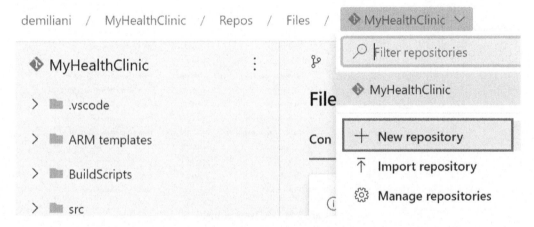

Figure 3.10 – New repository

A repository can be renamed or deleted easily from Azure DevOps.

In this section, we learned how to create a new project in Azure DevOps and how to create code repositories for your project.

In the next section, we'll learn how to manage a complete source code management flow with Azure DevOps, from cloning a remote repository to committing code on it.

Cloning a remote repository

To show you how to work with a code repository in Azure DevOps, I will start from a project where I have my web application source code stored in a Git repository in Azure DevOps. The following screenshot shows the code hosted remotely in the **master** branch:

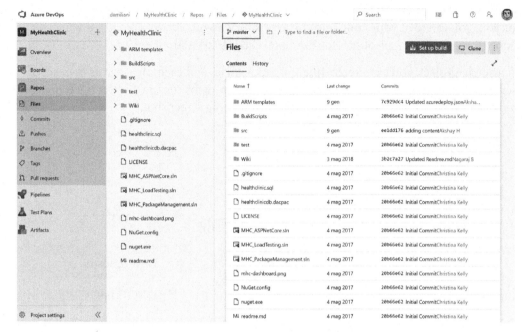

Figure 3.11 – Master branch

Every developer that must work with this code has to clone this repository locally. To do that, you can click on the **Clone** button, as shown in the following screenshot:

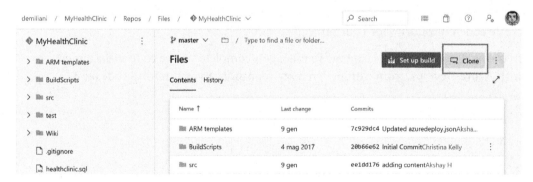

Figure 3.12 – Cloning the repository

From here, you'll see a window that shows you the clone repository's URL. You can clone this repository by using the `git clone <Repository URL>` command or directly in Visual Studio or Visual Studio Code by using one of the options shown in the following screenshot:

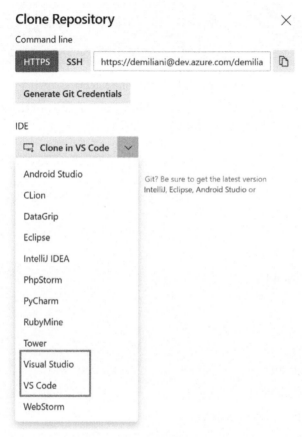

Figure 3.13 – Cloning options

Here, I'm cloning the project to Visual Studio Code. Azure DevOps prompts me to select a folder where I will save the project (local folder on your development machine), then opens Visual Studio Code and starts cloning the remote repository:

Figure 3.14 – Cloning in Visual Studio Code

In Visual Studio Code, you can also clone a repository by going to the Command Palette (*Ctrl + Shift + P*), selecting the Git:Clone command, and then pasting the repository URL into the URL window that will be prompted to you:

Figure 3.15 – The Git:Clone command

Once the cloning process has finished, you will have a local copy of the master branch of the remote repository in the selected folder:

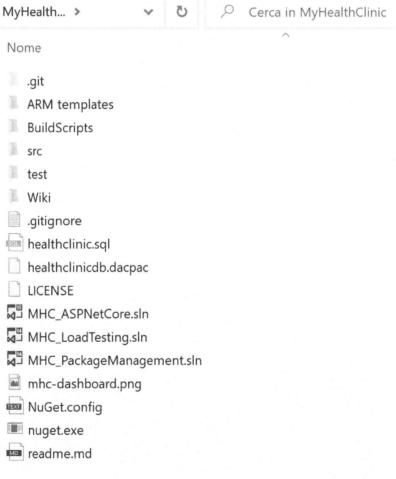

Figure 3.16 – Local copy of the remote repository

In order to work with remote repositories on Azure DevOps with Visual Studio Code more efficiently, I recommend that you install an extension (from the Visual Studio Code Marketplace) called **Azure Repos**:

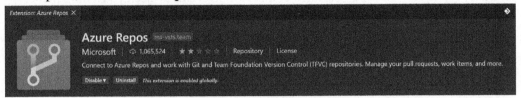

Figure 3.17 – Azure Repos extension

Once Azure Repos has been installed, if you go to the Command Palette and search for the word `teams`, you will see a new set of available commands to interact with in Azure DevOps, as follows:

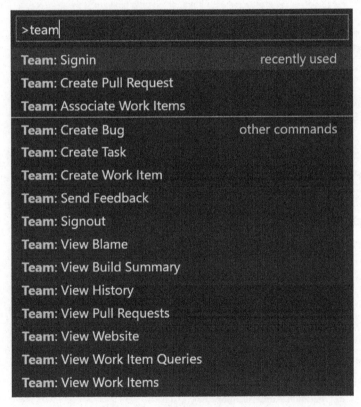

Figure 3.18 – Azure Repos commands

We'll use some of these commands later in this chapter.

In the next section, we'll learn how to import a GitHub repository into Azure DevOps.

Importing a GitHub repository into Azure DevOps

With Azure DevOps, you can also import a GitHub repository inside **Repos**. If you select an empty repository that you've created in an Azure DevOps project, you'll have the option to import a repository, as shown in the following screenshot:

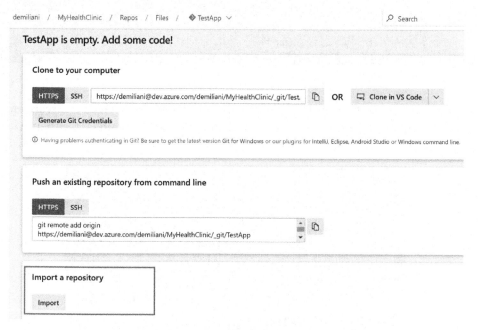

Figure 1.19 – Import a repository

Here, you can select the GitHub repository to import (by entering the source type and the GitHub repository's cloning URL):

Figure 1.20 – Import a Git repository

When you click the **Import** button, the remote GitHub repository import process will start and you will see an image showing its progress:

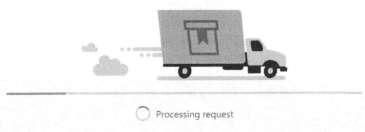

On its way!

Processing request

Importing https://github.com/demiliani/afzipdeployment.git

We'll send you a notification when it's ready. For now, you can work on some other project or just take a moment to sit back, relax and enjoy your day.

Figure 3.21 – Processing the import repository request

Once the import process has finished, you'll have the code available in Azure Repos. Please remember that when importing a repository from GitHub, the history and revision information is also imported into Azure DevOps for complete traceability:

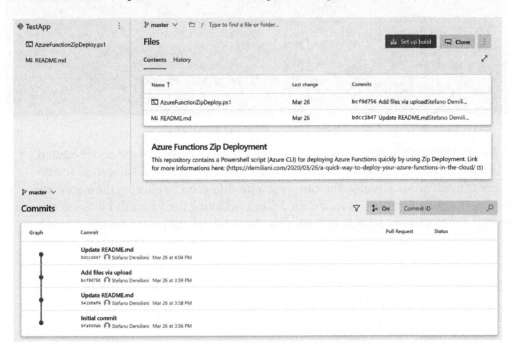

Figure 3.22 – History of the imported repository

Working with commits, pushes, and branches

Once you've cloned the remote repository to your local Git repository, you can start coding (create new files or modify new files).

Every time you create or change a file, Git records the changes in the local repository. You'll see the Visual Studio Code source control icon start signaling that a file has been modified. In the following screenshot, for example, I've added a comment to a file in my project. After saving this file, the Git engine says that I have an uncommitted file:

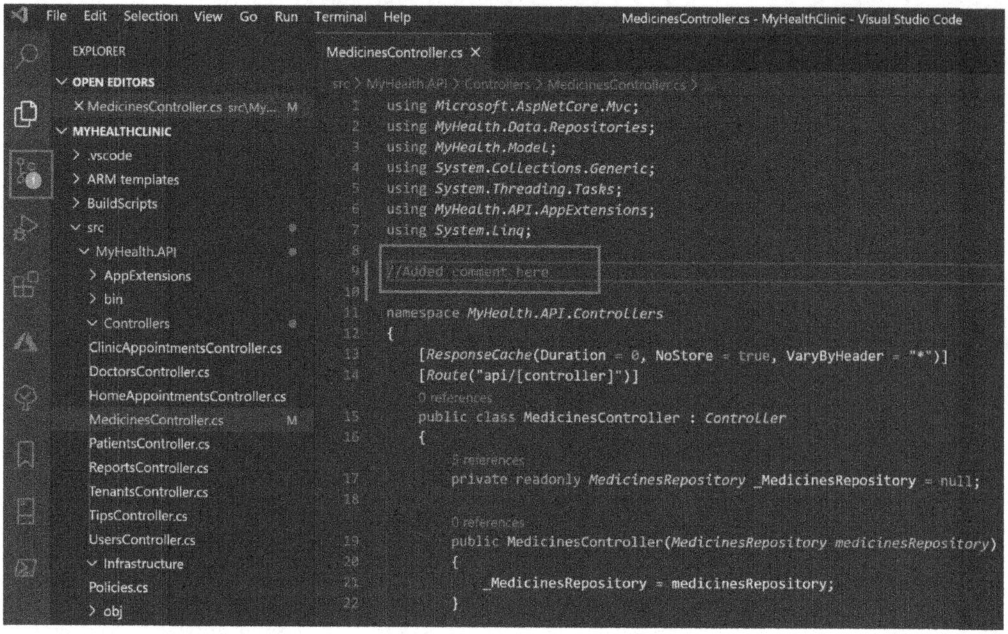

Figure 3.23 – Uncommitted file alert

If you click on the **Source Control** icon in the left bar, you will see the uncommitted file. From here, you can select the changes that you want to commit and stage them. Every commit is done locally. You can stage a modification by clicking the + icon and then perform a commit of all your staged files by clicking the **Commit** button in the top toolbar. Every commit must have a message that explains the reason for this commit:

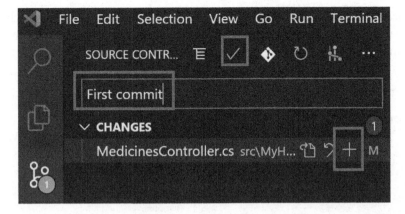

Figure 3.24 – Commit message

Now, the files are locally committed into your local `master` branch (although it's not recommended to do this, as explained later). To sync these modifications to the online repository in Azure DevOps, you can click the **Synchronize Changes** button on the bottom bar in Visual Studio Code (this visually indicates that you have some modifications that must be pushed online), as highlighted in red in the following screenshot:

Figure 3.25 – Modifications to be pushed online

Alternatively, you can select the `Git : push` command from the command bar, as follows:

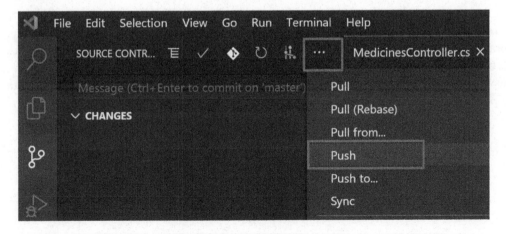

Figure 3.26 – The Git:Push command

Now, all the code modifications have been pushed online to the `master` branch. If you go to Azure DevOps in the **Repos** hub and select the **Commits** menu, you will see the history of every commit for the selected branch:

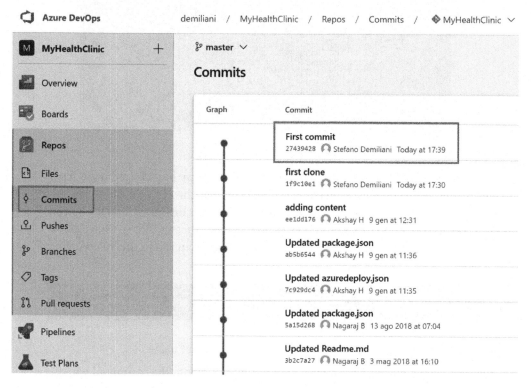

Figure 3.27 – Commit history

In this way, we're directly working on the `master` branch. This is not how you work in a real team of developers because if every developer commits directly to the `master` branch, you cannot guarantee that this branch will be always stable. The best way to work is by using the previously explained GitHub Flow. So, you should create a new branch, work on this newly created branch, and only when the work is finished should you create a `pull` request to merge your branch to the `master` branch.

You can create a new branch in Azure DevOps or directly from Visual Studio Code. To create a new branch, follow these steps:

1. From Azure DevOps, select **Branches** and then click on **New branch**:

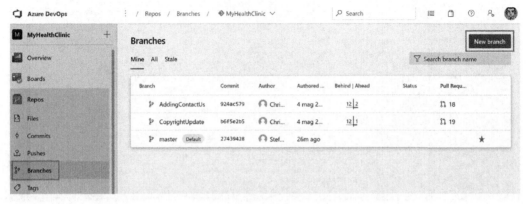

Figure 3.28 – New branch

2. Then, provide a branch name. You need to select the branch that your new branch will be created from, as shown in the following screenshot:

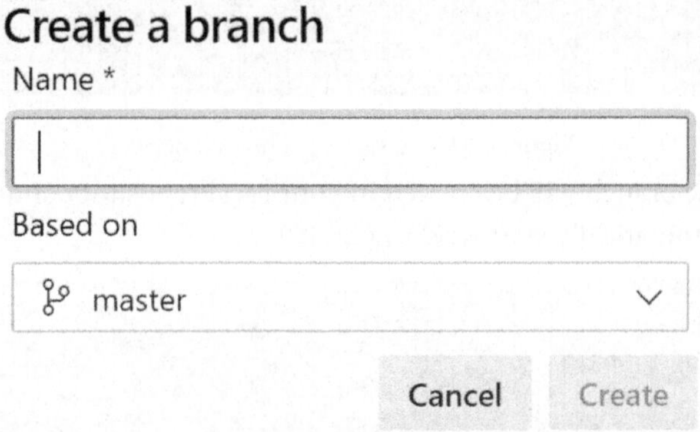

Create a branch

Name *

| |

Based on

| ⅄ master ∨ |

Cancel   Create

Figure 3.29 – Create a branch

To create a new branch directly from Visual Studio Code, just click on the branch name on the bottom bar and select **Create new branch…**:

Figure 3.30 – Create new branch… option in Visual Studio Code

3. Now, select the name for the new branch (here, it's called `development`):

Figure 1.31 – Assigning a branch name

With that, the branch will be created in your local repository and Visual Studio Code will automatically start working on it:

Figure 3.32 – Working on the new branch

4. Now, you can work on your code (maybe for developing a new set of features) and make commits on this new branch without affecting the `master` branch (it will continue to have the actually released version of your code base).

As an example, here, I have added a new modification to the `MedicineController.cs` file. I can stage and commit the modification on the `development` branch locally:

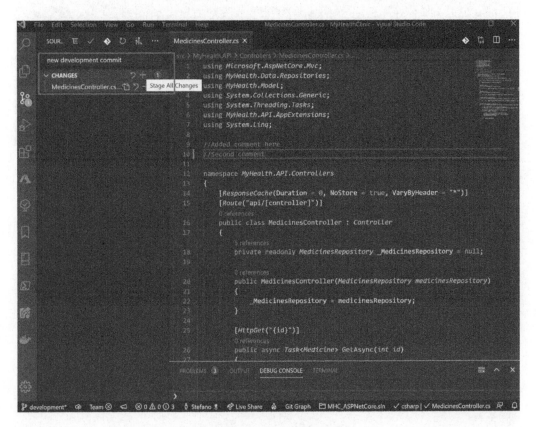

Figure 3.33 – Staging changes

5. Then, I can push these modifications to the remote repository on Azure DevOps. When pushed online, if this is the first time the **development** branch is being created, you will receive a message that looks as follows:

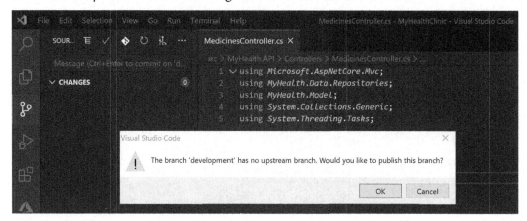

Figure 3.34 – Automatic branch creation and publishing

6. When finished, the **development** branch will be created on the remote repository and your code will be pushed online:

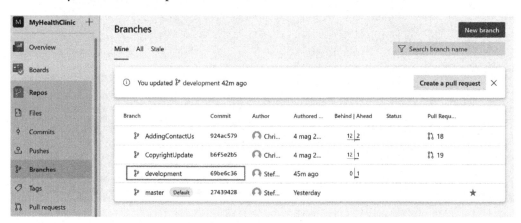

Figure 3.35 – Branch created on the remote repository

7. If you go to the **Commits** section in the **Repos** hub in Azure DevOps, you will see the history of your commits. By selecting a specific commit, you can view the file changes that were made (by comparing the previous version to the current version after the specific commit):

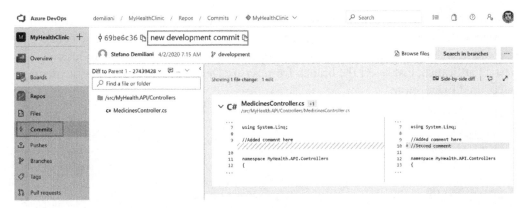

Figure 3.36 – Details of a commit

This action can also be done directly from Visual Studio Code with the **Azure Repos** extension by using the `Team:View History` command:

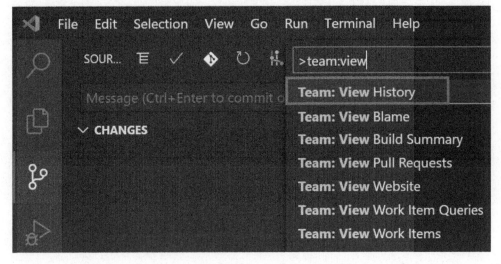

Figure 3.37 – The Team:View History command from Visual Studio Code

A branch can be deleted (manually or automatically after a pull request), restored from accidental deletion, and also be locked (in order to be placed in a read-only state or to avoid new commits on this branch affecting a merging that is in place). To lock a particular branch, just select the branch from Azure DevOps and then, from the menu, select the **Lock** option:

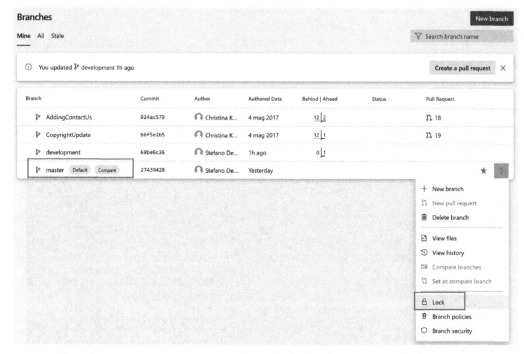

Figure 3.38 – Locking a branch

To unlock a locked branch, just select the **Unlock** action. It's important to note that locking a branch does not prevent cloning or fetching this branch locally.

Protecting branches with policies

When working with different developers and when using branches, it is extremely important to protect the critical branches you have in your repository (such as the master branch) with rules that can guarantee that the branch will always be in a healthy state.

For this scope, Azure DevOps permits you to specify a set of policies for your critical branches.

Branch policies in Azure DevOps permit you to do the following:

- Limit the contributors to a specific branch
- Specify who can create branches
- Specify a set of naming conventions for branches
- Automatically include code reviewers for every code change in the branch
- Enforce the use of pull requests
- Start a build pipeline before committing the code to the branch

To specify the branch policies for a particular branch, go to the **Branch** section in Azure DevOps, select your branch, and then select the **Branch policies** menu:

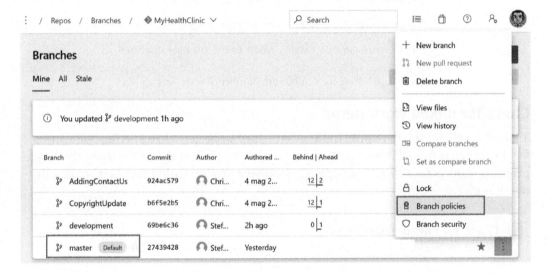

Figure 3.39 – Branch policies

Here, you have a set of options that you can set to control your selected branch. We'll look at each of these options in detail in the following sections.

Require a minimum number of reviewers

This option allows you to specify the number of reviewers that can approve a code modification. If any reviewer rejects the code changes, the modifications are not approved, and the code changes are discarded. If you select **Allow completion even if some reviewers vote to wait or reject**, then the pull request can be completed. The **Requestors can approve their own changes** option enables the creator of a pull request to approve its own code changes:

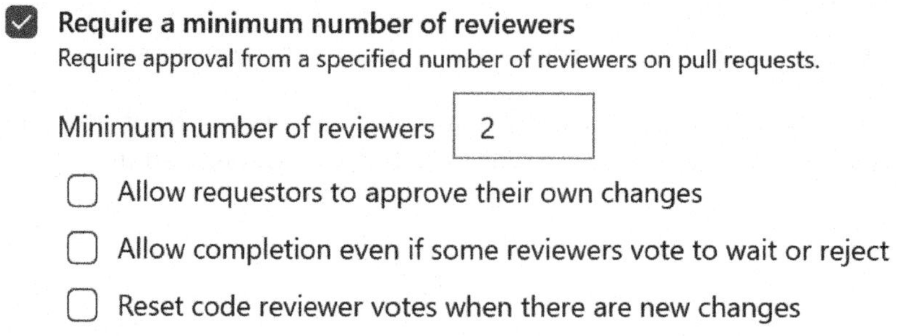

☑ **Require a minimum number of reviewers**
Require approval from a specified number of reviewers on pull requests.

Minimum number of reviewers   2

☐ Allow requestors to approve their own changes

☐ Allow completion even if some reviewers vote to wait or reject

☐ Reset code reviewer votes when there are new changes

Figure 3.40 – Require a minimum number of reviewers option

Check for linked work items

This option allows you to require the associations of work items to a specific pull request for the complete traceability of activities and tasks. This is useful if you're using the project planning features (as shown in *Chapter 2, Managing Projects with Azure DevOps Boards*, of this book):

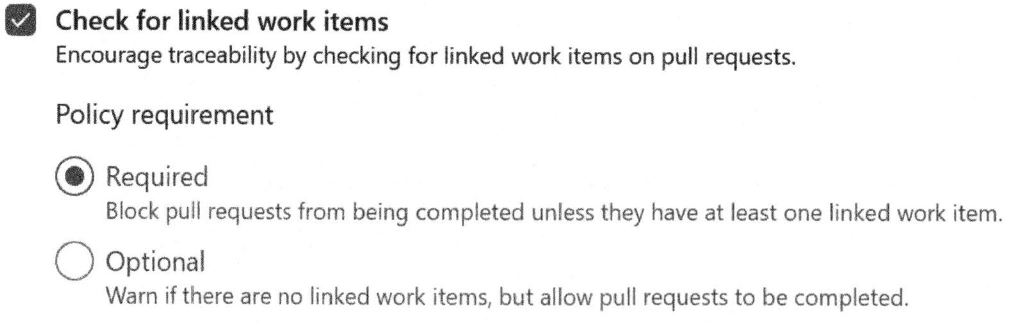

☑ **Check for linked work items**
Encourage traceability by checking for linked work items on pull requests.

Policy requirement

⦿ Required
Block pull requests from being completed unless they have at least one linked work item.

◯ Optional
Warn if there are no linked work items, but allow pull requests to be completed.

Figure 3.41 – Check for linked work items option

Check for comment resolution

This option allows you to specify a rule where all comments must be resolved so that the pull request can be performed:

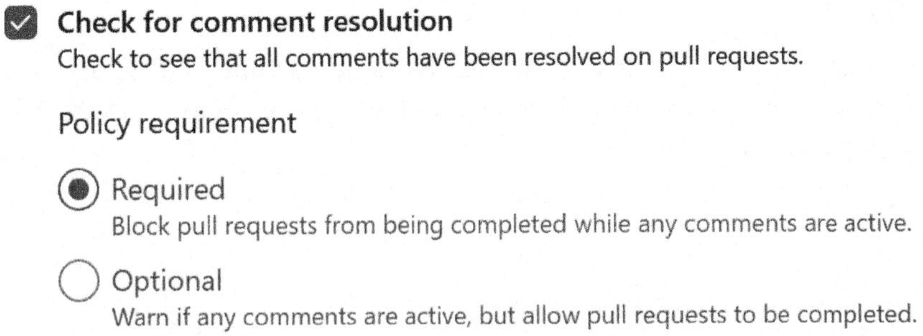

✅ Check for comment resolution
Check to see that all comments have been resolved on pull requests.

Policy requirement

◉ Required
Block pull requests from being completed while any comments are active.

○ Optional
Warn if any comments are active, but allow pull requests to be completed.

Figure 3.42 – Check for comment resolution option

Limit merge types

This option allows you to enforce a branch strategy when a pull request is completed. The available options are as follows:

- **Basic merge (no fast-forward)**: This option merges the commit history of the source branch and creates a merge commit in the target branch. The complete non-linear history of commits that occurs during development is preserved.

- **Squash merge**: This creates a single commit in the target branch by compressing the source branch commits (linear history).

- **Rebase and fast-forward**: A rebase allows the integration of a pull request branch into the master branch. Each commit on the pull request is merged into the target branch individually (linear history).

- **Rebase with merge commit**: This creates a semi-linear history by replacing the source branch commits in the target branch and then creating a merge commit.

All these options can be seen in the following screenshot:

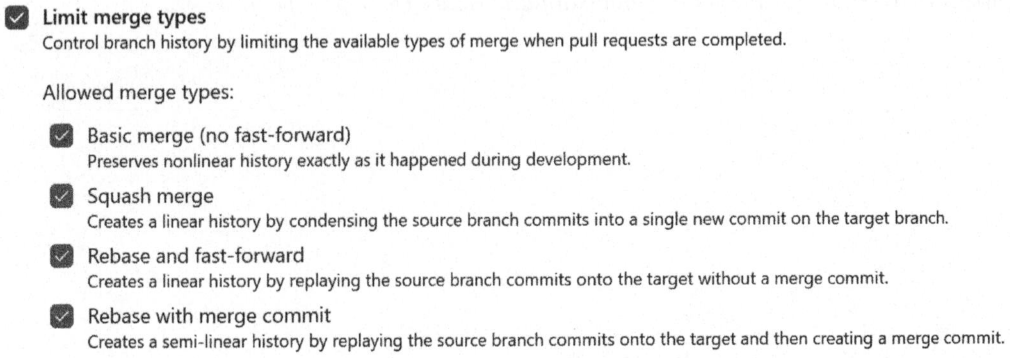

✅ Limit merge types
Control branch history by limiting the available types of merge when pull requests are completed.

Allowed merge types:

✅ Basic merge (no fast-forward)
Preserves nonlinear history exactly as it happened during development.

✅ Squash merge
Creates a linear history by condensing the source branch commits into a single new commit on the target branch.

✅ Rebase and fast-forward
Creates a linear history by replaying the source branch commits onto the target without a merge commit.

✅ Rebase with merge commit
Creates a semi-linear history by replaying the source branch commits onto the target and then creating a merge commit.

Figure 3.43 – Limit merge types option

Build validation

This section allows you to specify a set of rules for building your code before the pull request can be completed (useful for catching problems early). Upon clicking **Add build policy**, a new panel appears:

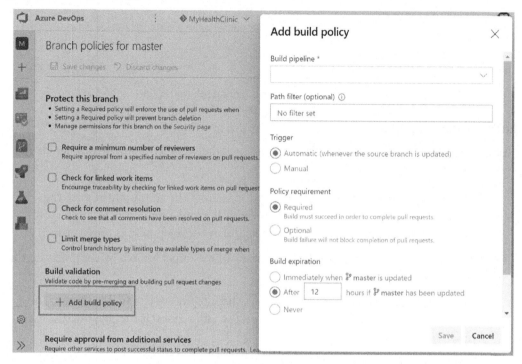

Figure 3.44 – Add build policy

Here, you can specify what build pipeline definition you wish to apply and if it must be triggered automatically when the branch is updated or manually. We'll talk about build pipelines in detail in *Chapter 4, Understanding Azure DevOps Pipelines*.

Require approval from additional services

This option allows you to connect external services (via Azure DevOps pull request APIs) in order to participate in the pull request flow:

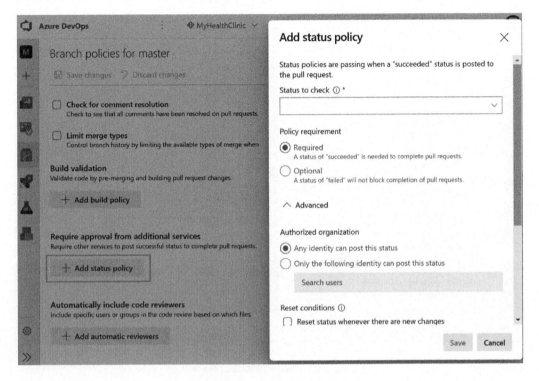

Figure 3.45 – Add status policy

Automatically include code reviewers

This policy allows you to include specific users or groups in the code review process:

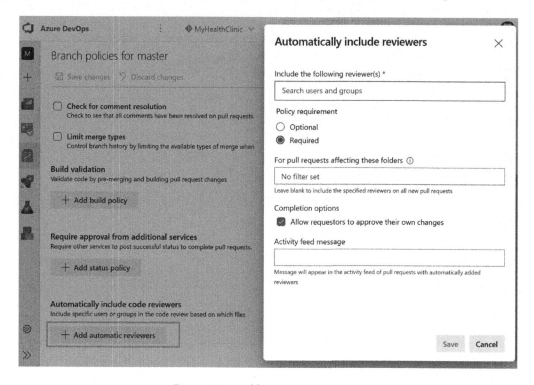

Figure 3.46 – Add automatic reviewers

Cross-repo policies

Instead of defining a policy for each branch you create manually, Azure DevOps allows you to define cross-repository policies (which will be automatically applied to all the branches that you create for your project).

To define a policy that will be valid for each repository you'll create, you need to go to **Project settings** and then select **Cross-repo policies**, as shown in the following screenshot:

Figure 3.47 – Cross-repo policies

From here, you can add a branch protection policy and select one of these options:

- **Protect the default branch of each repository** (for example, the master branch of each repo).

- **Protect current and future branches matching a specified pattern**. Here, you can define a pattern for filtering branches and the policy will be applied to all the branches that apply to this pattern.

As an example, if you want to define a policy that will be automatically applied to all the branches you create for your project, do the following:

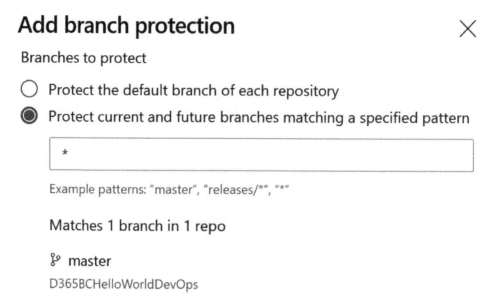

Figure 3.48 – Add branch protection

As you can see, here, we have selected the * key as a pattern to identify all the branches in our project.

Working with pull requests

Pull requests allow you to notify your team members that a new implementation has been completed and must be merged with a specified branch. By using pull requests, members of your team can review your code (by stepping through files and see the modifications that a particular commit introduces), provide review comments on minor issues, and approve or reject those modifications. This is the recommended practice to use when using source control management with Azure DevOps.

You can view the incoming pull requests for a specific repository on Azure DevOps by selecting the **Pull requests** menu from the **Repos** hub, as shown in the following screenshot:

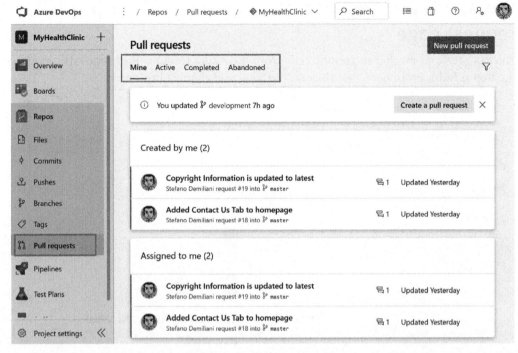

Figure 3.49 – Pull requests view

You can also filter this list to view only your pull requests or only the **Active**, **Completed**, or **Abandoned** pull requests.

A pull request can be created in different ways, as follows:

- Manually from the Azure DevOps pull request page
- From a work item linked to a branch (the **Development** tab)
- When you push an update to a feature branch
- From Visual Studio Code or Visual Studio directly
- From the Azure DevOps Services CLI

In the following sections, we'll learn how to start pull requests in each of these situations.

Creating a pull request from the Azure DevOps pull request page

You can create a new pull request directly from the Azure DevOps **Pull requests** menu (in the **Repos** hub). From here, just click on the **New pull request** button:

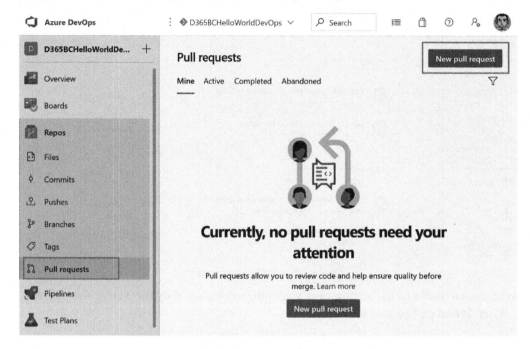

Figure 3.50 – New pull request

You can now enter details about the pull request you wish to create (we'll look at this later in this chapter).

Creating a pull request from a work item

From the **Backlogs** view of your team's work items, you can select a work item with a linked branch (a work item with a commit associated with a branch), go to the **Development** area of the selected work item, and create a **Create pull request** action:

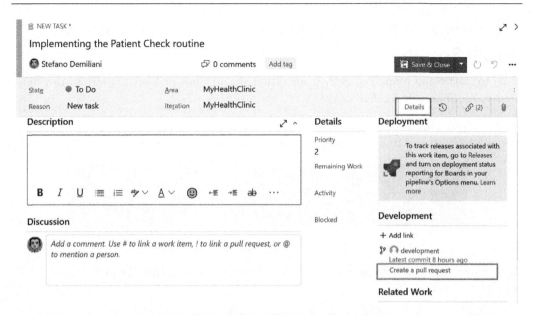

Figure 3.51 – Creating a pull request from a work item

Creating a pull request after pushing a branch

When you commit code to a `development` (secondary) branch to Azure DevOps, you're automatically prompted to create a pull request (you can see this prompt by going to the **Files** or **Pull requests** menu in the **Repos** hub). As you may recall, I previously committed a new code into a branch called **development** to Azure DevOps. Now, if we go to the **Files | History** section, we will see that there's a prompt for creating a new pull request:

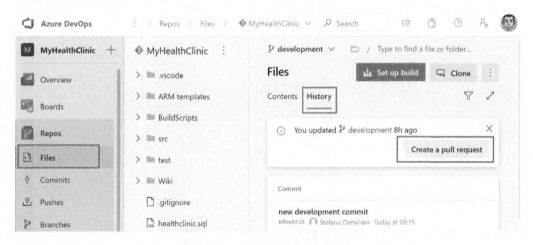

Figure 3.52 – Creating a pull request after a commit on a branch

Creating a pull request from Visual Studio Code or Visual Studio

You can start a pull request directly from Visual Studio Code or Visual Studio from where your project has been loaded.

To start a pull request from Visual Studio Code, launch the `Team:Create pull request` command from the Command Palette (*Ctrl + Shift + P*):

Figure 3.53 – Creating a pull request from Visual Studio Code

This will prompt you to open Azure DevOps. After confirming this, the pull request window will open.

From Visual Studio, select the **Team Explorer** panel. From here, you can click on **Pull Requests** to start a pull request:

Figure 3.54 – Creating a pull request from Visual Studio

Handling a pull request

All the different ways to handle a pull request that we've described converge to a unique point: in Azure DevOps, the **Pull requests** window opens, and you need to fill in the details of your pull request activity. As an example, this is the pull request that we started after the previous commit on the **development** branch:

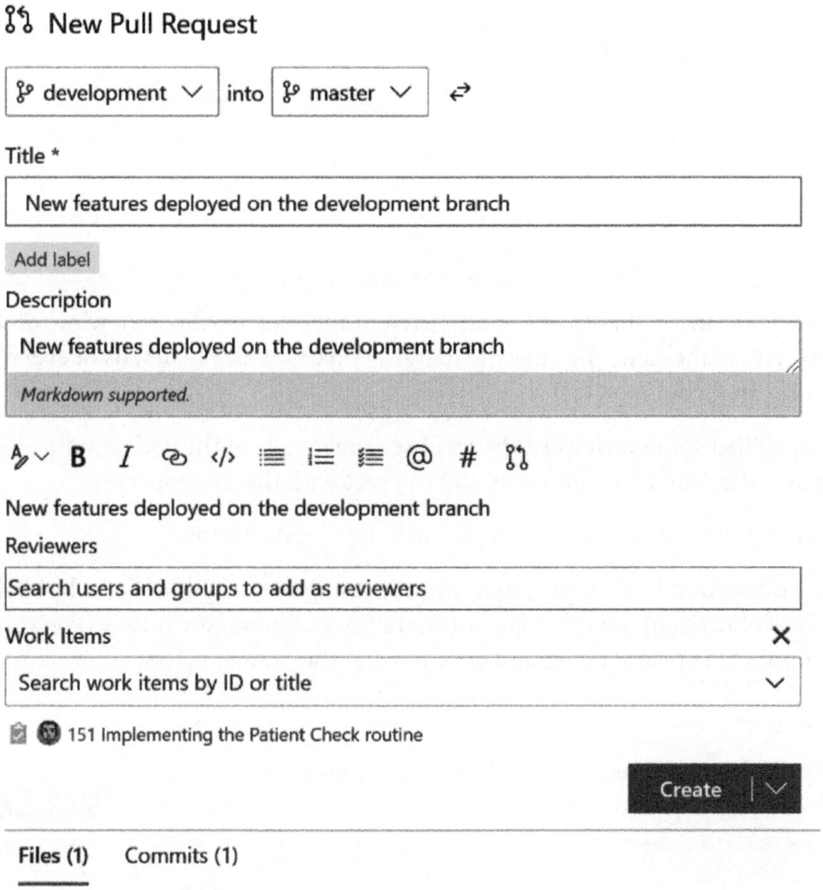

Figure 3.55 – New pull request window

Here, you can immediately see that the pull request merges a branch into another branch (in my case, **development** will be merged into **master**). You need to provide a title and a description of this pull request (that clearly describes the changes and the implementations you made in the merge), as well as attach links and add team members (users or groups) that will be responsible for reviewing this pull request. You can also include work items (this option will be automatically included if you completed a commit attached to a work item previously).

In the **Files** section, you can see what this pull request will do in the destination branch (for every file). As an example, this is what my pull request shows me:

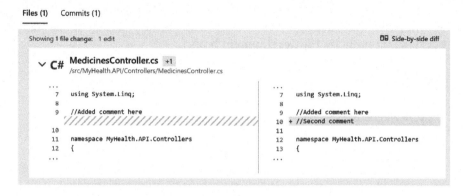

Figure 3.56 – Code modifications view in a pull request

On the left, you can see that the file committed in the `master` branch, while on the right, you can see the same file after the merging phase (with the details of every modification applied).

If you've specified some reviewers, they will see the details of the code modifications, which means they can add comments and interact with the developers.

To create the pull request process, simply click the **Create** button.

Once the pull request has been created, you can complete the pull request by clicking on the **Complete** button in the top-right corner of the pull request window (you can do this after the optional approval phase and after passing the branch rules):

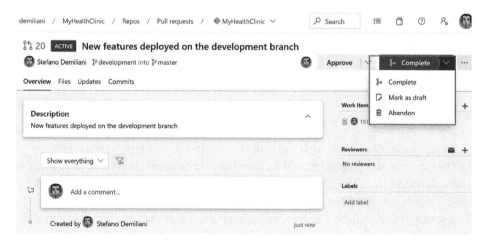

Figure 3.57 – Completing a pull request

From here, you can do the following:

- **Complete** the pull request.
- **Mark as draft**: This is like a "work in progress". If a pull request is marked as a draft, required reviewers are not automatically added, voting is not permitted, and build policies (if activated) are not automatically executed.
- **Abandon**: The pull request will be closed, and your code will not be merged.

When you click on **Complete**, you'll be prompted to fill in the **Complete pull request** window, which looks as follows:

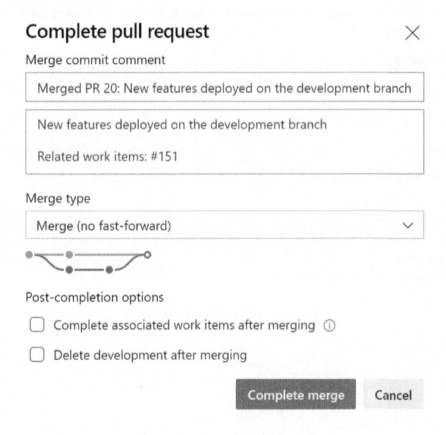

Figure 3.58 – Complete pull request

Here, you can insert a title and a description for the merge operation, select the merge type to apply, and select the post-completion operation to apply (if the associated work items should be marked as completed after merging and if the source branch must be deleted after the merge operation).

Regarding the type of merge operation to apply, you can choose from the following options:

- **Merge (no fast-forward)**: Non-linear history preserving all commits
- **Squash commit**: Linear history with only a single commit on the target
- **Rebase and fast-forward**: Rebase source commits on a target and fast-forward
- **Semi-linear merge**: Rebase source commits on a target and create a two-parent merge

Azure DevOps gives you a nice animated graph to show the final result of the merge. To complete the pull request, click on **Complete merge**. You need to resolve any merge conflicts if something happens. With this, the merging phase starts:

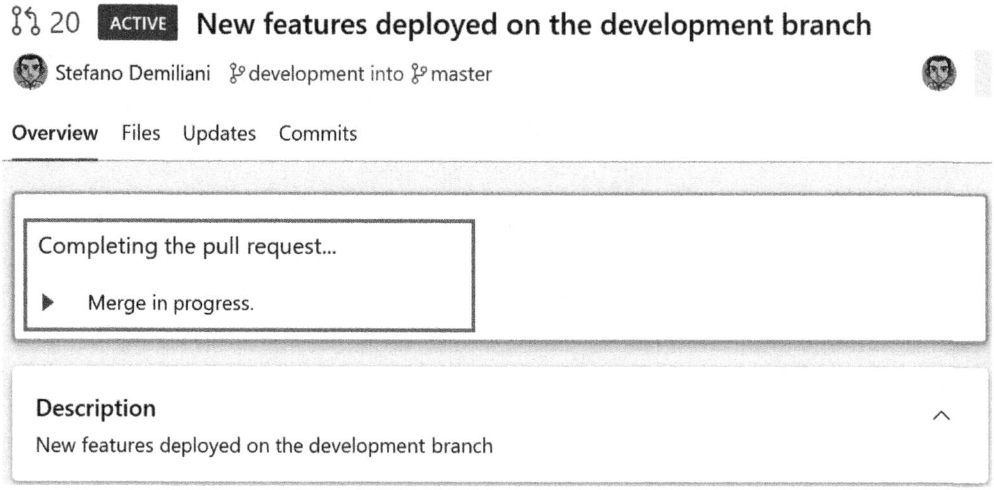

Figure 3.59 – Completing the pull request.

If you have an automatic build policy on the target branch (the `master` branch here), the build pipeline is executed and then the merge operation is completed:

Figure 3.60 – Pull request completed

In the next section, we'll learn how to use tags on branches to immediately identify the status of the code inside the repository.

Tagging a release

Git Tags are references that point to specific points in the **Git** history. **Tags** are used in Azure DevOps for marking a particular release (or branch) with an identifier that will be shared internally in your team to identify, for example, the "version" of your code base.

As an example, in the previous section, we merged the `development` branch into the `master` branch by using a **pull request**. Now, the `master` branch contains our latest release of the code, which we're now ready to share internally.

To use tags for your branches, in the **Repos** hub in Azure DevOps, go to the **Tags** menu:

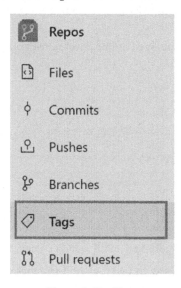

Figure 3.61 – Tags

From here, you can create a tag for this release by going to **Tags** and clicking on **New Tag**.

Here, you're prompted to insert a tag name (an identifier that cannot contain spaces), provide a description for this tag, and select the branch that the tag will be applied to:

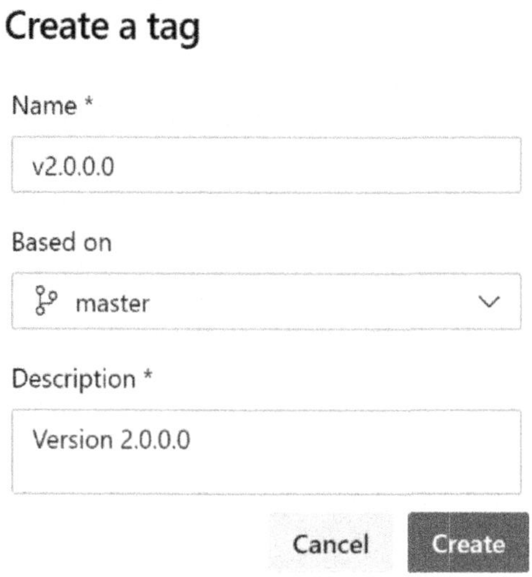

Create a tag

Name *

v2.0.0.0

Based on

master

Description *

Version 2.0.0.0

Cancel   Create

Figure 3.62 – Create a tag

When you click on **Create**, the tag will be applied to your branch:

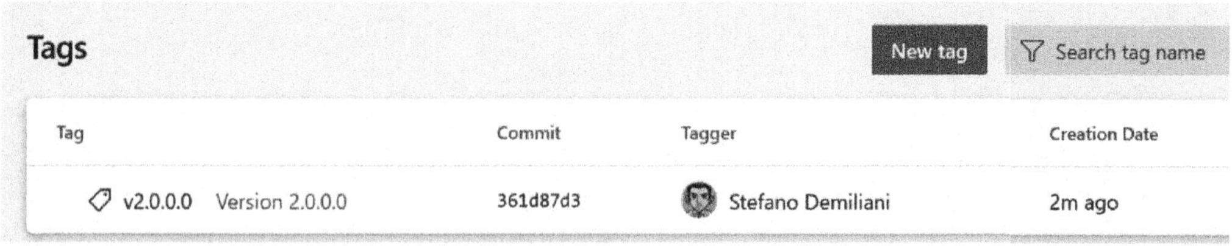

Figure 3.63 – Tag applied to a branch

Summary

In this chapter, we learned how to handle source control management with Azure DevOps and why it's so important when working in teams when developing code.

We looked at the basic concepts of source control management and Git, the possible strategies to apply when merging code, how to use Azure DevOps to apply SCM, and how to handle repositories, commits, branches, and pull requests from Azure DevOps and development tools such as Visual Studio Code and Visual Studio. We also learned how to apply better policies to control the source code releases in order to improve the SCM life cycle, how to protect branches and how to use tags for a branch.

In the next chapter, we'll learn how to create build pipelines with Azure DevOps for implementing CI/CD practices.

4

Understanding Azure DevOps Pipelines

When adopting **Azure DevOps** in your organization, one of the main important decisions you must make is how to define the **pipeline** of your development process. A pipeline is a company-defined model that describes the steps and actions that a code base must support, from building to the final release phase. It's a key part of any DevOps architecture.

In this chapter, we'll learn how to define and use pipelines with Azure DevOps for building code.

We will cover the following topics:

- Implementing a CI/CD process
- An overview of Azure Pipelines
- Creating and using build agents
- Overview of the YAML format
- Creating a CI/CD pipeline with Azure DevOps

- Retention of builds
- Multi-stage pipeline
- Build pipeline with GitHub repositories
- Using container jobs in Azure Pipelines
- Let's get started!

Technical requirements

To follow this chapter, you need to have the following:

- A valid organization in Azure DevOps
- An Azure subscription where you can create an Azure VM or a local machine on one of these environments so that you can install the build agent software
- Visual Studio or Visual Studio Code as your development environment
- Access to the following GitHub repository for cloning the project: `https://github.com/Microsoft/PartsUnlimited`

Implementing a CI/CD process

When adopting DevOps in a company, implementing the right DevOps tools with the right DevOps processes is essential and crucial. One of the fundamental flows in a DevOps implementation is the **continuous integration** (**CI**) and **continuous delivery** (**CD**) process, which can help developers build, test, and distribute a code base in a quicker, structured, and safer way.

CI is a software engineering practice where developers in a team integrate code modifications in a central repository a few times in a day. When a code modification integrated into a particular branch (normally with a pull request, as explained in the previous chapter), a new build is triggered in order to check the code and detect integration bugs quickly. Also, automatic tests (if available) are executed during this phase to check for breakages.

CD is the process that comes after the CI process. In this process, the output of the CI phase is packaged and delivered to the production stage without bugs. This is extremely helpful so that we always have a master branch that is tested, consistent, and ready to be deployed.

In DevOps, you can also have a **continuous deployment** process in place, where you can automate the deployment of your code modifications to the final production environments without manual intervention.

The typical DevOps CI/CD loop is represented in the following famous "loop" diagram:

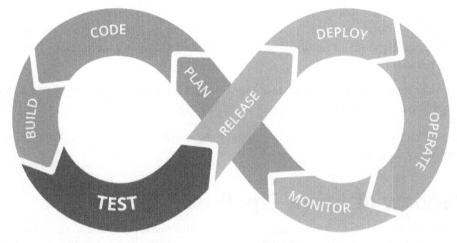

Figure 4.1 – DevOps CI/CD loop

A typical CI/CD pipeline implementation contains the following stages:

- **Commit stage**: Here, new code modifications are integrated into the code base and a set of unit tests are performed in order to check code integrity and quality.

- **Build stage**: Here, the code is automatically built and then the final results of the build process (artifacts) are pushed to the final registry.

- **Test stage**: The build code will be deployed to preproduction, where the final testing will be performed and then go to production deployment. Here, the code is tested by adopting alpha and beta deployments. The alpha deployment stage is where developers check the performance of their new builds and the interactions between builds. In the Beta deployment stage, developers execute manual testing in order to double-check whether the application is working correctly.

- **Production deployment stage**: This is where the final application, after successfully passing all the testing requirements, goes live to the production stage.

There are lots of benefits of implementing a CI/CD process in your organizations. The main benefits are as follows:

- **Improved code quality and early bug detection**: By adopting automated tests, you can discover bugs and issues at an early stage and fix them accordingly.

- **Complete traceability**: The whole build, test, and deployment process is tracked and can be analyzed later. This guarantees that you can inspect which changes in a particular build are included and the impact that they can have on the final tests or release.

- **Faster testing and release phases**: Automating building and testing of your code base on every new commit (or before a release).

In the next section, we'll provide an overview of the service offered by the Azure platform for implementing CI/CD: Azure Pipelines.

Overview of Azure Pipelines

Azure Pipelines is a cloud service offered by the Azure platform that allows you to automate the building, testing, and releasing phases of your development life cycle (CI/CD). Azure Pipelines works with any language or platform, it's integrated in Azure DevOps, and you can build your code on Windows, Linux, or macOS machines.

Azure Pipelines is free for public projects, while for private projects, you have up to 1,800 minutes' (30 hours) worth of pipelines for free each month. More information about pricing can be found here:

```
https://azure.microsoft.com/en-us/pricing/details/devops/
azure-devops-services/
```

Some important feature of Azure Pipelines can be summarized as follows:

- It's platform and language independent, which means you can build code on every platform using the code base you want.

- It can be integrated with different types of repositories (Azure Repos, GitHub, GitHub Enterprise, BitBucket, and so on).

- Lots of extensions (standard and community-driven) are available for building your code and for handling custom tasks.

- Allows you to deploy your code to different cloud vendors.

- You can work with containerized applications such as Docker, Azure Container Registry, or Kubernetes.

To use Azure Pipelines, you need the following:

- An organization in Azure DevOps, where you can create public or private projects

- A source code stored in a version control system (such as Azure DevOps Repos or GitHub)

Azure Pipelines works with the following schema:

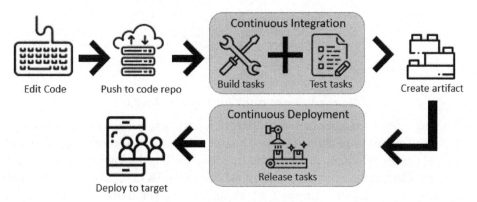

Figure 4.2 – Azure Pipelines schema

When your code is committed to a particular branch inside a repository, the **build pipeline** engine starts, build and test tasks are executed, and if all is successfully completed, your app is built and you have the final output (artifact). You can also create a **release pipeline** that takes the output of your build and releases it to the target environment (staging or production).

To start using Azure Pipelines, you need to create a **pipeline**. A pipeline in Azure DevOps can be created in the following two ways:

- **Using the Classic interface**: This allows you to select some tasks visually from a list of possible tasks. You only need to fill in the parameters for these tasks.

- **Using a scripting language called YAML**: The pipeline can be defined by creating a YAML file inside your repository with all the needed steps.

Using the classic interface can be easier initially, but remember that many features are only available on YAML pipelines. A YAML pipeline definition is a file, and this can be versioned and controlled just like any other file inside a repository. You can easily move the pipeline definition between projects (this is not possible with the Classic interface).

An Azure Pipeline can be represented as follows (courtesy of Microsoft):

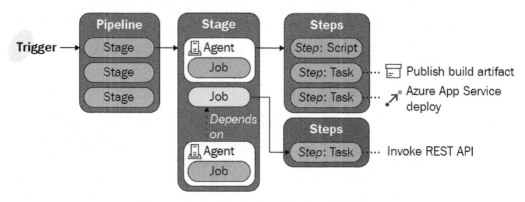

Figure 4.3 – Representation of an Azure Pipeline

A pipeline starts from a **trigger** (a manual trigger, a push inside a repository, a pull request, or a schedule). A pipeline is normally composed of one or more **stages** (logical separation of concerns in a pipeline, such as building, testing, deployment, and so on; they can run in parallel), and each stage contains one or more **jobs** (a set of steps that can also run in parallel). Every pipeline contains at least one stage if you don't explicitly create it. Each job runs on an **agent** (service or piece of software that executes the job). Every step is composed of a **task** that performs some action on your code (sequentially). The final output of a pipeline is an **artifact** (collection of files or packages published by the build).

When creating a pipeline, you need to define a set of jobs and tasks for automating your builds (or multi-phased builds). You have native support for testing integration, release gates, automatic reporting, and so on.

When defining multiple jobs within a pipeline, these jobs are executed in parallel. A pipeline that contains multiple jobs is called a **fan-out** scenario:

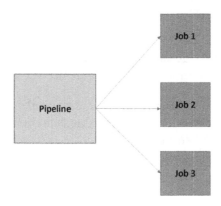

Figure 4.4 – Fan-out pipeline

A pipeline with multiple jobs in a single stage can be represented as follows:

```
pool:
  vmImage: 'ubuntu-latest'
jobs:
- job: job1
  steps:
  - bash: echo "Hello!"
  - bash: echo "I'm job 1"
- job: job2
  steps:
  - bash: echo "Hello again…"
  - bash: echo "I'm job 2"
```

If you're using stages when defining your pipeline, this is what is called a fan-out/fan-in scenario:

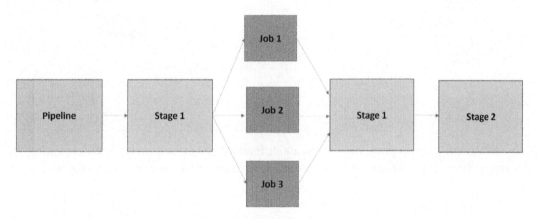

Figure 4.5 – Fan-out pipeline

Here, each stage is a fan-in operation, where all the jobs in the stage (which can consist of multiple tasks that run in sequence) must be finished before the next stage can be triggered (only one stage can be executing at a time). We'll talk about multi-stage pipelines later in this chapter.

Understanding build agents

To build and deploy your code using Azure Pipelines, you need at least one agent. An agent is a service that runs the jobs defined in your pipeline. The execution of these jobs can occur directly on the agent's host machine or in containers.

When defining agents for your pipeline, you have essentially two types of possible agents:

- **Microsoft-hosted agents**: This is a service totally managed by Microsoft and it's cleared on every execution of the pipeline (on each pipeline execution, you have a fresh new environment).

- **Self-hosted agents**: This is a service that you need to set up and manage by yourself. This can be a custom virtual machine on Azure or a custom on-premise machine inside your infrastructure. In a self-hosted agent, you can install all the software you need for your builds, and this is persisted on every pipeline execution. A self-hosted agent can be on Windows, Linux, macOS, or in a Docker container.

Microsoft-hosted agents

Microsoft-hosted agents is the simplest way to define an agent for your pipeline. Azure Pipelines provides a Microsoft-hosed agent pool by default called **Azure Pipelines**:

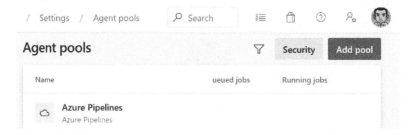

Figure 4.6 – Azure Pipelines default agent pool

By selecting this agent pool, you can create different virtual machine types for executing your pipeline. At the time of writing, the available standard agent types are as follows:

Image	Classic Editor Agent Specification	YAML VM Image Label
Windows Server 2019 with Visual Studio 2019	windows-2019	windows-latest OR windows-2019
Windows Server 2016 with Visual Studio 2017	vs2017-win2016	vs2017-win2016
Ubuntu 18.04	ubuntu-18.04	ubuntu-latest OR ubuntu-18.04
Ubuntu 16.04	ubuntu-16.04	ubuntu-16.04
macOS X Mojave 10.14	macOS-10.14	macOS-10.14
macOS X Catalina 10.15	macOS-10.15	macOS-latest OR macOS-10.15

Table 1.1

Each of these images has its own set of software automatically installed. You can install additional tools by using the pre-defined Tool Installer task in your pipeline definition. More information can be found here:

```
https://docs.microsoft.com/en-us/azure/devops/pipelines/
tasks/?view=azure-devops#tool.
```

When you create a pipeline using a Microsoft-hosted agent, you just need to specify the name of the virtual machine image to use for your agent from the preceding table. As an example, this is the definition of a hosted agent that's using Windows Server 2019 with a Visual Studio 2019 image:

```
- job: Windows
  pool:
    vmImage: 'windows-latest'
```

When using a Microsoft-hosted agent, you need to remember the following:

- You cannot sign in on the agent machine.

- The agent runs on a Standard DS2v2 Azure Virtual Machine and you cannot increase that capacity.

- It runs as an administrator user on the Windows platform and as a *passwordless sudo* user on the Linux platform.

- For public projects, you have 10 free Microsoft-hosted parallel jobs that can run for up to 360 minutes each time, with no overall time limit per month.

- For private projects, you have one free parallel job that can run for up to 60 minutes each time, with the maximum being 1,800 minutes (30 hours) per month. If you need more capacity, you can pay for additional parallel jobs. By doing this, you can run each job for up to 360 minutes.

- The Microsoft-hosted agent runs in the same Azure geography as your Azure DevOps organization, but it's not guaranteed that it will run in the same region too (an Azure geography contains one or more regions).

Self-hosted agents

While Microsoft-hosted agents are a SaaS service, self-hosted agents are private agents that you can configure as per your needs by using Azure virtual machines or directly using your on-premise infrastructure. You are responsible for providing all the necessary software and tools to execute your pipeline and you're responsible for maintaining and upgrading your agent.

A self-hosted agent can be installed on the following platforms:

- Windows
- Linux
- macOS
- Docker

Creating a self-hosted agent involves completing the following activities:

- Prepare the environment
- Prepare permissions on Azure DevOps
- Download and configure the agent
- Start the agent

These steps are similar for all the environments. Next, we'll learn how to create a self-hosted Windows agent.

Creating a self-hosted Windows agent

A self-hosted Windows agent is used to build and deploy applications built on top of Microsoft's platforms (such as .NET applications, Azure cloud apps, and so on) but also for other types of platforms, such as Java and Android apps.

The first step to perform when creating an agent is to register the agent in your Azure DevOps organization. To do so, you need to sign into your DevOps organization as an administrator and from the **User Settings** menu, click on **Personal access tokens**:

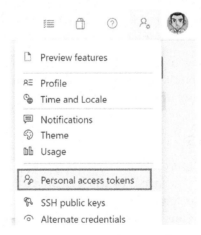

Figure 4.7 – Personal access tokens

Here, you can create a new personal access token for your organization with an expiration date and with full access or with a custom defined access level (if you select the custom defined scope, you need to select the permission you want for each scope). To see the complete list of available scopes, click on the **Show all scopes** link at the bottom of this window:

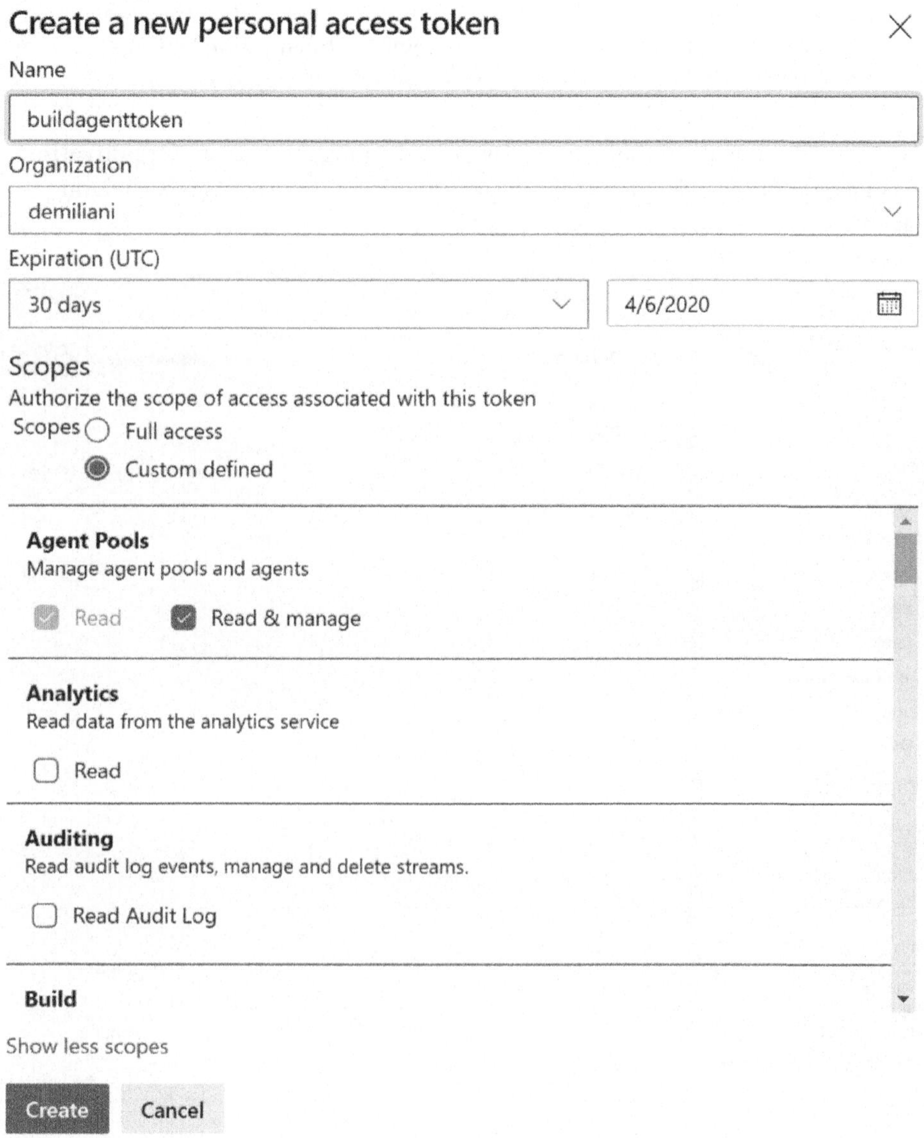

Create a new personal access token   ✕

Name

buildagenttoken

Organization

demiliani   ⌄

Expiration (UTC)

| 30 days   ⌄ | 4/6/2020   🗓 |

Scopes

Authorize the scope of access associated with this token

Scopes ◯ Full access

◉ Custom defined

Agent Pools
Manage agent pools and agents

☑ Read   ☑ Read & manage

Analytics
Read data from the analytics service

☐ Read

Auditing
Read audit log events, manage and delete streams.

☐ Read Audit Log

Build

Show less scopes

Create   Cancel

Figure 4.8 – Create a new personal access token

Please check that the **Agent Pools** scope has the **Read & manage** permission enabled.

When finished, click on **Create** and then copy the generated token before closing the window (it will only be shown once).

> **Important Note**
>
> The user that you will be using for the agent must be a user with permissions to register the agent. You can check this by going to **Organization Settings | Agent pools**, selecting the **Default** pool, and clicking on **Security**.

Now, you need to download the agent software and configure it. From **Organization Settings | Agent Pools**, select the **Default** pool and from the **Agents** tab, click on **New agent**:

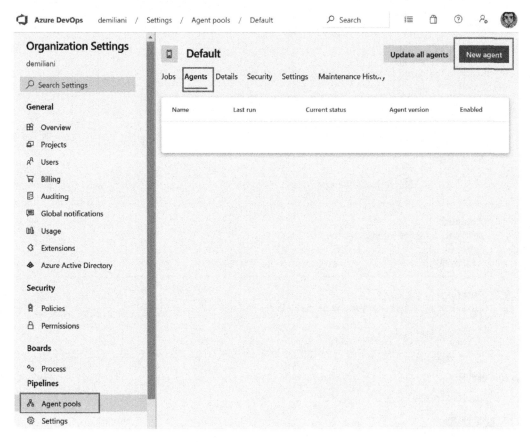

Figure 4.9 – Creating a new agent

The **Get the agent** window will open. Select **Windows** as the target platform, select **x64** or **x86** as your target agent platform (machine) accordingly, and then click on the **Download** button:

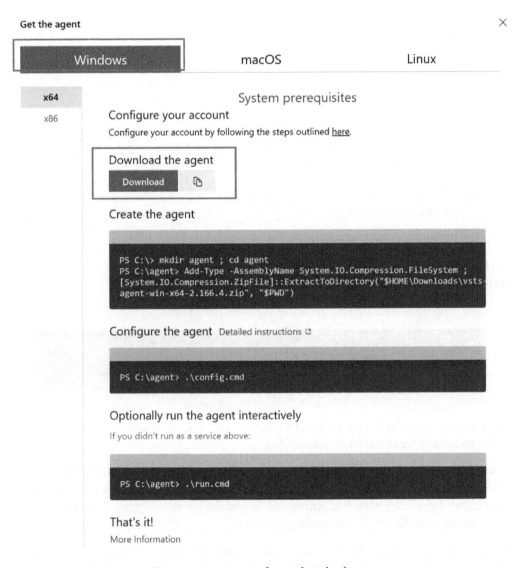

Figure 4.10 – Agent software download page

This procedure will download a package (normally called `vsts-agent-win-x64-2.166.4.zip`). You need to run this package (`config.cmd`) on the agent machine (an Azure VM or your on-premise server, which will act as an agent for your builds):

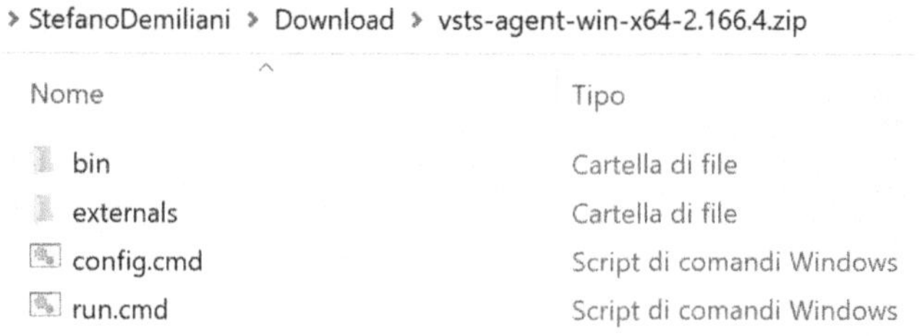

Figure 4.11 – Agent software package

The setup will ask you for the following:

- The URL of your Azure DevOps organization (`https://dev.azure.com/ {your-organization}`)

- The personal access token to use (created previously)

When running the agent (interactively or as a service), it's recommended to run it as a service if you want to automate builds.

After inserting these parameters, the setup registers the agent:

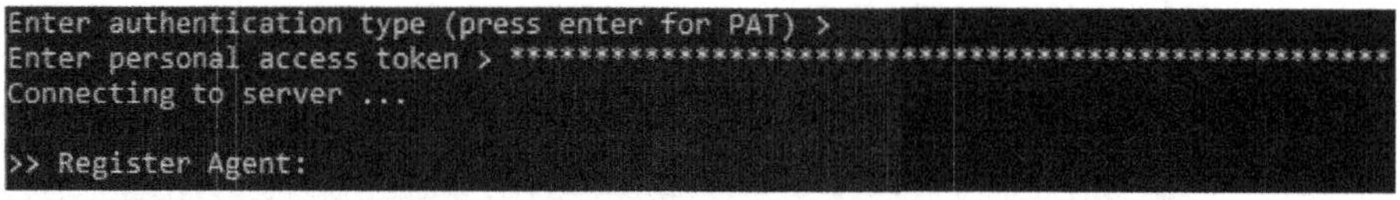

Figure 4.12 – Agent registration

To register the agent, you need to insert the agent pool, the agent name, and the work folder (you can leave the default value as-is).

Finally, you need to decide whether your agent must be executed *interactively* or *as a service*. As we mentioned previously, running the agent as a service is recommended, but in many cases, the interactive option can be helpful because it gives you a console where you can see the status and running UI tests.

In both cases, please be aware of the user account you select for running the agent. The default account is the built-in Network Service user, but this user normally doesn't have all the needed permissions on local folders. Using an administrator account can help you solve a lot of problems.

If the setup has been completed successfully, you should see a service running on your agent machine and a new agent that pops up on your agent pool in Azure DevOps:

4.13 – New agent created

If you select the agent and then go to the **Capabilities** section, you will be able to see all its capabilities (OS version, OS architecture, computer name, software installed, and so on):

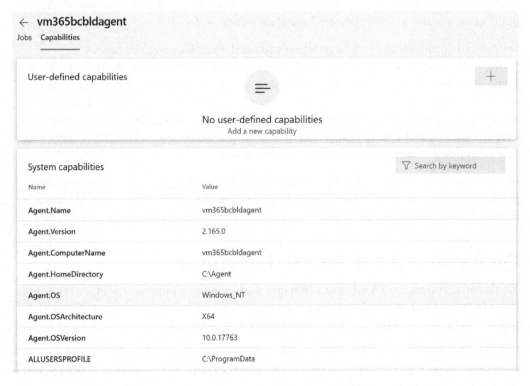

Figure 4.14 – Agent capabilities

The agent's capabilities can be automatically discovered by the agent software or added by you (user-defined capabilities) if you click on the **Add a new capability** action. Capabilities are used by the pipeline engine to redirect a particular build to the correct agent according to the required capabilities for the pipeline (demands).

When the agent is online, it's ready to accept your code build, which should be queued.

Remember that you can also install multiple agents on the same machine (for example, if you want the possibility to execute core pipelines or handle jobs in parallel), but this scenario is only recommended if the agents will not share resources.

When to use a Microsoft-hosted or a self-hosted agent

Microsoft-hosted agents are normally useful when you have a standard code base and you don't need particular software or environment configuration to build your code. If you're in this scenario, using a Microsoft-hosted agent is recommended because you don't have to worry about creating environments. As an example, if you need to build an Azure Function project, normally, you don't have the need to install custom software on the build agent and the Microsoft-hosted agent can work perfectly.

Self-hosted agents are the way to go when you need a particular environment configuration, when you need a particular piece of software or tools installed on the agent, and when you need more power for your builds. Self-hosted agents are also the way to go when you need to preserve the environment between each run of your builds. A self-hosted agent is normally the right choice when you need to have better control of your agent or you wish to deploy your build to on-premise environments (not accessible externally). It also normally allows you to save money.

Now that we've discussed about the possible build agents that you can use for your build pipelines, in the next section, we'll provide an overview of YAML, the scripting language that allows you to define a pipeline.

Overview of the YAML language

YAML, an acronym for **YAML Ain't Markup Language**, is a human-readable scripting language used for data serialization and normally used for handling configurations definitions for applications. It can be considered a superset of JSON.

YAML uses indentation for handling the structure of the object's definitions, and it's insensitive to quotation marks and braces. It's simply a data representation language and is not used for executing commands.

With Azure DevOps, YAML is extremely important because it allows you to define a pipeline by using a script definition instead of a graphical interface (that cannot be ported between projects).

The official YAML website can be found here:

```
http://yaml.org/
```

A YAML structure is based on key-value elements:

```
Key: Value    # This is a comment
```

In the following sections, we'll learn how to define objects in YAML.

Scalars

As an example, the following are scalar variables that have been defined in YAML:

```
Number: 1975
quotedText: "some text description"
notQuotedtext: strings can be also without quotes
boolean: true
nullKeyValue: null
```

You can also define multi-line keys by using ?, followed by a space, as follows:

```
? |
  This is a key
  that has multiple lines
: and this is its value
```

Collections and lists

This is a YAML definition for a collection object:

```
Cars:
  - Fiat
  - Mercedes
  - BMW
```

You can also define nested collections:

```
- Drivers:
    name: Stefano Demiliani
    age: 45
    Driving license type:
      - type: full car license
        license id: ABC12345
        expiry date: 2025-12-31
```

Dictionaries

You can define a `Dictionary` object by using YAML in the following way:

```
CarDetails:
    make: Mercedes
    model: GLC220
    fuel: Gasoline
```

Document structure

YAML uses three dashes, `- - -`, to separate directives from document content and to identify the start of a document. As an example, the following YAML defines two documents in a single file:

```
- - -
# Products purchased
- item     : Surface Book 2
  quantity: 1
- item     : Surface Pro 7
  quantity: 3
- item     : Arc Mouse
  quantity: 1

# Product out of stock
- - -
- item     : Surface 4
- item     : Microsoft Trackball
```

Complex object definition

As an example of how to define a complex object in YAML, the following is the representation used for an `Invoice` object:

```
- - -
invoice: 20-198754
date    : 2020-05-27
bill-to: C002456
    Name    : Stefano Demiliani
```

```
      address:
          lines:
              Viale Pasubio, 21
              c/o Microsoft House
          city    : Milan
          state   : MI
          postal  : 20154
  ship-to: C002456
  product:
      - itemNo      : ITEM001
        quantity    : 1
        description : Surface Book 2
        price       : 1850.00
      - sku         : ITEM002
        quantity    : 2
        description : Arc Mouse
        price       : 65.00
  tax   : 80.50
  total: 1995.50
  comments:
      Please deliver on office hours.
      Leave on the reception.
```

Now that we've provided a quick overview of the YAML syntax, in the next section, we'll learn how to create a build pipeline with Azure DevOps.

Creating a build pipeline with Azure DevOps

Having a build pipeline in place is a fundamental step if you want to implement continuous integration for your code (having your code automatically built and tested on every commit).

The prerequisite to creating a build pipeline with Azure DevOps is obviously to have some code stored inside a repository.

To create a build pipeline with Azure DevOps, you need to go to the **Pipelines** hub and select the **Pipelines** action:

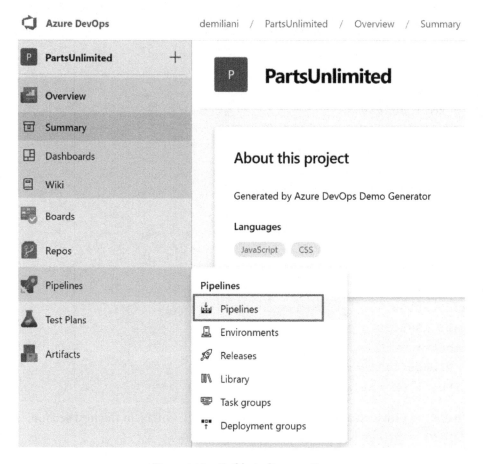

Figure 4.15 – Build pipeline creation

From here, you can create a new build pipeline by selecting the **New pipeline** button. When pressed, you will see the following screen, which asks you for a code repository:

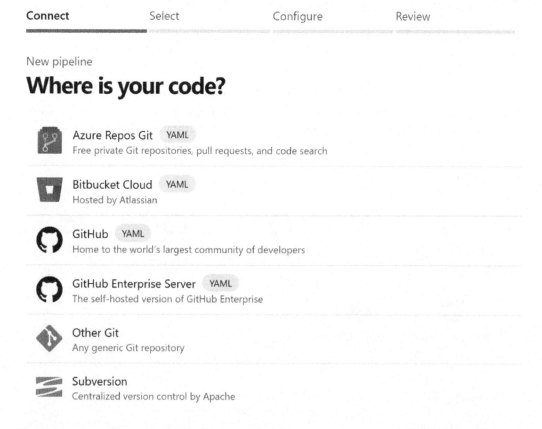

Figure 4.16 – Selecting a repository

This screen is extremely important. From here, you can start creating a build pipeline in two possible ways (described previously):

1. Using a YAML file to create your pipeline definition. This is what happens when you select the repository in this window.

2. Using the classic editor (graphical user interface). This is what happens when you click on the **Use the classic editor** link at the bottom of this page.

In the next section, we'll learn how to create a build pipeline by using these two methods.

Pipeline definition with the classic editor

The classic editor permits you to define a build pipeline for your project graphically by selecting pre-defined actions. As we mentioned previously, a pipeline definition created in this way is not under source control.

When you click on the **Use the classic editor** link, you need to select the repository where your code is stored (**Azure Repos Git, GitHub, GitHub Enterprise Server, Subversion, TFVC, Bitbucket Cloud,** or **Other Git**) and the branch that the build pipeline will be connected to:

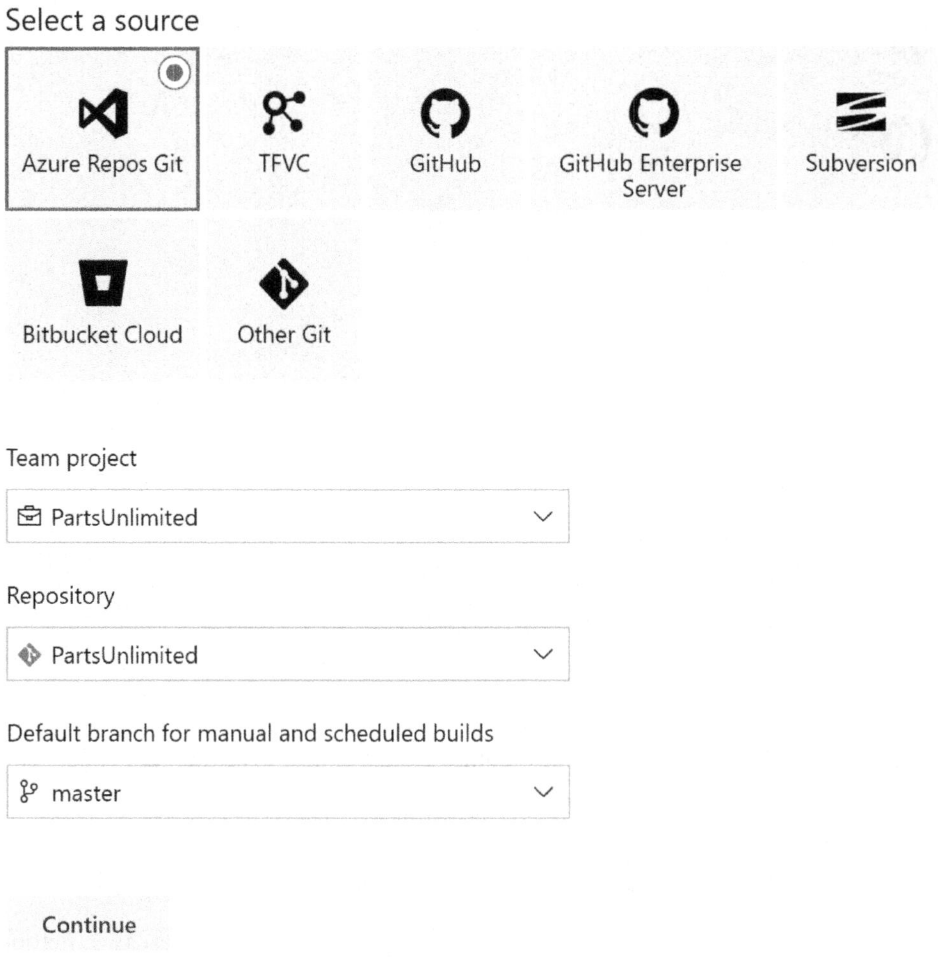

Select a source

Azure Repos Git   TFVC   GitHub   GitHub Enterprise Server   Subversion

Bitbucket Cloud   Other Git

Team project

PartsUnlimited

Repository

PartsUnlimited

Default branch for manual and scheduled builds

master

Continue

Figure 4.17 – Classic editor pipeline definition

Then, you need to choose a template for the kind of app you're building. You have a set of predefined templates to choose from (that you can customize later), but you can also start from an empty template:

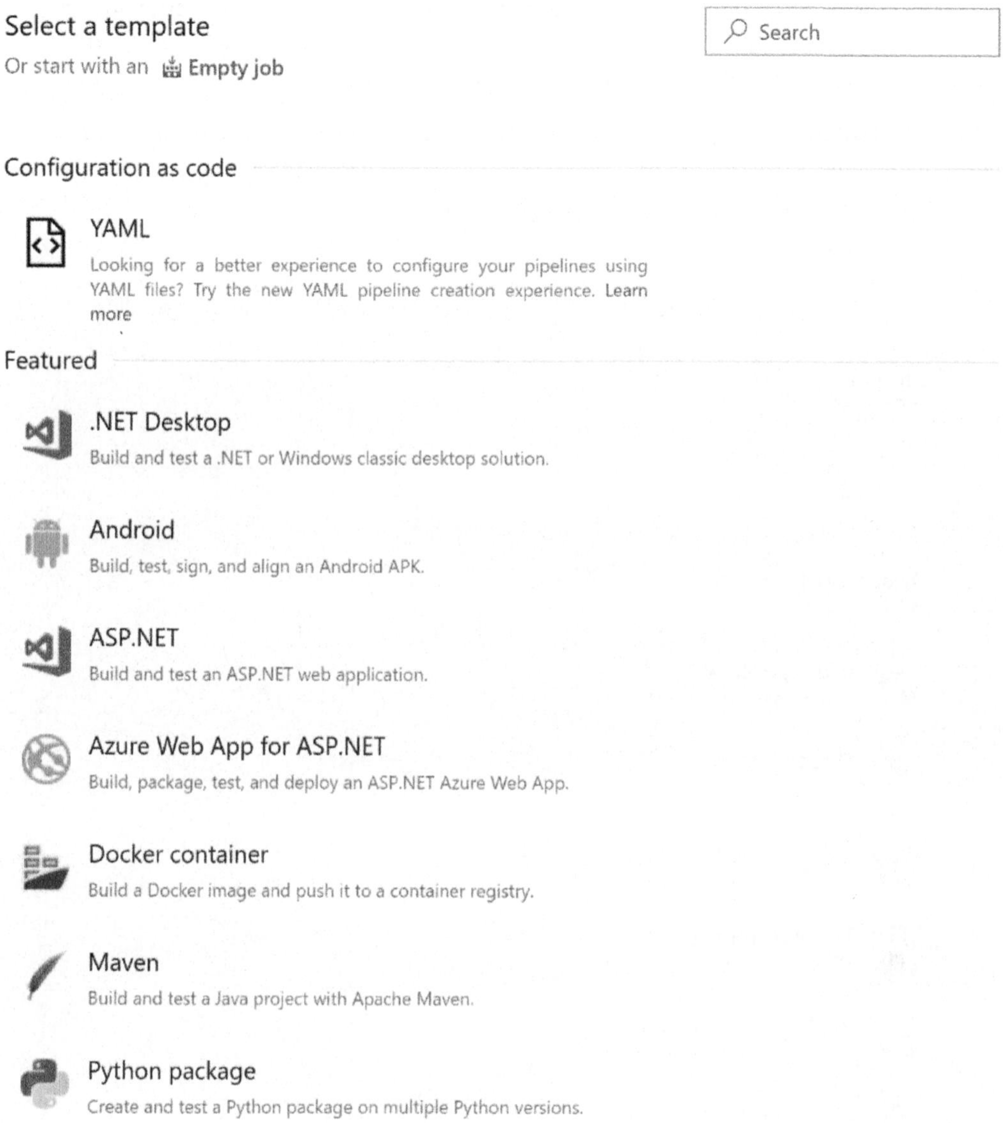

Select a template

Or start with an 🏗 Empty job

🔍 Search

Configuration as code ──────────

YAML

Looking for a better experience to configure your pipelines using YAML files? Try the new YAML pipeline creation experience. Learn more

Featured ──────────

.NET Desktop

Build and test a .NET or Windows classic desktop solution.

Android

Build, test, sign, and align an Android APK.

ASP.NET

Build and test an ASP.NET web application.

Azure Web App for ASP.NET

Build, package, test, and deploy an ASP.NET Azure Web App.

Docker container

Build a Docker image and push it to a container registry.

Maven

Build and test a Java project with Apache Maven.

Python package

Create and test a Python package on multiple Python versions.

Figure 4.18 – Pipeline template selection

If predefined templates fit your needs, you can start by using them; otherwise, it's recommended to create a custom pipeline by selecting the actions you need.

Here, my application that's stored in the Azure DevOps project repository is an ASP.NET web application (an e-commerce website project called PartsUnlimited; you can find the public repository at the following URL: https://github.com/Microsoft/PartsUnlimited), so I've selected the ASP.NET template.

When selected, this is the pipeline template that will be created for you automatically:

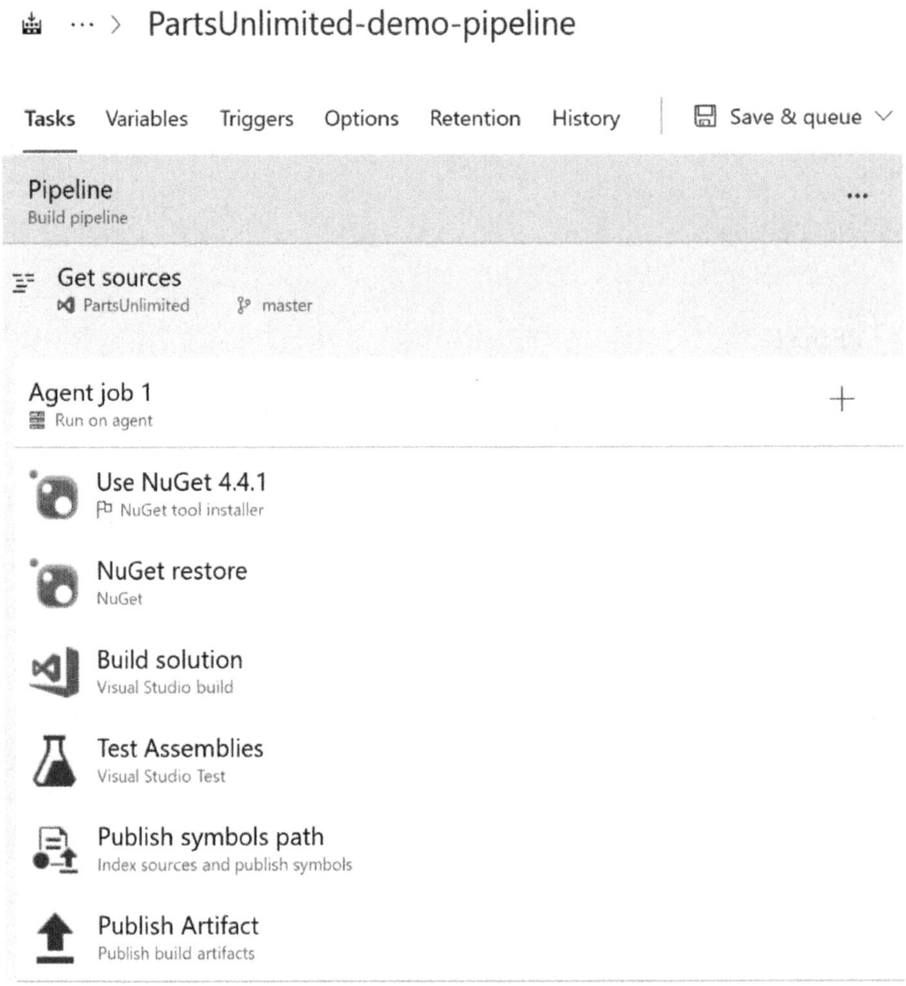

Figure 4.19 – Pipeline created from a template

Let's check every section of the pipeline in detail.

The pipeline (here, this is called `PartsUnlimited-demo-pipeline`) runs on a Microsoft-hosted agent (Azure Pipelines agent pool) based on the **vs2017-win2016** template (Windows Server 2016 with Visual Studio 2017), as shown in the following screenshot:

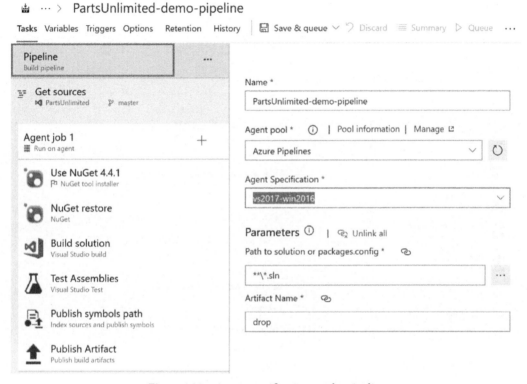

Figure 4.20 – Agent specification on the pipeline

The agent job starts by installing the NuGet package manager and restoring the required packages for building the project in the selected repository. For these actions, the pipeline definition contains the tasks that you can see in the following screenshot:

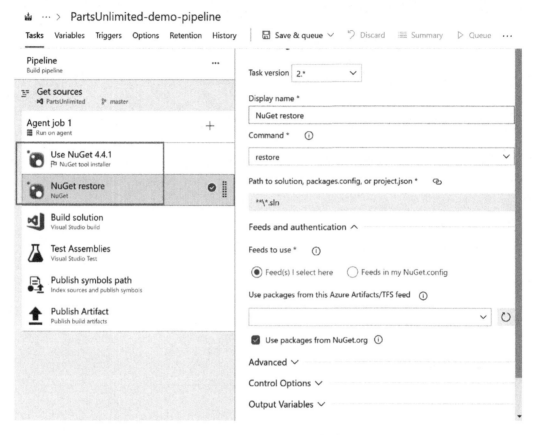

Figure 4.21 – NuGet tasks

Then, there's a task for building the solution:

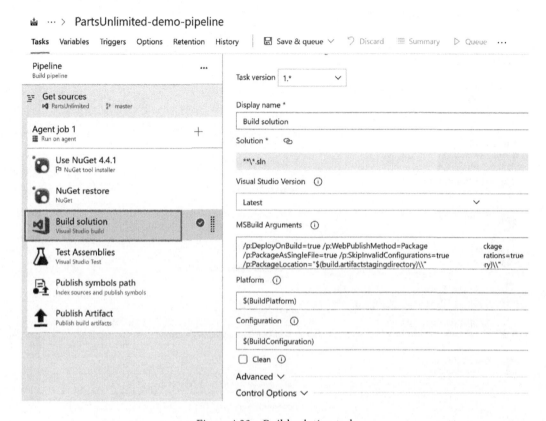

Figure 4.22 – Build solution task

There's also a task for testing the solution and publishing the test results:

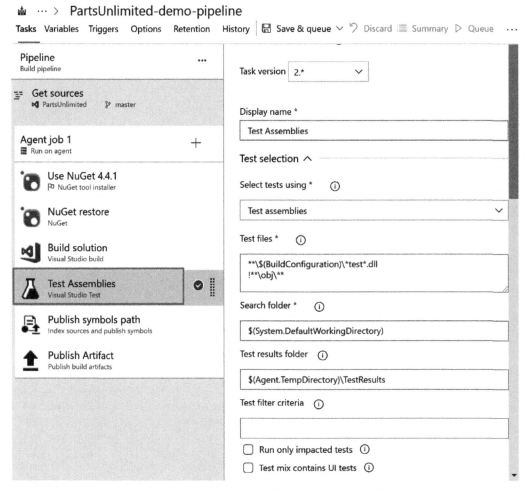

Figure 4.23 – Test Assemblies task

The last steps are for publishing the sources of the build process as artifacts (output of the build):

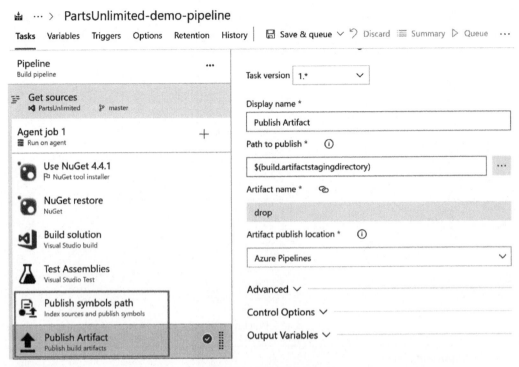

Figure 4.24 – Publishing tasks

If you select the **Variables** tab, you will see that there are some parameters that are used during the build process. Here, you can create your own variables to use inside the pipeline if needed:

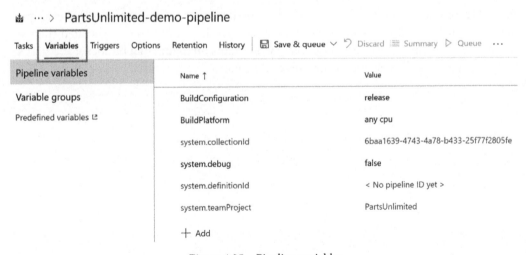

Figure 4.25 – Pipeline variables

The next section is called **Triggers**. Here, you can define what triggers start your pipeline. By default, no triggers are published initially, but here, you can enable CI to automatically start your pipeline on every commit on the selected branch:

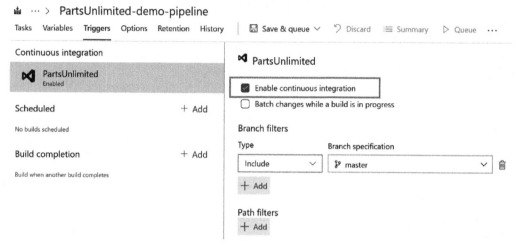

Figure 4.26 – Pipeline triggers

Important Note

Enabling CI is a recommended practice if you want every piece of code that's committed on a branch (for example, on the **master** branch) to always be tested and safely controlled. In this way, you can be assured that the code is always working as expected.

In the **Option** tab, you can set some options related to your build definition. For example, here, you can create links to all the work items so that they're linked to associated changes when a build completes successfully, create work items on failure of a build, set the status badge for your pipeline, specify timeouts, and so on:

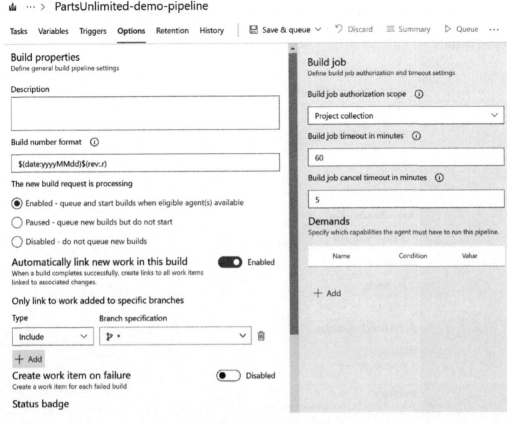

Figure 4.27 – Pipeline options

The **Retention** tab, on the other hand, is used for configuring the retention policy for this specific pipeline (how many days to keep artifacts for, the number of days to keep runs and pull requests for, and so on). Doing this will override the general retention settings. We'll talk about them later in the *Retention of builds* section.

Once you've finished defining the pipeline, you can click **Save & queue** to save your definition. By clicking on **Save and run**, the pipeline will be placed in a queue and wait for an agent:

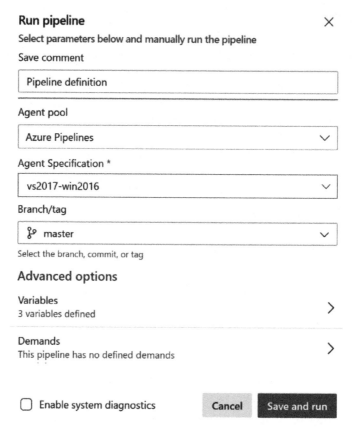

Figure 4.28 – Run pipeline

When the agent is found, the pipeline is executed and your code is built:

Figure 4.29 – Pipeline execution starting

You can follow the execution of each step of the pipeline and see the related logs. If the pipeline ends successfully, you can view a summary of its execution:

Figure 4.30 – Pipeline – final result

You can also select the **Tests** tab to review the test execution status:

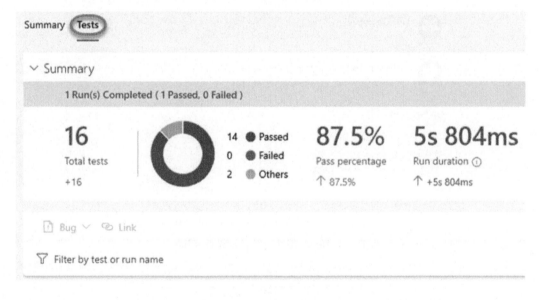

Figure 4.31 – Pipeline tests result

In the next section, we'll learn how to create a YAML pipeline for this application.

YAML pipeline definition

As previously explained, when you start creating a build pipeline with Azure DevOps, the wizard creates a YAML-based pipeline by default.

To start creating a YAML pipeline, go to the **Pipeline** section in Azure DevOps and click on **New Pipeline**.

Here, instead of selecting the classic editor (as we did in the previous section), just select the type of repository where your code is located (**Azure Repos Git**, **GitHub**, **BitBucket**, and so on):

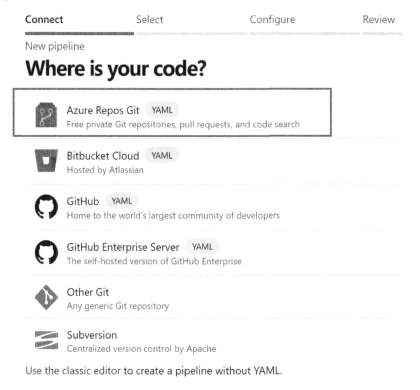

Figure 4.32 – YAML pipeline definition

Then, select your repository from the available repositories list:

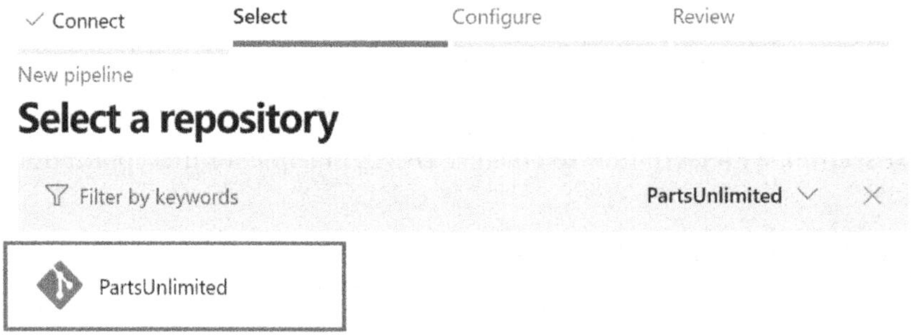

Figure 4.33 – YAML pipeline – repository selection

The system now analyzes your repository and proposes a set of available templates according to the code stored in the repository itself. You can start from a blank YAML template or you can select a template. Here, I'm selecting the ASP.NET template:

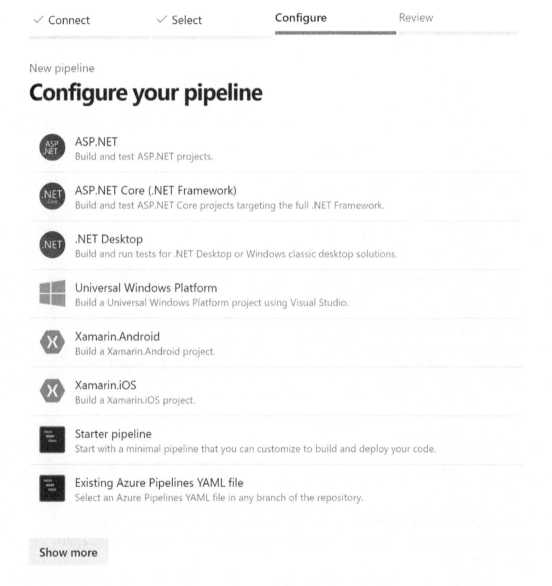

Figure 4.34 – YAML pipeline – template selection

The system creates a YAML file (called `azure-pipelines.yml`), as shown in the following screenshot:

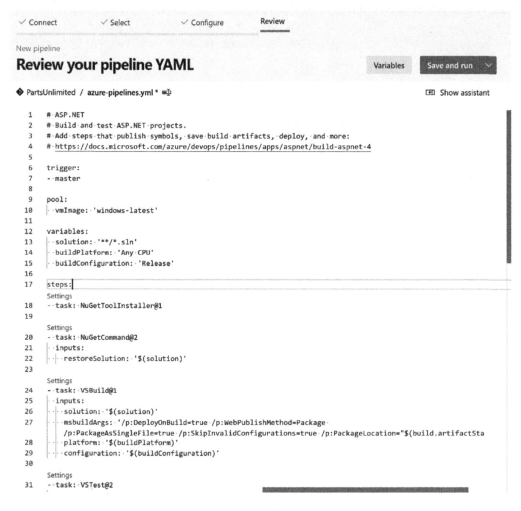

Figure 4.35 – YAML pipeline definition

The generated YAML definition contains a set of tasks, just like in the previous example, but here, these tasks are in their YAML definition. The complete generated file is as follows:

```
# ASP.NET
# Build and test ASP.NET projects.
# Add steps that publish symbols, save build artifacts,
  deploy, and more:
```

```
# https://docs.microsoft.com/azure/devops/pipelines/
apps/aspnet/build-aspnet-4

trigger:
- master

pool:
  vmImage: 'windows-latest'

variables:
  solution: '**/*.sln'
  buildPlatform: 'Any CPU'
  buildConfiguration: 'Release'

steps:
- task: NuGetToolInstaller@1

- task: NuGetCommand@2
  inputs:
    restoreSolution: '$(solution)'

- task: VSBuild@1
  inputs:
    solution: '$(solution)'
    msbuildArgs: '/p:DeployOnBuild=true /
p:WebPublishMethod=Package /p:PackageAsSingleFile=true
/p:SkipInvalidConfigurations=true /p:PackageLocation="$(build.
artifactStagingDirectory)"'
    platform: '$(buildPlatform)'
    configuration: '$(buildConfiguration)'

- task: VSTest@2
  inputs:
    platform: '$(buildPlatform)'
    configuration: '$(buildConfiguration)'
```

Here I add two more tasks for publishing the symbols and the

```
final artifacts of the pipeline:
task: PublishSymbols@2
  displayName: 'Publish symbols path'
  inputs:
    SearchPattern: '**\bin\**\*.pdb'
    PublishSymbols: false
  continueOnError: true

- task: PublishBuildArtifacts@1
  displayName: 'Publish Artifact'
  inputs:
    PathtoPublish: '$(build.artifactstagingdirectory)'
    ArtifactName: '$(Parameters.ArtifactName)'
  condition: succeededOrFailed()
```

As you can see, the YAML file contains the trigger that starts the pipeline (here, this is a commit on the master branch), the agent pool to use, the pipeline variables, and the sequence of each task to execute (with its specific parameters).

Click on Save and run as shown in the previous screenshot to queue the pipeline and have it executed. The following screenshot shows the executed YAML pipeline.

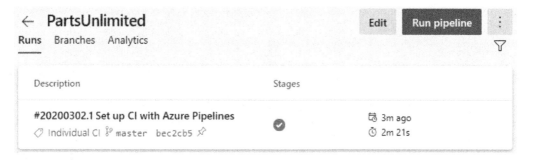

Figure 4.36 – YAML pipeline executed

To add new tasks, it's useful to use the assistant tool on the right of the editor frame. It allows you to have a **Tasks** list where you can search for a task, fill in the necessary parameters, and then have the final YAML definition:

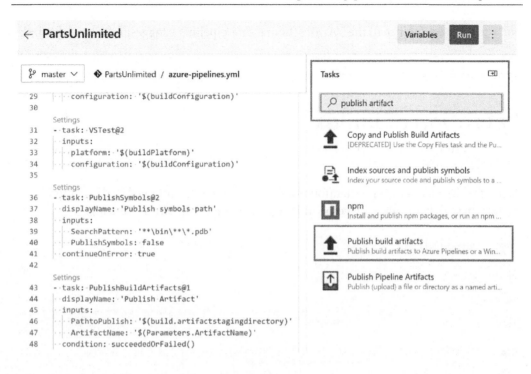

Figure 4.37 – YAML pipeline task selection

When you choose to create a pipeline with YAML, Azure DevOps creates a file that's stored in the same repository that your code is stored in:

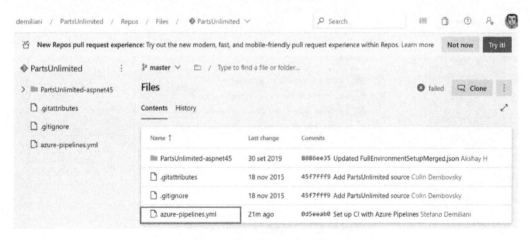

Figure 4.38 – YAML pipeline file created

This file is under source control and versioned on every modification.

For a complete reference to the YAML schema for a pipeline, I suggest following this link:

`https://docs.microsoft.com/en-us/azure/devops/pipelines/yaml-schema?view=azure-devops&tabs=schema%2Cparameter-schema`

Retention of builds

When you run a pipeline, Azure DevOps logs each step's execution and stores the final artifacts and tests for each run.

Azure DevOps has a default retention policy for pipeline execution of 30 days. You can change these default values by going to **Project settings | Pipelines | Settings**:

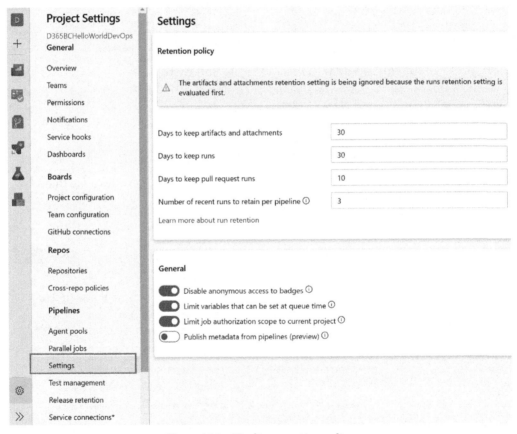

Figure 4.39 – Pipeline retention policy

You can also use the **Copy files** task to store your build and artifacts data in external storage so that you can preserve them for longer than what's specified in the retention policy:

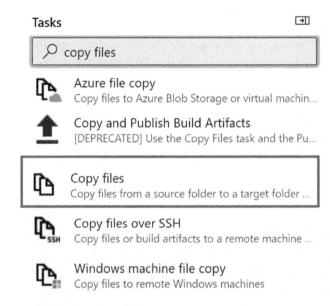

Figure 4.40 – Copy files task

The YAML definition for this task is as follows:

```yaml
- task: CopyFiles@2
  displayName: 'Copy files to shared network'
  inputs:
    SourceFolder: '$(Build.SourcesDirectory)'
    Contents: '**'
    TargetFolder: '\\networkserver\storage\$(Build.
BuildNumber)'
```

> **Important Note**
>
> Remember that any data saved as artifacts with the **Publish Build Artifacts** task is periodically deleted.

More information about the **Copy files** task can be found here:

https://docs.microsoft.com/en-us/azure/devops/pipelines/tasks/
utility/copy-files?view=azure-devops&tabs=yaml.

Multi-stage pipeline

As we explained previously, you can organize the jobs in your pipeline into `stages`. `Stages` are logical boundaries inside a pipeline flow (units of works that you can assign to an agent) that allow you to isolate the work, pause the pipeline, and execute checks or other actions. By default, every pipeline is composed of one stage, but you can create more than one and arrange those stages into a dependency graph.

The basic YAML definition of a multi-stage pipeline is as follows:

```
stages:
    - stage: Build
      jobs:
      - job: BuildJob
        steps:
        - script: echo Build!
    - stage: Test
      jobs:
      - job: TestOne
        steps:
        - script: echo Test 1
      - job: TestTwo
        steps:
        - script: echo Test 2
    - stage: Deploy
      jobs:
      - job: Deploy
        steps:
        - script: echo Deployment
```

As an example of how to create a multi-stage pipeline with YAML, let's look at a pipeline that builds code in your repository (with .NET Core SDK) and publishes the artifacts as NuGet packages. The pipeline definition is as follows. The pipeline uses the `stages` keyword to identify that this is a multi-stage pipeline.

In the first stage definition (`Build`), we have the tasks for building the code:

```
trigger:
    - master
    stages:
```

```
    - stage: 'Build'
      variables:
        buildConfiguration: 'Release'
      jobs:
      - job:
        pool:
          vmImage: 'ubuntu-latest'
        workspace:
          clean: all
        steps:
        - task: UseDotNet@2
          displayName: 'Use .NET Core SDK'
          inputs:
            packageType: sdk
            version: 2.2.x
            installationPath: $(Agent.ToolsDirectory)/dotnet

        - task: DotNetCoreCLI@2
          displayName: "NuGet Restore"
          inputs:
            command: restore
            projects: '**/*.csproj'

        - task: DotNetCoreCLI@2
          displayName: "Build Solution"
          inputs:
            command: build
            projects: '**/*.csproj'
            arguments: '--configuration (buildConfiguration)'
```

Here, we installed the .NET Core SDK by using the **UseDotnet** standard task template that's available in Azure DevOps (more information can be found here: https://docs. microsoft.com/en-us/azure/devops/pipelines/tasks/tool/dotnet- core-tool-installer?view=azure-devops). After that, we restored the required NuGet packages and built the solution.

Now, we have the task of creating the release version of the NuGet package. This package is saved in the packages/release folder of the artifact staging directory. Here, we will use `nobuild = true` because in this task, we do not have to rebuild the solution again (no more compilation):

```
- task: DotNetCoreCLI@2
  displayName: 'Create NuGet Package - Release Version'
  inputs:
    command: pack
    packDirectory: '$(Build.ArtifactStagingDirectory)/
packages/releases'
    arguments: '--configuration $(buildConfiguration)'
    nobuild: true
```

As the next step, we have the task of creating the prerelease version of the NuGet package. In this task, we're using the `buildProperties` option to add the build number to the package version (for example, if the package version is 2.0.0.0 and the build number is 20200521.1, the package version will be 2.0.0.0.20200521.1). Here, a build of the package is mandatory (for retrieving the build ID):

```
- task: DotNetCoreCLI@2
  displayName: 'Create NuGet Package - Prerelease Version'
  inputs:
    command: pack
    buildProperties: 'VersionSuffix="$(Build.BuildNumber)"'
    packDirectory: '$(Build.ArtifactStagingDirectory)/
packages/prereleases'
    arguments: '--configuration $(buildConfiguration)'
```

The next task publishes the package as an artifact:

```
- publish: '$(Build.ArtifactStagingDirectory)/packages'
  artifact: 'packages'
```

Next, we need to define the second stage, called `PublishPrereleaseNuGetPackage`. Here, we skip the checkout of the repository and the download step downloads the `packages` artifact that we published in the previous build stage. Then, the `NuGetCommand` task publishes the prerelease package to an internal feed in Azure DevOps called `Test`:

```yaml
- stage: 'PublishPrereleaseNuGetPackage'
  displayName: 'Publish Prerelease NuGet Package'
  dependsOn: 'Build'
  condition: succeeded()
  jobs:
  - job:
    pool:
      vmImage: 'ubuntu-latest'

    steps:
    - checkout: none

    - download: current
      artifact: 'packages'

    - task: NuGetCommand@2
      displayName: 'Push NuGet Package'
      inputs:
        command: 'push'
        packagesToPush: '$(Pipeline.Workspace)/packages/
prereleases/*.nupkg'
        nuGetFeedType: 'internal'
        publishVstsFeed: 'Test'
```

Now, we have to define the third stage, called `PublishReleaseNuGetPackage`, which creates the release version of our package for NuGet:

```
- stage: 'PublishReleaseNuGetPackage'
  displayName: 'Publish Release NuGet Package'
  dependsOn: 'PublishPrereleaseNuGetPackage'
  condition: succeeded()
  jobs:
  - deployment:
    pool:
      vmImage: 'ubuntu-latest'
    environment: 'nuget-org'
    strategy:
     runOnce:
       deploy:
         steps:
         - task: NuGetCommand@2
           displayName: 'Push NuGet Package'
           inputs:
             command: 'push'
             packagesToPush: '$(Pipeline.Workspace)/packages/
releases/*.nupkg'
             nuGetFeedType: 'external'
             publishFeedCredentials: 'NuGet'
```

This stage uses a deployment job to publish the package to the configured environment (here, this is called `nuget-org`). An environment is a collection of resources inside a pipeline.

In the `NuGetCommand` task, we specify the package to push and that the feed where we're pushing the package to is external (`nuGetFeedType`). The feed is retrieved by using the `publishFeedCredentials` property, set to the name of the service connection we created.

For this stage, we have created a new environment:

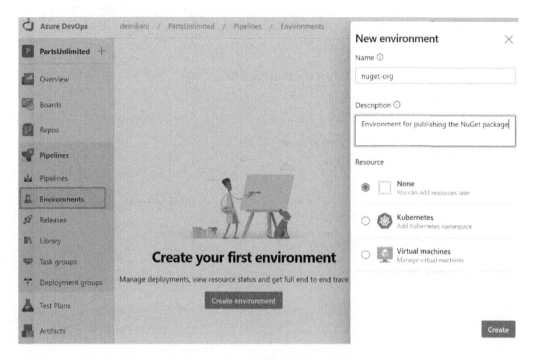

Figure 4.41 – Creating a new environment

Once the environment has been created, in order to publish it to NuGet, you need to create a new service connection by going to **Project Settings | Service Connections | Create Service Connection**, selecting **NuGet** from the list of available service connection types, and then configuring the connections according to your NuGet account:

New NuGet service connection   ✕

Authentication method

◉ ApiKey

○ External Azure DevOps Server

○ Basic Authentication

Feed URL

https://api.nuget.org/v3/index.json

URL for the feed. This will generally end with 'index.json'. For nuget.org, use
https://api.nuget.org/v3/index.json

Authentication

ApiKey

ApiKey (only for push).

Details

Service connection name

NuGet

Description (optional)

Security

☑ Grant access permission to all pipelines

Learn more

Troubleshoot   **Back**   Save

Figure 4.42 – New NuGet service connection

With that, we have created a multi-stage build pipeline. When the pipeline is executed and all the stages terminate successfully, you will see a results diagram that looks as follows:

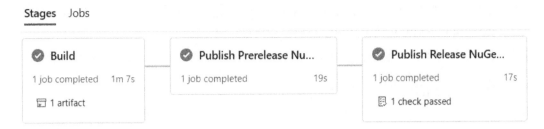

Figure 4.43 – Multi-stage build pipeline executed

Now that we have understood what a multi-stage pipeline is, we'll create some pipelines with GitHub repositories in the next section.

Building a pipeline with GitHub repositories

GitHub is one of the most popular platforms for source control management and often, it's quite common to have scenarios where the code is stored inside a GitHub repository and you want to use Azure DevOps for managing CI/CD.

By using Azure DevOps and the Azure Pipeline service, you can also create pipelines for a repository stored on GitHub, thus triggering a build pipeline on every commit in a branch inside the GitHub repository. We will do this by following these steps:

1. To use Azure Pipelines to build your GitHub repository, you need to add the **Azure DevOps** extension to your GitHub account. From your GitHub page, select the **Marketplace** link from the top bar and search for `Azure Pipelines`. Select the **Azure Pipelines** extension and click on **Set up a plan**, as shown in the following screenshot:

Figure 4.44 – Azure Pipelines on GitHub – setup

2. Select the **Free** plan, click the **Install it for free** button, and then click **Complete order and begin installation**.

3. Now, the Azure Pipelines installation will ask you if this app should be available for all your repositories or only for selected repositories. Select the desired option and click on **Install**:

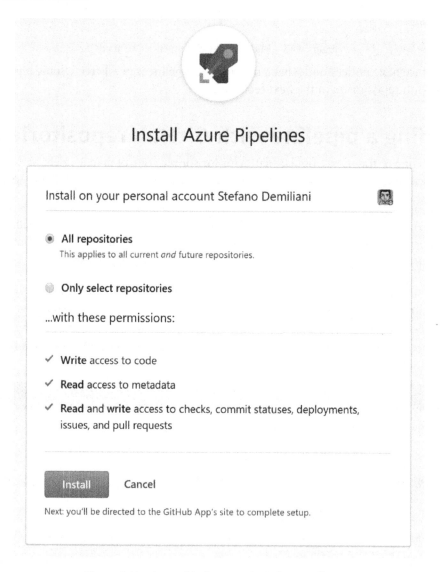

Figure 4.45 – Azure Pipelines on GitHub – installation

4. You will now be redirected to Azure DevOps, where you can create a new project (or select an existing one) for handling the build process. Here, I'm going to create a new project:

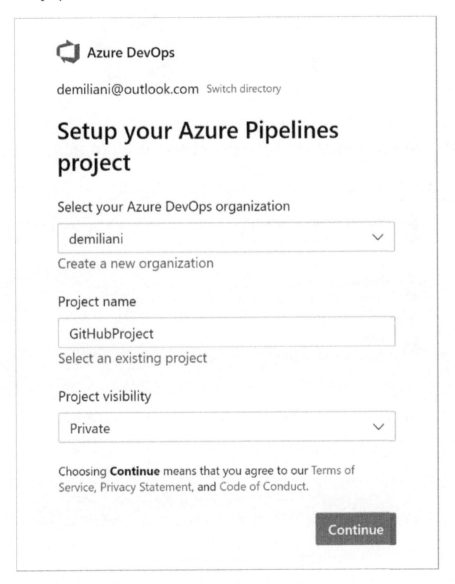

Figure 4.46 – Setting up your Azure Pipelines project

5.   Now, you need to authorize Azure Pipelines so that it can access your GitHub account:

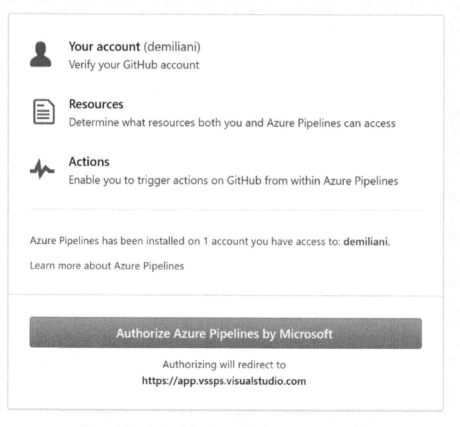

Figure 4.47 – Authorizing Azure Pipelines to access GitHub

When the necessary authorization is given, the project will be created for you on Azure DevOps and the pipeline creation process will start. You'll be immediately prompted to select a GitHub repository for the build from the list of available GitHub repositories in your account:

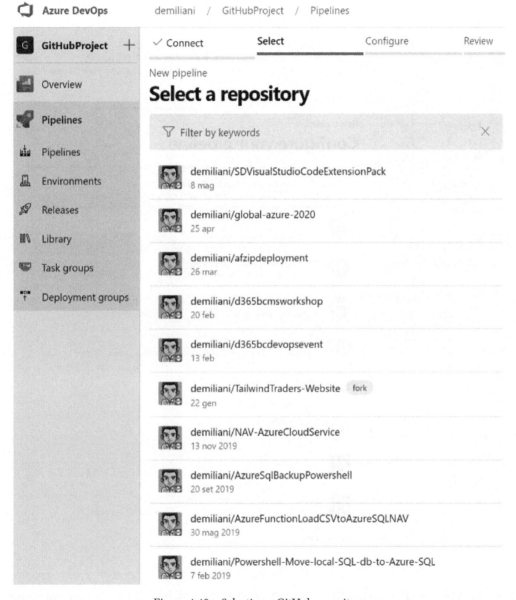

Figure 4.48 – Selecting a GitHub repository

6. Here, I'm selecting a repository where I have an Azure Function project. As you can see, Azure Pipelines has recognized my project and proposed a set of available templates for the pipeline (but you can also start from a blank template or from a YAML file that you have in any branch of the repository). Here, I will select **.NET Core Function App to Windows on Azure**:

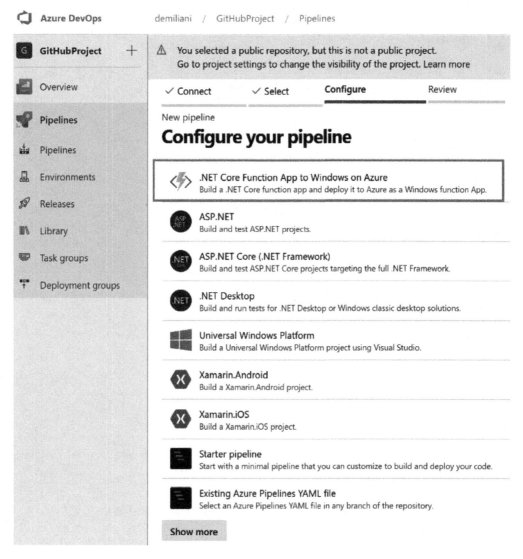

Figure 4.49 – Configuring the pipeline

A multi-stage YAML pipeline (Build and Deploy stages) will be created for you and saved as a YAML file (`azure-pipelines.yml`) inside your GitHub repository:

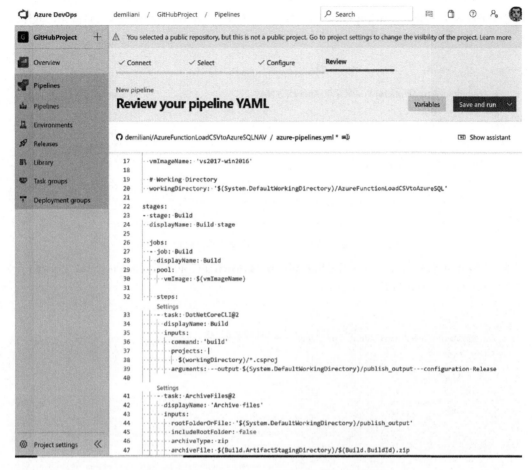

Figure 4.50 – multi.stage YAML pipeline definition

This pipeline is triggered on every commit on the master branch.

7. Click the **Save and run** button. Here, the pipeline will be queued and waiting for an agent, then executed.

Every time you commit code inside your GitHub repository, the build pipeline on Azure DevOps will be triggered automatically.

If you're building a public repository on GitHub, it's quite useful to show all your users that the code inside this repository has been checked and tested with a build pipeline. Then, you can show the result of the build. You can do that by placing a badge in your repository.

A badge is a dynamically generated image that reflects the status of a build (never built, success, or fail) and it's hosted on Azure DevOps.

8. To do so, select your pipeline in Azure DevOps, click on the three dots on the right, and select **Status badge**:

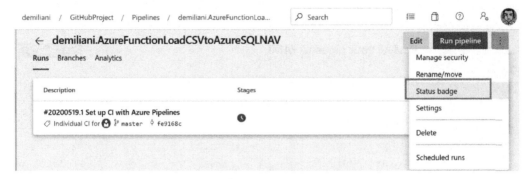

Figure 4.51 – Status badge definition

9. From here, you can copy the **Sample markdown** string and place it in the Readme. md file on your GitHub repository:

Figure 4.52 – Build status badge markdown

Every time a user accesses your repository, they will be able to see the status of the latest build via a graphical badge:

Status badge

Figure 4.53 – Build pipeline Status badge

Next, let's look at how to execute jobs in parallel.

Executing jobs in parallel in an Azure Pipeline

Within an Azure Pipeline, you can also execute jobs in parallel. Each job can be independent of other jobs and can also be executed on a different agent. This will allow you to speed up your build time and improve your pipeline's performance.

As an example of how to handle parallel jobs in a pipeline, consider a simple pipeline where you have to execute three PowerShell scripts called **Task 1**, **Task 2**, and **Final Task**. **Task 1** and **Task 2** can be executed in parallel, while **Final Task** can only be executed when the previous two tasks are completed.

When you start creating a new pipeline (I'm using the classic editor here for simplicity), Azure DevOps creates an agent job (here, this is called **Agent Job 1**). You can add your task to this agent. By selecting the agent job, you can specify the agent pool where this task runs. Here, I want this task to be executed on a Microsoft-hosted agent pool:

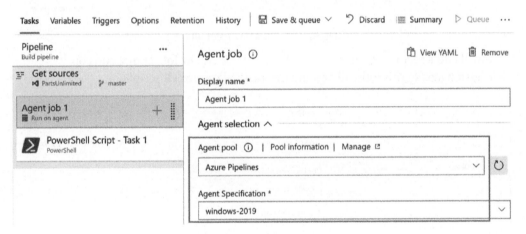

Figure 4.54 – Agent specification

Then, to add a new agent pool to your pipeline (for executing the other task independently), click the three dots beside the pipeline and select **Add an agent job**:

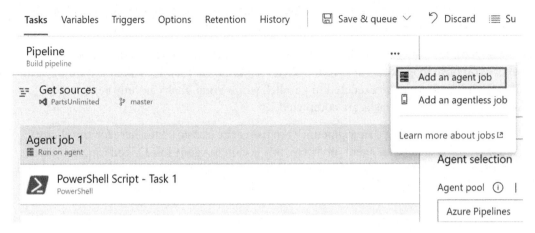

Figure 4.55 – Add an agent job

Now, we'll add a second agent job (here, this is called **Agent job 2**) that runs on a self-hosted agent. This job will execute the **Task 2** PowerShell script:

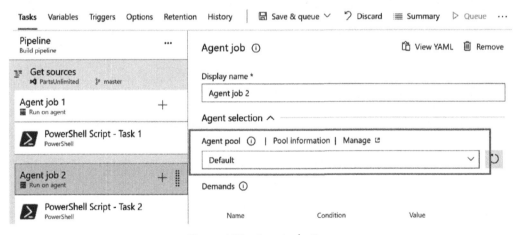

Figure 4.56 – Agent selection

Finally, we'll add a new agent job (here, this is called **Agent Job 3**) to execute the **Final Task** that will run on a Microsoft-hosted agent. However, this job has dependencies from **Agent Job 1** and **Agent Job 2**:

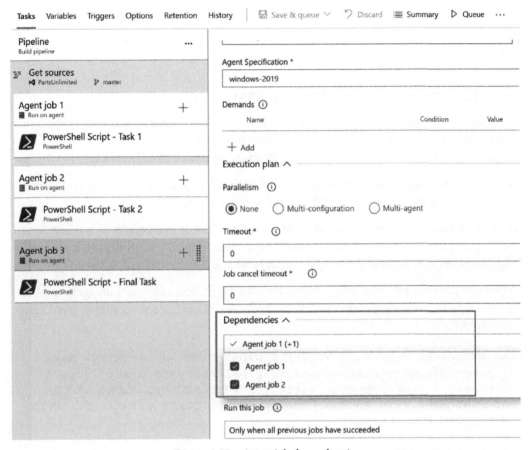

Figure 4.57 – Agent job dependencies

In this way, the first two tasks start in parallel and the final job will wait until the two previous tasks are executed.

For more information about parallel jobs in an Azure pipeline, I recommend that you check out this page:

`https://docs.microsoft.com/en-us/azure/devops/pipelines/process/phases?view=azure-devops&tabs=yaml`

Agents on Azure Container Instances

If standard Microsoft-hosted agents don't fit your needs (requirements, performance, and so on), there's also the possibility to create a self-hosted agent for Azure DevOps that runs inside a Docker container on the **Azure Container Instances** (**ACI**) service.

You can create a build agent running on Azure Container Instances by using a custom image or by reusing one of Microsoft's available images.pipe

To create a build agent running on ACI, you need to create a **personal access token** for your Azure DevOps organization. To do so, from your Azure DevOps organization home page, open the user settings (top-right corner) and select **Personal access tokens**.

When you have the personal access token for your agent, you can create an agent on ACI by executing the following command from the Azure CLI (after connecting to your Azure subscription):

```
az container create -g RESOURCE_GROUP_NAME -n CONTAINER_NAME
--image mcr.microsoft.com/azure-pipelines/vsts-agent --cpu 1
--memory 7 --environment-variables VSTS_ACCOUNT=AZURE_DEVOPS_
ACCOUNT_NAME VSTS_TOKEN=PERSONAL_ACCESS_TOKEN VSTS_AGENT=AGENT_
NAME VSTS_POOL=Default
```

Here, we have the following:

- `RESOURCE_GROUP_NAME` is the name of your resource group in Azure where this resource will be created.

- `CONTAINER_NAME` is the name of the ACI container.

- `AZURE_DEVOPS_ACCOUNT_NAME` is the name of your Azure DevOps account.

- `PERSONAL_ACCESS_TOKEN` is the personal access token you created previously.

- `AGENT_NAME` is the name of the build agent that you want to create. This will be displayed on Azure DevOps.

In this command, there are also other two important parameters:

- `--image` is used to select the name of the Azure Pipelines image for creating your agent, as described here: `https://hub.docker.com/_/microsoft-azure-pipelines-vsts-agent`.

- `VSTS_POOL` is used to select the agent pool for your build agent.

Remember that you can start and stop an ACI instance by using the `az container stop` and `az container start` commands. This can help you save money.

Using container jobs in Azure Pipelines

In this chapter, we saw that when you create a pipeline, you define jobs, and that when the pipeline is executed, these jobs runs on the host machine where the agent is installed.

If you're using Windows or Linux agents, you can also run a job inside a container (in an isolated way from the host). To run a job inside a container, you need to have Docker installed on the agent and your pipeline must have permission to access the Docker daemon. If you're using Microsoft-hosted agents, running jobs in containers is actually supported on the `windows-2019` and `ubuntu-16.04` pool images.

As an example, this is a YAML definition for using a container job in a Windows pipeline:

```yaml
pool:
  vmImage: 'windows-2019'


container: mcr.microsoft.com/windows/servercore:ltsc2019


steps:
- script: date /t
  displayName: Gets the current date
- script: dir
  workingDirectory: $(Agent.BuildiDirectory)
  displayName: list the content of a folder
```

As we mentioned previously, to run a job inside a Windows container, you need to use the windows-2019 image pool. It's required that the kernel version of the host and the container match, so here, we're using the ltsc2019 tag to retrieve the container's image.

For a Linux-based pipeline, you need to use the ubuntu-16.04 image:

```
pool:
  vmImage: 'ubuntu-16.04'

container: ubuntu:16.04

steps:
- script: printenv
```

As you can see, the pipeline creates a container based on the selected image and runs the command (steps) inside that container.

Summary

In this chapter, we provided an overview of the Azure Pipelines service and we saw how to implement a CI/CD process by using Azure DevOps. We also saw how to create a pipeline for code hosted in a repository by using the graphical interface and by using YAML, as well as how to use and create build agents. We then looked at how to create a build pipeline by using the classic editor and by using a YAML definition. We also saw an example of a multi-stage pipeline and how to use Azure DevOps pipelines to build code inside a GitHub repository, before looking at how to use parallel tasks in a build pipeline to improve build performance. Finally, we learned how to create a build agent on Azure Container Instances and how to use a container's jobs.

In the next chapter, we'll learn how to execute quality tests for our code base in a build pipeline.

5
Running Quality Tests in a Build Pipeline

In the previous chapter, we introduced Azure Pipelines and learned how to implement a CI/CD process using Azure DevOps, GitHub, and containers.

In this chapter, we are going to cover how to run quality tests in a build pipeline. We will begin by explaining what the benefits of automatic testing are. Then, we will look at how to run unit tests in a build pipeline, how to perform code coverage testing, and how to view the test results. Finally, we will cover how to use Feature Flags to test code in production.

The following topics will be covered in this chapter:

- Benefits of automatic testing
- Introduction to unit testing
- Running unit tests in a build pipeline
- Introduction to code coverage testing

- Performing code coverage testing

- Assigning test results to work items

- Introduction to Feature Flags

- Using Feature Flags to test in production

Technical requirements

To follow this chapter, you need to have an active Azure DevOps organization. The organization that will be used in this chapter is called the Parts Unlimited organization. It was created in *Chapter 1, Azure DevOps Overview*. You also need to have Visual Studio 2019 installed, which can be downloaded from `https://visualstudio.microsoft.com/downloads/`. For the latest demo, you will need Visual Studio Code with the C# extension installed and the .NET Core SDK, version 3.1 or later.

The source code for our sample application can be downloaded from the following link:

```
https://github.com/PacktPublishing/Learning-Azure-DevOps---B16392/tree/master/Chapter%205/RazorFeatureFlags
```

Benefits of automatic testing

After adding a new feature to your application, you want to know if it will work correctly, given all the possible interactions. You also don't want to break any other features with this new functionality and want to know if the code is easily understood by others, as well as being maintainable.

All of this can be tested manually. But as the project and code base grows over time, testing all these features manually can become repetitive and error-prone. This is where automatic testing comes in.

There has always been a great deal of controversy around automatic testing. Many people believe that testing is too expensive to create and maintain. This is indeed true when tests are created badly. But when automatic tests are created properly, it will absolutely lower the amount of time and costs compared to frequent manual testing or releasing poor-quality software. Using automatic testing, your project will benefit from the ability to release software more frequently. It can be reused and run repeatedly, delivering faster results and feedback to the team. The earlier a bug is detected, the more cost-effective it is to fix it.

In conjunction with CI, where the code is automatically pushed into production, automatic testing will protect teams from releasing bugs into their software. However, there is a trade-off. Developers need to dedicate more time to writing and maintaining test code. However, by investing this extra time, the outcome will be higher quality code, and code that has been proven to function completely as expected.

There are different types of automated testing you can perform; for instance, you can run regression, acceptance, and security tests. In this chapter, we are going to focus on **development testing**, which is also used in CI and can be done directly from the build pipeline.

Visual Studio and Azure DevOps both offer features for testing. They are test framework-agnostic, so you can plug in your own framework and bring third-party tools as well. You can easily add test adapters in order to run the tests and explore the results. This can make testing part of your daily software build process.

In the upcoming sections, we will cover unit testing and code coverage testing, which is part of development testing. First, we will describe how to run an automatic unit test from a build pipeline, and then how to perform code coverage and UI tests from a build pipeline.

Introduction to unit testing

With unit testing, you break up code into small pieces, called units, that can be tested independently from each other. These units can consist of classes, methods, or single lines of code. The smaller the better works best here. This will give you a better view of how your code is performing and allows tests to be run fast.

In most cases, unit tests are written by the developer that writes the code. There are two different ways of writing unit tests: before you write the actual production code, or after. Most programmers write it afterwards, which is the traditional way of doing things, but if you are using **test-driven development** (TDD), you will typically write them beforehand. Unit testing will also make code documentation easier. It encourages better coding practices and you can leave code pieces to describe the code's functionality behind. Here, you will focus more on updating a system of checks.

In the next section, we are going to cover how to run unit tests in a build pipeline.

Running unit tests in a build pipeline

Our **Parts Unlimited** test project already has unit tests created. So, this is a good pick for this demo. First, we are going to look at the application and the tests that are created. Therefore, we have to clone the repository to our local filesystem and open the solution in Visual Studio.

Downloading the source code

We are going to create unit tests for the web application for Parts Unlimited. First, we need to clone the repository from Azure DevOps to our filesystem. This will allow us to add the unit tests to it using Visual Studio Code. Therefore, we must take the following steps:

1. Open a web browser and navigate to `https://dev.azure.com/`.

2. Log in with your Microsoft account and select the **Parts.Unlimited** project. Then, from the left menu, select **Repos**. This will let you navigate to the source code of the project.

3. From the top-right menu, select **Clone**:

Figure 5.1 – Search result

4. On the next screen, make sure that **Clone in Visual Studio** is selected and click the button shown as follows:

Figure 5.2 – Clone repository

5. Now, Visual Studio will open. From here, we will take a brief look at the test classes that are already in the project. For this, open the **Solution Explorer** window and navigate to **test > PartsUnlimited.UnitTests**:

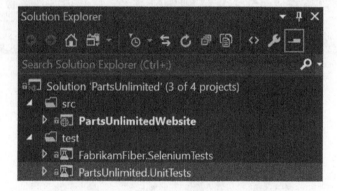

Figure 5.3 – Unit test project

6. There are different test projects available in this project. Take some time to become familiar with what is actually being tested. The default testing framework for Visual Studio is being used here, which is **MS Test**.

7. From Visual Studio, you will be able to build and run the application. To do this, press *F5*. Alternatively, from the top menu, select **Debug** > **Start Debugging**:

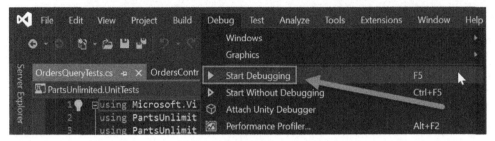

Figure 5.4 – Unit test project

8. Once the project has been built, the website will look as follows:

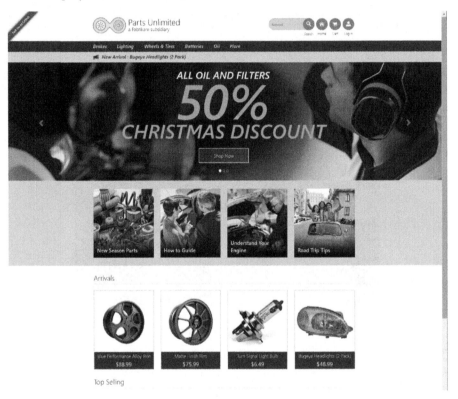

Figure 5.5 – Sample website

9. Go back to Visual Studio and stop the debugger.

Now that everything is working, we can start creating a build pipeline, which includes running the unit test projects.

Creating the pipeline

To create the pipeline, we need to go back to Azure DevOps. From there, follow these steps:

1. From the left-hand menu, select **Pipelines**.

2. At the top-right of the screen, find and click **New pipeline**:

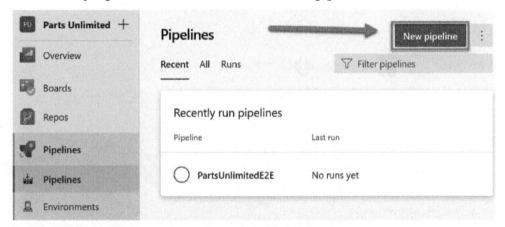

Figure 5.6 – Creating a new pipeline

3. The wizard for creating a build pipeline will appear. On the first screen, select **Use the classic editor** to create a pipeline using the designer:

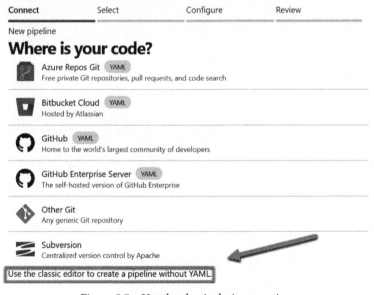

Figure 5.7 – Use the classic designer option

4. On the next screen, make sure that **Azure Repos Git** is selected. Keep the default settings as they are and click **Continue**:

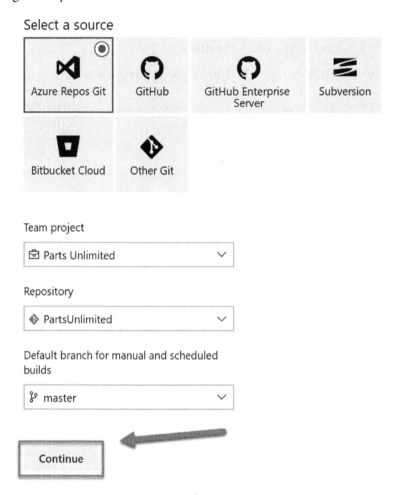

Figure 5.8 – Pipeline source settings

5. Next, we need to select a template. Select **ASP.NET** from the overview and click **Apply**:

Select a template

Or start with an ⛏ **Empty job**

🔍 Search

Configuration as code

YAML

Looking for a better experience to configure your pipelines using YAML files? Try the new YAML pipeline creation experience. Learn more

Featured

.NET Desktop

Build and test a .NET or Windows classic desktop solution.

Android

Build, test, sign, and align an Android APK.

ASP.NET

Build and test an ASP.NET web application.

Apply

Azure Web App for ASP.NET

Build, package, test, and deploy an ASP.NET Azure Web App.

Docker container

Build a Docker image and push it to a container registry.

Figure 5.9 – Selecting the ASP.NET template

6. With that, the pipeline will be created. Various tasks are added to the pipeline by default. We are going to use these tasks here. For this demo, we are going to focus on the **Test Assemblies** task. Click on this task and make sure that version **2** is selected. Under **Test selection**, you will see the following settings:

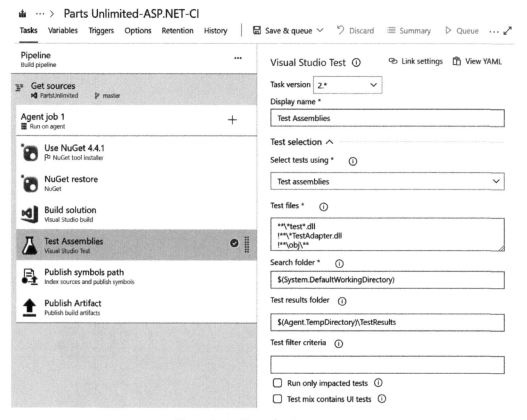

Figure 5.10 – Test selection settings

7. By default, **Test assemblies** will be selected under **Select tests using**. Keep that selected. Since we want to run our unit tests automatically, this is the option we need to choose. Unit tests are usually stored inside an assembly.

8. Also, by default, there are some assemblies already filled in. You can make changes to them if needed. For this demo, we will keep the default settings as they are because the task looks for assemblies in different folders that have `test` in them. Our test project is called **PartsUnlimited.UnitTests**, so this will be picked up by the task.

9. The search folder is the folder that's used to search for test assemblies. In this case, this is the default working directory.

10. The **test results** folder is where test results are stored. The results directory will always be cleaned before the tests are run.

11. We are now ready to run the test. Click on **Save & queue** from the top menu and then again on the **Save & queue** sub-menu item to execute the build pipeline:

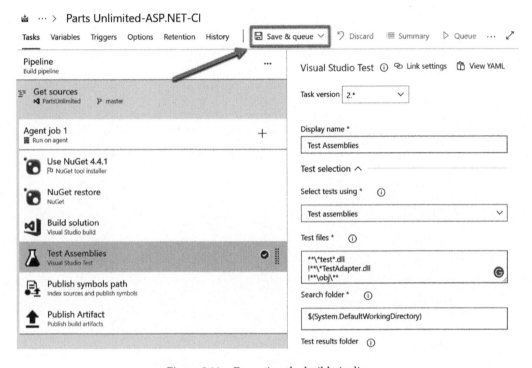

Figure 5.11 – Executing the build pipeline

12. The wizard for running the pipeline will open. Here, you can specify a comment and then select an **Agent Pool**, **Agent Specification**, and which **Branch/tag** you would like to use:

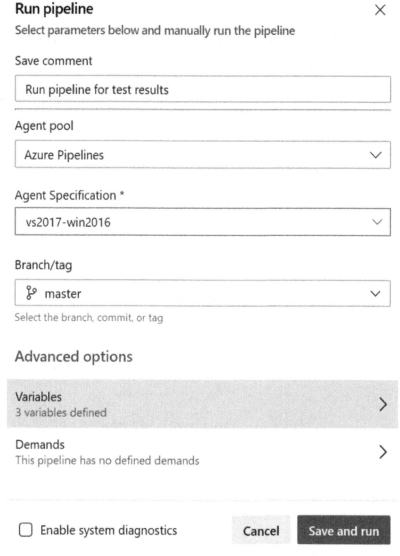

Figure 5.12 – Parameters for running a pipeline

13. Click **Save and run** to queue the pipeline.

The overview page of the job will be displayed, which is where you can view the status of the execution:

Figure 5.13 – Overview of our jobs

14. After a couple of minutes, the pipeline will have completed. From the right-top menu, under **Tests and coverage**, you will be able to see the pass percentage for the tests for this build. You can click on this to navigate to the test results (alternatively, you can navigate to it by clicking **Tests** from the top-left menu:

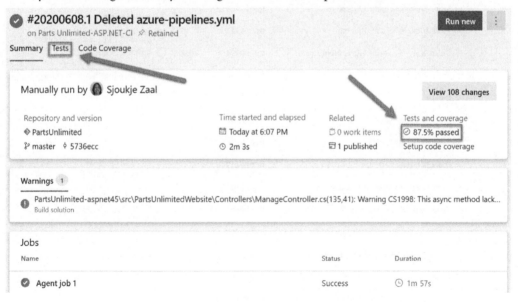

Figure 5.14 – Tests overview

15. On the **Tests** screen, you will see the number of tests you have, as well as the tests that passed and failed. You can also see the duration of the run from here.

16. At the bottom of the screen, you can filter by specific tests. For instance, you can filter for tests that have been **Passed**, **Failed**, and **Aborted**:

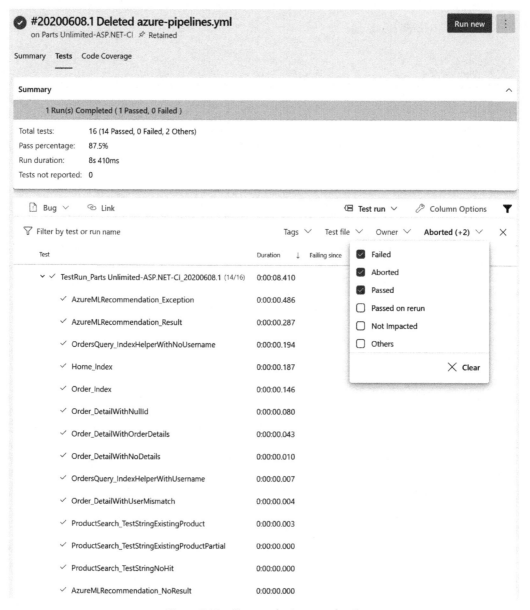

Figure 5.15 – Test results in more detail

In this demonstration, we have created a build pipeline that includes automatic unit testing for our source code. In the next section, we are going to look at code coverage testing.

Introduction to code coverage testing

With code coverage testing, you can measure what source code for an application is going to be tested. Code coverage testing measures how many lines, blocks, and classes are executed while automated tests, such as unit tests, are running.

The more code that's tested, the more confident teams can be about their code changes. By reviewing the outcome of the code coverage tests, teams can identify what code is not covered by these tests. This information is very helpful as it reduces test debt over time.

Azure DevOps supports code coverage testing from the build pipeline. The **Test Assemblies** task allows us to collect code coverage testing results. There is also a separate task, called **Publish Code Coverage Results**, that can also publish these results. This task offers out-of-the-box support for popular coverage results formats such as Cobertura and JaCoCo.

> **Important Note**
>
> Cobertura and JaCoCo are both Java tools that calculate the percentage of code that's accessed by tests. For more information about Cobertura, you can refer to `https://cobertura.github.io/cobertura/`. For more information about JaCoCo, you can refer to `https://www.eclemma.org/jacoco/`.

In the next section, we are going to look how to perform code coverage testing by using Azure DevOps.

Performing code coverage testing

To perform code coverage testing, we need to open the build pipeline that we created in the previous demo. Let's get started:

1. With the build pipeline open, select the **Edit** button in the right-hand corner:

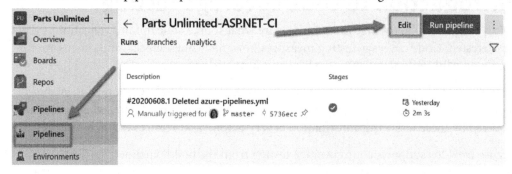

Figure 5.16 – Editing the pipeline from the previous demo

2. Navigate to the **Test Assemblies** task to open the settings.

   Under **Execution** settings, check the **Code coverage enabled** box:

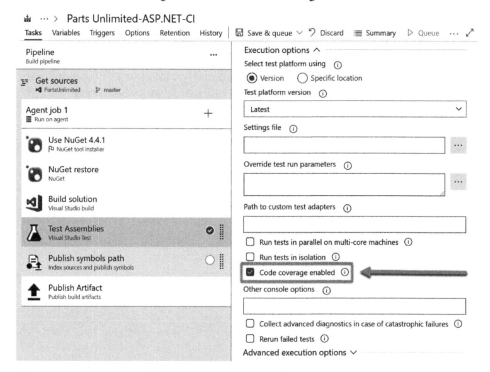

Figure 5.17 – Enabling code coverage testing

3. Now, **Save and queue** the build, specify a save comment, and wait until the pipeline is fully executed. The Visual Studio Test task creates an artifact that contains `.coverage` files that can be downloaded and used for further analysis in Visual Studio.

4. After executing the pipeline, on the overview page of the build, select **Code Coverage** from the top menu and click on **Download code coverage results**. A file with the `.coverage` extension will be downloaded to your local filesystem.

5. Double-click the downloaded file so that it opens in Visual Studio. From here, you can drill down into the different classes and methods to get an overview of the test results:

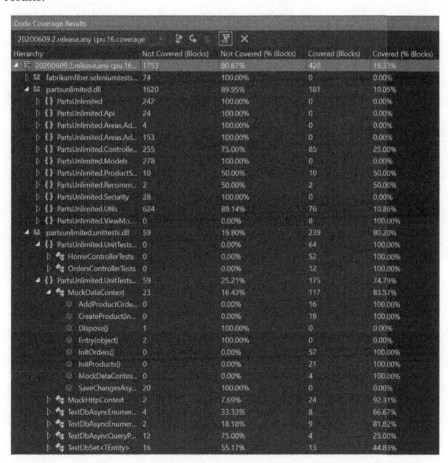

Figure 5.18 – Code coverage testing results in Visual Studio

In this demonstration, we enabled code coverage testing from our build pipeline. In the next section, we are going to assign these test results to the User Stories.

Assigning test results to work items

Once the test has run automatically and the build process has finished, you can assign the results to work items that have been added to the backlog and sprint. For this, you must perform the following steps:

1. Go back to the build pipeline and select the pipeline that ran last. Click **Test** from the top menu.

2. For the results table, make sure that **Passed** is selected and that **Failed** and **Aborted** have been deselected:

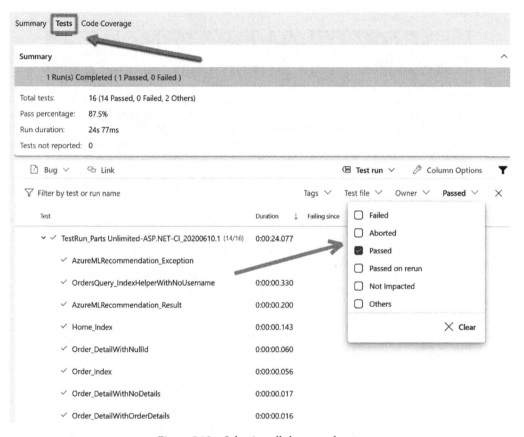

Figure 5.19 – Selecting all the passed tests

3. Then, select a couple of tests. After doing this, from the top menu, click **Link**:

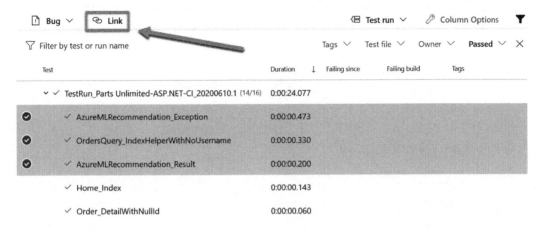

Figure 5.20 – Linking the items

4. Search for As a tester and select the work item that is displayed as a search result:

Figure 5.21 – Selecting the work item

5. Click **Associate** to link the work item to the test result.

6. Now, click on one of the test results that's linked to the work item. This will show the details for this item. From here, you can click on **work items** from the top menu. This will display the work item that we linked in the previous step:

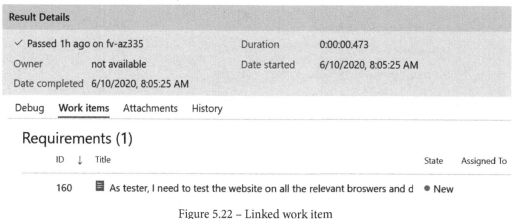

Figure 5.22 – Linked work item

7. By clicking on that work item, you can look at its details.

In this demonstration, we covered how to link test results to work items. In the next section, we are going to cover how to use Feature Flags to test in production.

Introduction to Feature Flags

You can use a Feature Flag to turn features in your code, such as specific methods or sections in your code, on or off. This can be extremely helpful when you want to hide (disable) and expose (enable) features in a solution. Features that are not complete and ready for release yet can be hidden or exposed in the solution. This allows us to test code in production for a subset of users. You can enable the code for a subset of users, for instance, based on the login name of the user and let them test the features before releasing them to others. However, there is a drawback to Feature Flags: they introduce more complexity in your code, so it is better to constrain the number of toggles in your application.

The recommended approach when creating Feature Flags is to keep them outside the application. For instance, a web or app configuration file is a good place to add Feature Flags because you can change them easily, without the need to redeploy the application again.

In the next section, we are going to implement a Feature Flag in a .NET Core solution.

Using Feature Flags to test in production

In this demonstration, we are going to create a new .NET Core application in Visual Studio Code. Then, we are going to implement a Feature Flag for this application.

We are going to add a very basic Feature Flag that changes the welcome message from *Welcome* to *Welcome to Learn Azure DevOps*. This is only going to be tested by a subset of users. Therefore, we need to open **Visual Studio Code** and create a new `Razor` application with .NET Core. I have created a new folder on my local filesystem called `FeatureFlags` for this. Open this folder in Visual Studio Code. Check the next section for the detailed steps.

Creating a new .NET Core application

To create a new .NET Core application, follow these steps:

1. With **Visual Studio Code** open, click on **Terminal** > **New terminal** from the top menu.

2. In the Terminal, add the following line of code to create a new project:

    ```
    dotnet new webapp -o RazorFeatureFlags
    code -r RazorFeatureFlags
    ```

3. The newly created project will now open. Open the Terminal once more and add the following line of code to test the project:

    ```
    dotnet run
    ```

    The output of running this code will look as follows:

```
AzureAD+SjoukjeZaal@SZ-Desktop MINGW64 ~/RazorFeatureFlags
$ dotnet run
info: Microsoft.Hosting.Lifetime[0]
      Now listening on: https://localhost:5001
info: Microsoft.Hosting.Lifetime[0]
      Now listening on: http://localhost:5000
info: Microsoft.Hosting.Lifetime[0]
      Application started. Press Ctrl+C to shut down.
info: Microsoft.Hosting.Lifetime[0]
      Hosting environment: Development
info: Microsoft.Hosting.Lifetime[0]
      Content root path: C:\Users\SjoukjeZaal\RazorFeatureFlags
```

Figure 5.23 – Output in the Terminal

4. Navigate to the .NET Core application by clicking on one of the localhost URLs in the Terminal output. You will then see the following:

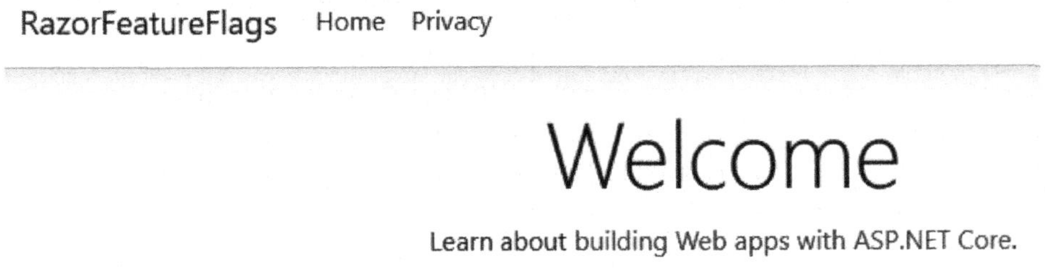

RazorFeatureFlags   Home   Privacy

Welcome

Learn about building Web apps with ASP.NET Core.

Figure 5.24 – Running the new project

5. The next step is to add the `Microsoft.FeatureManagement` NuGet package to the project. Therefore, add the following line of code to the Terminal:

```
dotnet add package Microsoft.FeatureManagement
```

6. Once the package has been installed, open the `Program.cs` class and add the following `using` statement:

```
using Microsoft.FeatureManagement;
```

7. Now, open the `appsettings.json` file. We are going create a `FeatureManagement` section in this file. Replace the code inside the file with the following:

```
{
  'Logging': {
    'LogLevel': {
      'Default': 'Information',
      'Microsoft': 'Warning',
      'Microsoft.Hosting.Lifetime': 'Information'
    }
  },
  'FeatureManagement': {
    'ChangeBanner': false
  },
  'AllowedHosts': '*'
}
```

8. Then, open the `Startup.cs` class. Here, add the `using` statement again and add the following to the `ConfigureServices` method:

```
public void ConfigureServices(IServiceCollection
services)
    {
        //...
        services.AddFeatureManagement();
    }
```

9. Now, we can inject this into a controller, for instance. Open the code behind the home page of the application, which can be found in the `Index.cshtml.cs` file, and add the `using` statement again. Then, replace the `IndexModel` class with the following code:

```
public class IndexModel : PageModel
    {
        private readonly IFeatureManager _featureManager;
        public IndexModel(IFeatureManager featureManager)
        {
            _featureManager = featureManager;
        }
        public static string WelcomeMessage { get; set; }

        public async Task OnGetAsync()
        {
            WelcomeMessage = await _featureManager.
IsEnabledAsync('ChangeBanner') ? 'Welcome to Learn Azure
DevOps' : 'Welcome';
        }
    }
}
```

10. The `Index.cshtml.cs` class will look as follows:

```
Pages > C# Index.cshtml.cs > {} RazorFeatureFlags.Pages
 1    using System;
 2    using System.Collections.Generic;
 3    using System.Linq;
 4    using System.Threading.Tasks;
 5    using Microsoft.AspNetCore.Mvc;
 6    using Microsoft.AspNetCore.Mvc.RazorPages;
 7    using Microsoft.Extensions.Logging;
 8    using Microsoft.FeatureManagement;
 9
10    namespace RazorFeatureFlags.Pages
11    {
          6 references
12        public class IndexModel : PageModel
13        {
              2 references
14            private readonly IFeatureManager _featureManager;
              0 references
15            public IndexModel(IFeatureManager featureManager)
16            {
17                _featureManager = featureManager;
18            }
              1 reference
19            public static string WelcomeMessage { get; set; }
20
              0 references
              public async Task OnGetAsync()
21            {
22                WelcomeMessage = await _featureManager.IsEnabledAsync("ChangeBanner")
23                    ? "Welcome to Learn Azure DevOps" : "Welcome";
24            }
25        }
26    }
```

Figure 5.25 – Overview of the Index.cshtml.cs file

11. Finally, open the `Index.cshtml` file and replace the code inside it with the following:

```
<div class='text-center'>
    <h1 class='display-4'>@IndexModel.WelcomeMessage</h1>
    <p>Learn about <a href='https://docs.microsoft.com/aspnet/
core'>building Web apps with ASP.NET Core</a>.</p>
</div>
```

12. This will inject the welcome message into the web page.

13. Build and run the code by opening a new Terminal window and adding the following line of code to the Terminal:

```
dotnet run
```

14. Let the application open in the browser and open the appsettings.json file again in Visual Studio Code. Change the ChangeBanner Feature Flag to **true** and reload the website in your browser by pressing *F5*. This will result in the following output:

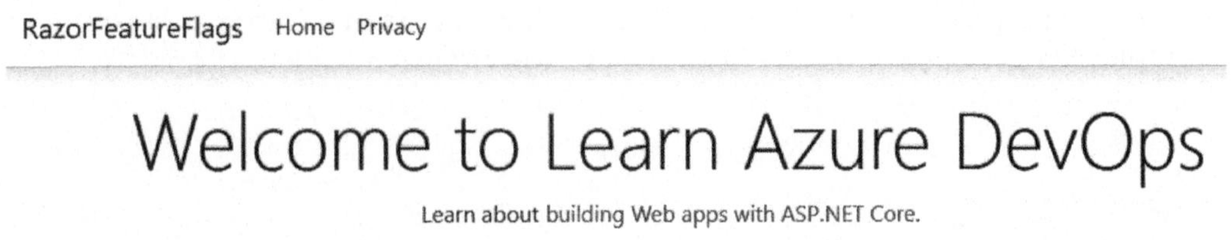

RazorFeatureFlags   Home   Privacy

Welcome to Learn Azure DevOps

Learn about building Web apps with ASP.NET Core.

Figure 5.26 – Welcome message changed based on the Feature Flag provided

In this demonstration, we added some Feature Flags to our application using the Featuremanagement NuGet package of Microsoft. Using these Feature Flags, we changed the welcome message for the home page of the application. This concludes this chapter.

Summary

In this chapter, we covered how to run quality tests in a build pipeline in more depth. With this, you can now run unit tests from the build pipeline and execute coverage tests from Azure DevOps. Lastly, we covered how to create Future Flags inside an application that you can use in your future projects as well.

In the next chapter, we are going to focus on how to host build agents in Azure Pipelines.

Further reading

Check out the following links for more information about the topics that were covered in this chapter:

- Unit test basics: `https://docs.microsoft.com/en-us/visualstudio/test/unit-test-basics?view=vs-2019`

- Run quality tests in your build pipeline by using Azure Pipelines: `https://docs.microsoft.com/en-us/learn/modules/run-quality-tests-build-pipeline/`

- Explore how to progressively expose your features in production for some or all users: `https://docs.microsoft.com/en-us/azure/devops/migrate/phase-features-with-feature-flags?view=azure-devops`

6
Hosting Your Own Azure Pipeline Agent

In the previous two chapters, we looked at setting up continuous integration through Azure Pipelines while using Microsoft-hosted agents. In this chapter, we'll be building a self-hosted agent and updating the pipeline to use our own agent, rather than using the Microsoft-hosted one.

We will first look at the types of pipeline agents available and then dive into the technical specifications of setting up the agent pools. We will also look at how you can use VM scale sets for large-scale Azure DevOps projects.

We'll be covering the following topics:

- Azure pipeline agent overview
- Understanding the types of agents in Azure Pipelines
- Planning and setting up your own pipeline agent in Azure
- Updating your Azure pipeline to use your self-hosted agent
- Using containers as your self-hosted agents
- Planning for scale – using Azure VM scale sets as self-hosted agents

Technical requirements

To follow this chapter, you need to have an active Azure DevOps organization and an Azure subscription to create a VM.

Getting the project pre-requisites ready: This section requires you to have the **PartsUnlimited** project ready in your own DevOps organization. If you are continuing from the previous chapter, *Chapter 5, Running Quality Tests in a Build Pipeline*, you should have it already.

If you do not have the project ready in your DevOps org, you can import it using Azure DevOps Demo Generator – `https://azuredevopsdemogenerator.azurewebsites.net/`:

1. Log in to the **Azure DevOps Demo Generator** website.

2. Enter a project name and select your **DevOps organization**.

3. Click on **Choose Template** and find **PartsUnlimited**.

4. Once you're ready, click **Create Project**:

Figure 6.1 – Creating a sample DevOps project

It will take a couple of minutes for the project to be imported; you can monitor the progress using the progress bar displayed.

5. Upon completion, click on **Navigate to project**:

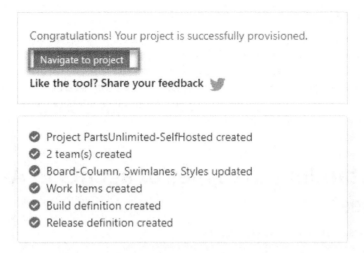

Figure 6.2 – Project successfully created

We'll be using this project throughout this chapter.

Azure pipeline agent overview

An Azure pipeline agent is the component responsible for executing the tasks defined in the pipeline definition. This agent typically runs inside a VM or container and includes the pre-requisites required for the pipeline to run successfully.

In most cases, you'll need to have an agent in order to run the pipeline. As your project size and the number of developers grows, you will need to have more agents to support the scale.

Each execution of a pipeline initiates a job on one of the agents, and one agent can only run one job at a time. Azure pipeline agents can be hosted in the cloud or on-premises in one of the following compute infrastructures:

- Server or client host (physical or virtual)
- Containers
- Azure VM scale sets (preview)

Azure pipeline agents are grouped into **agent pools**. You can create as many agent pools as you require.

> **Important note**
>
> Azure Pipelines supports running basic tasks, such as invoking the REST API or Azure Function without the need to have any agents. Please refer to `https://docs.microsoft.com/en-us/azure/devops/pipelines/process/phases?view=azure-devops&tabs=yaml#server-jobs` for more details about agentless execution of Azure Pipelines.

Understanding the types of agents in Azure Pipelines

Azure Pipelines offers two types of agents:

- Microsoft-hosted agents
- Self-hosted agents

Let's look at them in detail.

Microsoft-hosted agents

Microsoft-hosted agents are fully managed VMs, deployed and managed by Microsoft. You can choose to use a Microsoft-hosted agent with no additional pre-requisites or configurations. Microsoft-hosted agents are the simplest and are available at no additional cost.

Every time you execute a pipeline, you get a new VM for running the job, and it's discarded after one use.

Self-hosted agents

Self-hosted agents are servers owned by you, running in any cloud platform or data center owned by you. Self-hosted agents are preferred due to various reasons, including security, scalability, and performance.

You can configure your self-hosted agent to have the dependencies pre-installed, which will help you decrease the time for your pipeline execution.

Choosing between a Microsoft-hosted agent and self-hosted agents depends on various factors, such as the following:

- The size of the code base
- The number of developers
- The build and release frequency
- The dependencies and packages required for the build process
- Security and compliance requirements
- Performance

If your code base is small and the build pipeline is optimized, it's better to use Microsoft-hosted agents as it won't take much time to download all the dependencies on the fly. However, if you have a large code base with numerous amounts of dependencies, using a self-hosted agent will be a better option as you can eliminate various build pre-creation tasks from the pipeline by configuring them in your self-hosted environment in advance. Self-hosted agents would be the only option in the case of highly secure and customized build pipelines that interact with other services running in your network. If you need more CPU and memory than what is provided with Microsoft-hosted agents, you can use self-hosted agents with your customized sizing.

It is recommended to start with Microsoft-hosted agents and move to self-hosted at a later stage when the Microsoft-hosted agents become a bottleneck in your build and release process.

Planning and setting up your self-hosted Azure pipeline agent

In order to use a self-hosted agent with Azure Pipelines, you will need to set up a machine and configure it for your pipeline requirements. Typically, you would choose an OS version best suited for your project, considering the framework, libraries, and build tools compatibility.

For the purpose of this demonstration, we'll be setting up a VM in Azure and will configure it to use a self-hosted agent. You can choose to host your agent server in any cloud or on-premises environment.

Choosing the right OS/image for the agent VM

The first decision you take while setting up the VM is choosing the OS/image for the server depending on your target deployment. If you are deploying in an on-premises environment, you may just select one of the supported OS versions (such as Windows Server 2016) and install the necessary software. In the case of cloud deployments, you have multiple options provided in the form of images, which come in various combinations of OS version and pre-installed tools.

It is advised that you have the agent VM specifications planned with your developers to have them best suited for your project needs. Here is a recommended approach:

1. Identify whether your application is built to run on Windows, Linux, or macOS. If it's cross-platform, choose the one that runs it best and has support for the build tools you're using.

2. List down the underlying frameworks and external libraries/components used with their versions.

3. Select the latest version of the OS version from the top-level OS selected in *step 1*.

4. Identify whether it is compatible and supported by the **original equipment manufacturers** (**OEMs**) for all the dependencies listed in *step 2*.

5. Keep going one version down at a time and select the one that is compatible for all the required dependencies for your project.

Based on the specifications identified in this process, you can choose to start with a vanilla OS and install your required frameworks and build tools, or choose a pre-created image in the cloud.

OS support and pre-requisites for installing an Azure Pipelines agent

Azure supports various OS versions to use as a self-hosted agent; based on the OS you choose, there is a set of pre-requisites you'll need to complete before you can install the Azure Pipelines agent on your host.

Supported OSes

The following list shows the supported OSes:

- Windows-based:

  a) Windows 7, 8.1, or 10 (if you're using a client OS)

  b) Windows Server 2008 R2 SP1 or higher (Windows Server OS)

- Linux-based:

  a) CentOS 7, 6

  b) Debian 9

  c) Fedora 30, 29

  d) Linux Mint 18, 17

  e) openSUSE 42.3 or later

  f) Oracle Linux 7

  g) Red Hat Enterprise Linux 8, 7, 6

  h) SUSE Enterprise Linux 12 SP2 or later

  i) Ubuntu 18.04, 16.04

- ARM32:

  a) Debian 9

  b) Ubuntu 18.04

- macOS-based:

  a) macOS Sierra (10.12) or higher

Pre-requisite software

Based on the OS you choose, you will have to install the following pre-requisites before you can set up the host as an Azure pipeline agent:

- Windows-based:

    a) PowerShell 3.0 or higher

    b) .NET Framework 4.6.2 or higher

- Linux/ARM/macOS-based:

    a) Git 2.9.0 or higher.

    b) RHEL 6 and CentOS 6 require installing the specialized RHEL.6-x64 version of the agent.

The agent installer for Linux includes a script to auto-install the required pre-requisite. You can complete the pre-requisite by running `./bin/installdependencies.sh`, which is available in the downloaded agent directory. The downloading of the agent is covered in the following sections of this chapter.

> **Important note**
>
> Please note that the preceding pre-requisites are just to install the Azure Pipelines agent on the host; based on your application development requirements, you may need to install additional tools, such as Visual Studio build tools, a Subversion client, and any other frameworks that your application might need.

Now that we have understood the pre-requisites, we will create an agent VM for our sample project, **PartsUnlimited**.

Creating a VM in Azure for your project

The **PartsUnlimited** project is built using .NET Framework 4.5 and Visual Studio as the primary IDE tool. You can review that by browsing through the repository in the **PartsUnlimited** project in your Azure DevOps.

Looking at that, our best bet would be to use a Visual Studio-based server OS. Let's look in Azure to explore our options here:

1. Log in to the Azure portal and click **+ Create a resource**.

2. Search for **Visual Studio** and select the **Visual Studio images for Azure** option:

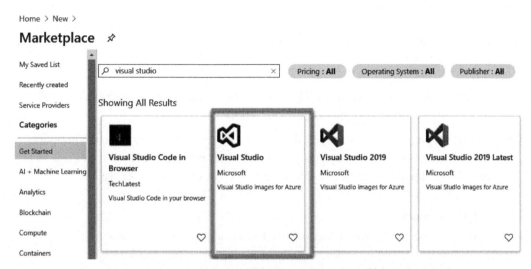

Figure 6.3 – Visual Studio in the Azure portal

3. Now, you'll be able to select from the various combinations available. We'll go with
    Visual Studio community 2017 on Windows Server 2016(x64):

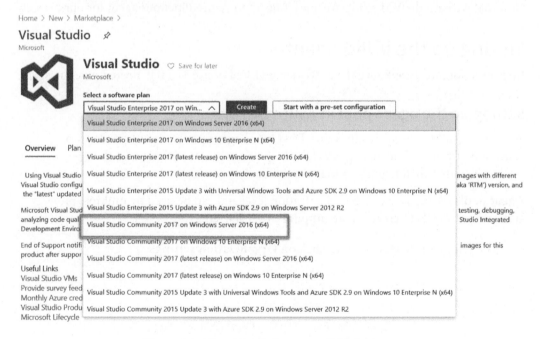

Figure 6.4 – Visual Studio images available in Azure

> **Important note**
> Visual Studio 2019-based images are available in the Azure portal directly in the search results.

4. Click **Create** to start creating a VM. Choose the required subscription, resource group, and other settings based on your preference.

5. In further pages, you can modify the settings to use a pre-created virtual network, as well as customize the storage settings and other management aspects. Please review the documentation to explore more on VM creation in Azure.

> **Important note**
> Please follow the Microsoft docs to learn more about creating a VM in Azure: `https://docs.microsoft.com/en-us/azure/virtual-machines/windows/quick-create-portal`.

6. Log in to the VM upon creation and install the required pre-requisites.

Now that we have the VM ready, we'll set it up as an Azure Pipelines agent for our project.

Setting up the build agent

In this section, we'll configure the newly created VM to use as a self-hosted pipeline agent.

Setting up the agent pool in Azure DevOps

You can organize your agents in Azure DevOps as **agent pools**. **Agent pools** are a collection of your self-hosted agents; they help you organize and manage the agents at the pool level, rather than managing them individually.

Agent pools are managed at the organization level and can be used by multiple projects at the same time. Let's create an **agent pool** to get started:

1. Log in to Azure DevOps and click on **Organization settings**:

Figure 6.5 – Azure DevOps Organization settings

2. Click on **Agent pools** under **Pipelines**:

Figure 6.6 – Azure DevOps Agent pools

3. You will see that there are two default agent pools created. Click on **Add pool** to create a new pool:

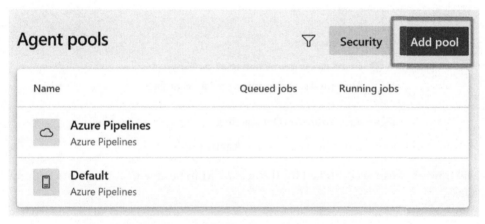

Figure 6.7 – Azure DevOps – adding an agent pool

4. Provide the pool type, name, description, and pipeline permissions. Under the permissions option, you can choose to make this pool available to all pipelines and projects at once. Click **Create** once you're ready:

a) --**Pool type: Self-hosted**

b) --**Name** and **Description**: Give a meaningful name that you can use to refer to later:

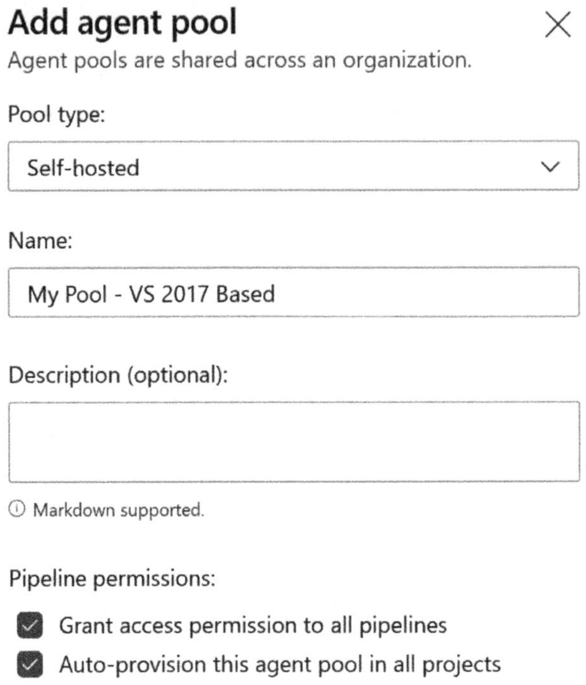

Add agent pool   ✕

Agent pools are shared across an organization.

Pool type:

| Self-hosted   ⌄ |

Name:

| My Pool - VS 2017 Based |

Description (optional):

| |
| |

ⓘ Markdown supported.

Pipeline permissions:

☑ Grant access permission to all pipelines
☑ Auto-provision this agent pool in all projects

Figure 6.8 – Azure DevOps – adding agent pool configuration

5.   Your agent pool should be listed under **Agent pools** now.

We will now set up an access token for the agent VM to be able to authenticate with Azure DevOps.

Setting up an access token for agent communication

In this task, you will create a personal access token that will be used by the Azure Pipelines agent to communicate with your Azure DevOps organization:

1.   Sign in to your Azure DevOps organization with the admin user account.

2.   Go to your user profile and click **Personal access tokens**:

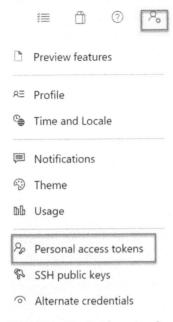

Figure 6.9 – Personal access token

3. Click on **New token**.

4. Provide the token specifications as given here:

   --**Name**: **Self-Hosted Agent Token**.

   --**Organization**: Your Azure DevOps organization.

   --**Expiration**: You can choose a date as per your choice. This is only for a one-time setup; you do **not** need to re-configure the agent once this token expires.

   --**Scope**: **Custom defined**.

5. On **Scope**, it is recommended to only give the permissions required to manage the agents. Click on **Show all scope** and select both the **Read** and **Read & manage** permissions:

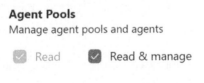

Figure 6.10 – Agent pool access

6. Review all the settings and click **Create**:

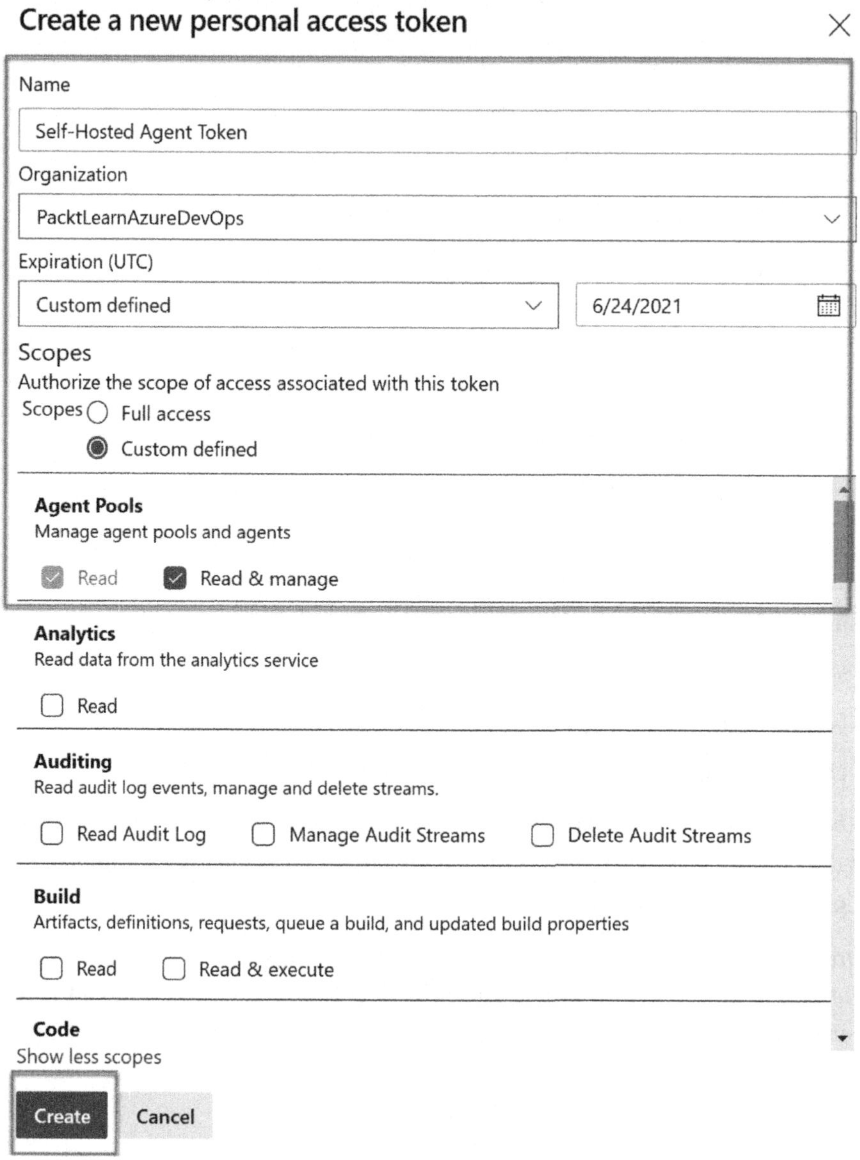

Create a new personal access token   ✕

Name

Self-Hosted Agent Token

Organization

PacktLearnAzureDevOps   ⌄

Expiration (UTC)

Custom defined   ⌄ | 6/24/2021   📅

Scopes
Authorize the scope of access associated with this token
Scopes ◯ Full access
       ◉ Custom defined

Agent Pools
Manage agent pools and agents

☑ Read   ☑ Read & manage

Analytics
Read data from the analytics service

☐ Read

Auditing
Read audit log events, manage and delete streams.

☐ Read Audit Log   ☐ Manage Audit Streams   ☐ Delete Audit Streams

Build
Artifacts, definitions, requests, queue a build, and updated build properties

☐ Read   ☐ Read & execute

Code
Show less scopes

[Create] Cancel

Figure 6.11 – Creating a personal access token for the agent pool

7. Once you click **Create**, Azure DevOps will display the personal access token. Please copy the token and save it in a secure location. If you happen to lose this token, you must create a new token for setting up new agents.

We will use this token when setting up the Azure Pipelines agent.

> **Important note**
>
> You will need to give additional permissions when creating a token if you plan to use deployment groups (more information here: `https://docs.microsoft.com/en-us/azure/devops/pipelines/release/deployment-groups/?view=azure-devops`).

Now that we have completed the agent pool setup in Azure DevOps, we can start installing the agent in the VM we created earlier.

Installing Azure Pipelines agents

You are now ready to install the Azure Pipelines agent on your VMs that you created earlier. Let's download the Azure Pipelines agent. Before you start, please log in to the VM created earlier using **Remote desktop**:

1. In your Azure DevOps account, browse to **Organization Settings** > **Agent Pools**.

2. Select your newly created agent pool and click on **New agent**:

Figure 6.12 – Add agent

3. On the next page, you can download the agent installer based on the OS and architecture (x64/x32). In our example, we're using a Windows Server 2016-based VM. We'll choose Windows and the x64 architecture. You can also copy the download URL and use it to download the agent directly inside your self-hosted agent machine. You can also choose to follow the installation steps given in the Azure DevOps portal based on the OS for your agent machine:

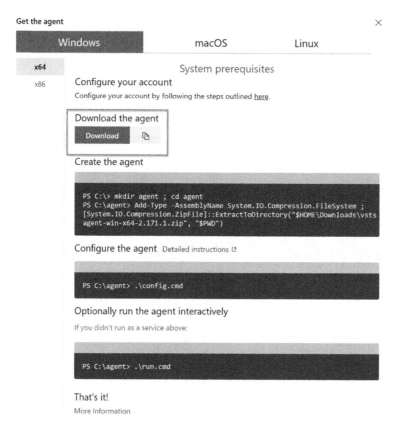

Figure 6.13 – Agent commands

> **Tip**
> If you are unable to download the agent file on your Visual Studio machine, you can use a different browser than Internet Explorer or disable **Enhanced IE Security** configuration from the server manager. You can refer to `https://www.wintips.org/how-to-disable-internet-explorer-enhanced-security-configuration-in-server-2016/` to learn how to disable enhanced Internet Explorer security configuration.

4. Launch an elevated PowerShell window and change to the C: directory root by running the cd C:\ command:

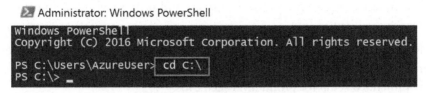

Figure 6.14 – Change directory

5. Run the following PowerShell commands to create an agent directory on the C drive and extract the agent files to the new directory. Please note that you may have to change the filename/path depending on the version of the agent you've downloaded and the directory where you saved the downloaded file:

```
mkdir agent ; cd agent
Add-Type -AssemblyName System.IO.Compression.
FileSystem ; [System.IO.Compression.
ZipFile]::ExtractToDirectory("$HOME\Downloads\vsts-agent-
win-x64-2.171.1.zip", "$PWD")
```

6. It will take a minute or two to extract the files. Please browse to the new directory once it's completed. You should see files as displayed in the following screenshot:

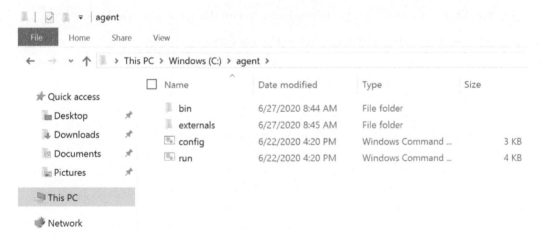

Figure 6.15 – Agent files

7. You can run the Azure pipeline agent in two modes:

    --**Run Once**: This will run the agent manually using the `run` batch file stored in the agent directory. Your agent will stop responding to pipelines if you stop the interactive authentication.

    --**Run as Service**: In this version, you configure the agent to run as a Windows service that will remain online all the time and auto-start on reboot. This is the recommended setup for production scenarios.

8. Let's configure the agent to run as a service. In your PowerShell window, run `.\config.cmd`.

    This will ask a series of questions about your Azure DevOps organization.

9. Enter your Azure DevOps organization as the server URL. Typically, this would be `https://dev.azure.com/YourOrganizationName`.

10. Press *Enter* to select **PAT** (**Personal access token**) as the authentication mechanism for Azure DevOps.

11. Provide your personal access token generated earlier.

12. Provide the agent pool name you created earlier.

13. Provide a name for this agent.

14. Provide a working directory for the agent to choose as default.

15. Finally, press *Y* and hit *Enter* to configure to run the agent as a Windows service.

16. You can accept the default account to run the service.

17. This will complete the agent setup; at the end, you should see a message stating that the services are started successfully:

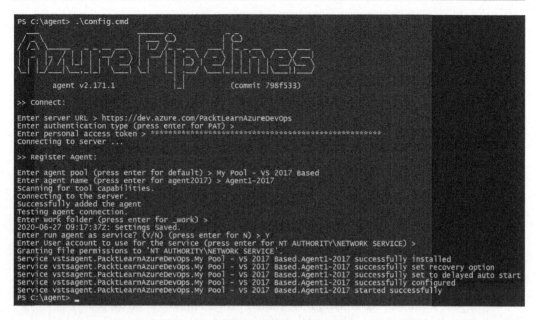

Figure 6.16 – Installing the agent

Now, if you look under your agent pool in the Azure DevOps portal, you should see this agent listed:

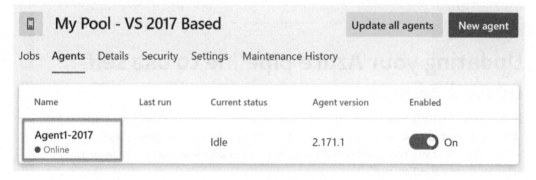

Figure 6.17 – Azure Pipelines agent listed

You now have a ready-to-use, self-hosted agent for your Azure pipelines! This self-hosted agent can be used to run your Azure pipeline jobs, and you can add as many agents as you want in a similar fashion. You may have various types of hosted agents in one pool; the appropriate agent for the job is automatically selected based on the pipeline requirements, or you can select an agent specifically at execution time. Typically, in a large environment, you'd pre-create an image of an agent server so that it is faster to provision additional agents whenever needed. In the next section, we will update our pipeline to leverage this newly set-up self-hosted agent. Please refer to this documentation if you wish to use a Linux-based hosted agent: `https://docs.microsoft.com/en-us/azure/devops/pipelines/agents/v2-linux?view=azure-devops`.

Refer to the following link for macOS-based agents: `https://docs.microsoft.com/en-us/azure/devops/pipelines/agents/v2-osx?view=azure-devops`.

Important note

If your self-hosted agent machine is behind a network firewall or proxy, you must define the proxy address while installing the Azure pipeline agent. You can do that by specifying the proxy URL, username, and password with a config command:

```
./config.cmd --proxyurl http://127.0.0.1:8888
--proxyusername "myuser" --proxypassword "mypass"
```

Updating your Azure pipeline to use self-hosted agents

In this section, we'll take the Azure pipeline scenario covered in the last chapters (**PartsUnlimited**) and modify it to use our newly created self-hosted agent. This will enable us to use our self-hosted agent to run the pipelines, rather than using Microsoft-provided agents.

Preparing your self-hosted agent to build the Parts Unlimited project

Before we can start using the self-hosted agent, we must prepare it to support building our sample project, **PartsUnlimited**. The **PartsUnlimited** project is built using Visual Studio leveraging .NET Framework, Azure development tools and .NET Core, Node.js, and so on. In order to use our self-hosted agent for building the solution, we must install the required dependencies prior to running the pipeline jobs:

1. Log in to your self-hosted agent VM.

2. Download the Visual Studio build tools with this link: `https://visualstudio.microsoft.com/thank-you-downloading-visual-studio/?sku=BuildTools&rel=16`.

    This will launch Visual Studio Installer.

3. Select **ASP.Net and Web Development** and **Azure Development**.

4. Click **Modify**. This will start installing the required framework and tools.

5. Once this is completed, please download and install .NET Core 2.2. You can download it from this link: `https://dotnet.microsoft.com/download/dotnet-core/thank-you/sdk-2.2.110-windows-x64-installer`.

    You can find all the .NET downloads here: `https://dotnet.microsoft.com/download`.

6. Install Azure PowerShell by running the following commands in an elevated PowerShell window:

    ```
    [Net.ServicePointManager]::SecurityProtocol = [Net.
    SecurityProtocolType]::Tls12
    Install-Module AzureRM -AllowClobber
    ```

7. Install Node.js version 6.x from `https://nodejs.org/download/release/v6.12.3`. You can download the file named `node-v6.12.3-x64.msi` and install it using the interactive installer.

Your host is now ready to build the **PartsUnlimited** solution.

Running the Azure pipeline

In this task, we'll now run the pipeline job to build the **PartsUnlimited** solution using our own self-hosted agents:

1. Log in to the **Azure DevOps** portal and browse to the **PartsUnlimited** project.

2. Browse to **Pipelines**:

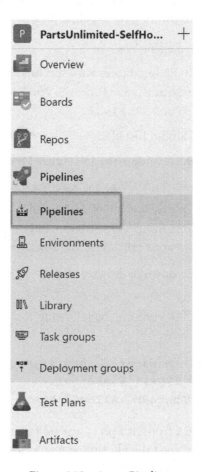

Figure 6.18 – Azure Pipelines

3. Open the pre-created pipeline named `PartsUnlimitedE2E`.

4. Click on **Edit Pipeline**.

5. In the pipeline, change the **agent pool** to your newly created agent pool:

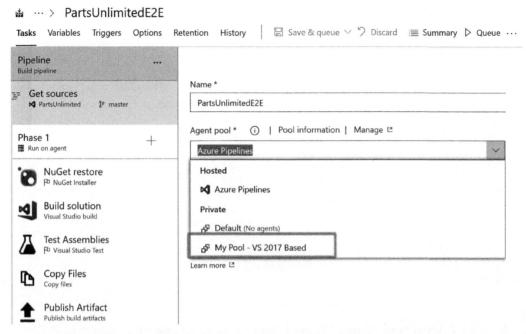

Figure 6.19 – Selecting an agent pool for the pipeline

6. Save the pipeline. You can also choose to run it after saving by selecting **Save & queue**:

Figure 6.20 – Saving the pipeline

7. Now, we are ready to execute the pipeline. Click on **Run pipeline**:

Figure 6.21 – Running the pipeline

8. Under **Agent pool**, change the pool name to the agent pool you configured in the previous section and click **Run**:

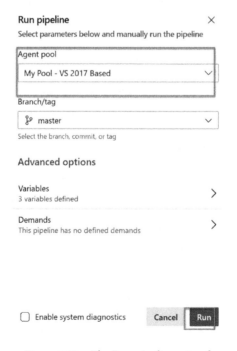

Figure 6.22 – The Run pipeline wizard

9. This will start executing the pipeline job on your self-hosted agent. This may take a few minutes to complete:

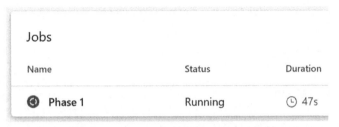

Figure 6.23 – The Azure pipeline Jobs logs

10. You can click on the job name to view the logs in real time.

You've now completed setting up an Azure pipeline, which is using a VM-based self-hosted pipeline agent for running the jobs.

Using containers as self-hosted agents

Azure Pipelines supports using Docker containers as the compute target for running pipeline jobs. You can use both Windows containers (Windows Server Core/Nano Server) and Linux containers (Ubuntu) to host your agents.

In order to connect the container to your Azure DevOps organization, you'll need to pass a few environment variables, such as the agent pool name, personal access token, and so on.

Setting up Windows containers as Azure pipeline agents

In order to use Windows containers as Azure pipeline agents, you need to build the container image first and then run it with your Azure DevOps organization environment variables. Let's look at the process.

Building the container image

Follow these steps to build the container image:

1. Launch Command Prompt and run the following commands:

```
mkdir C:\dockeragent
cd C:\dockeragent
```

2. Create a new file named `Dockerfile` (no extension) and update it with the following content. You can use Notepad to open the file:

```
FROM mcr.microsoft.com/windows/servercore:ltsc2019


WORKDIR /azp


COPY start.ps1 .


CMD powershell .\start.ps1
```

3. Create a new PowerShell file with the name `start.ps1` and copy the content from here: `https://github.com/PacktPublishing/Learning-Azure-DevOps---B16392/blob/master/Chapter-6/start.ps1`.

4. Run the following command to build the container image:

```
docker build -t dockeragent:latest.
```

Your container image is now ready to use. You can use `dockeragent` as the image name to refer to this image. Optionally, you can save this image in your container repository.

Running the Azure Pipelines agent container

Now that you have a container image ready, you can use it as the pipeline agent by running the container.

Launch a Command Prompt window and run the following command. Be sure to update the Azure DevOps organization URL, token, and agent name:

```
docker run -e AZP_URL=<Azure DevOps instance> -e AZP_TOKEN=<PAT
token> -e AZP_AGENT_NAME=mydockeragent dockeragent:latest
```

Your container-based Azure pipeline agent is now ready to use. If you want to use a container for one job and re-create it every time, you can use the `--once` flag to use one container for running one job **only** and use a container orchestrator such as Kubernetes to re-create the container as soon as it finishes executing the current job.

> **Important note**
>
> Refer to the Microsoft docs – `https://docs.microsoft.com/en-us/virtualization/windowscontainers/about/` – for additional details about Windows containers.

In the next section, we'll take a look at setting up Linux-based containers as Azure Pipelines agents.

Setting up Linux containers as Azure Pipelines agents

In order to use Linux containers as Azure pipeline agents, you can either use the Docker image published by Microsoft on Docker Hub or build your own Docker image.

Microsoft's Azure pipeline agent image is available here: `https://hub.docker.com/_/microsoft-azure-pipelines-vsts-agent`. You can directly run this image with environment variables, including information about your Azure DevOps organization:

```
docker run \
   -e VSTS_ACCOUNT=<name> \
   -e VSTS_TOKEN=<pat> \
   -it mcr.microsoft.com/azure-pipelines/vsts-agent
```

Alternatively, you can also choose to build your own Docker image to use for your Pipelines agents. The process is similar to building an image for Windows containers. Please refer to the Microsoft docs here – `https://docs.microsoft.com/en-us/azure/devops/pipelines/agents/docker?view=azure-devops` – for reference to the entry point script.

Using Azure Container Instances as agents

Azure Container Instances (**ACI**) is a managed service to run Windows and Linux containers in the Azure cloud. If standard Microsoft-hosted agents don't fit your needs (requirements, performances, and so on) and you do not have sufficient infrastructure to host the container on-premises, you can use ACI to create a self-hosted agent for Azure DevOps.

You can create a build agent running on ACI by using a custom image or reusing one of Microsoft's images that are available.

You'll need the Azure DevOps account name, personal access token, and agent name to run an Azure pipeline agent in ACI. When you have the required details, you can create an agent on ACI by executing the following command from the Azure CLI (after connecting to your Azure subscription):

```
az container create -g RESOURCE_GROUP_NAME -n CONTAINER_NAME
--image mcr.microsoft.com/azure-pipelines/vsts-agent --cpu 1
--memory 7 --environment-variables VSTS_ACCOUNT=AZURE_DEVOPS_
```

```
ACCOUNT_NAME VSTS_TOKEN=PERSONAL_ACCESS_TOKEN VSTS_AGENT=AGENT_
NAME VSTS_POOL=Default
```

Here, we have the following:

- `RESOURCE_GROUP_NAME` is the name of your resource group in Azure where you want to create this resource.

- `CONTAINER_NAME` is the name of the ACI container name.

- `AZURE_DEVOPS_ACCOUNT_NAME` is the name of your Azure DevOps account.

- `PERSONAL_ACCESS_TOKEN` is the personal access token previously created.

- `AGENT_NAME` is the name of the build agent that you want to create and that will be displayed on Azure DevOps.

In this command, there are also other two important parameters:

- The `--image` parameter is used to select the name of the Azure Pipelines image for creating your agent, as described here: `https://hub.docker.com/_/microsoft-azure-pipelines-vsts-agent`.

- The VSTS_POOL parameter is used to select the agent pool for your build agent.

Remember that you can start and stop an ACI instance by using the `az container stop` and `az container start` commands, and this can help you save money.

Let's take a look at some of the additional environment variables you can use with Azure pipeline agent-based containers.

Environment variables

Azure DevOps pipeline agents running on containers can be customized further by using additional environment variables. The environment variables and their purposes are described as follows:

- `AZP_URL`: The URL of the Azure DevOps organization

- `AZP_TOKEN`: Personal access token

- `AZP_AGENT_NAME`: The name of your Azure pipeline agent

- `AZP_POOL`: Agent pool name (default value is `Default`)

- `AZP_WORK`: Work directory (default value is `_work`)

In this section, we learned about using containers as your Azure pipeline agents for executing your pipeline jobs.

Planning for scale – Azure VM scale sets as Azure pipeline agents

Azure VM scale sets are an Azure service that allow you to create and manage hundreds of identical VMs with the ability to automatically or manually scale the number of VMs. Azure VM scale sets can be used as Azure pipeline agents in a large-scale project where you need elastic capacity based on your Azure pipeline job execution workload.

Azure VM scale sets support up to 1,000 VMs in one scale set.

Planning for scale

Azure VM scale set-based agents can be auto-scaled based on your Azure Pipelines jobs demand at a given time. There are several reasons why scale set agents can be a better option, rather than using dedicated agents:

- You need more computer power (CPU and memory) at a certain time and this requirement fluctuates based on workload.

- Microsoft-hosted agents are not able to meet your pipeline requirements.

- Your job runs for a long time or takes time to complete.

- You wish to use the same agent for various jobs consecutively to take advantage of caching and so on.

- You don't want to run dedicated agents all the time as these incur costs.

- You want to regularly update the image of VMs running jobs.

Azure VM scale sets can automatically increase/decrease the number of pipeline agents available based on the current demand of Azure Pipelines. This helps you save money, as well as supports your scaling requirements.

Creating an Azure VM scale set

In this section, we'll create an Azure VM scale set to use as an Azure pipeline agent. Please note that Azure Pipelines requires the scale set to be created with certain configurations, so you may not be able to use an existing scale set:

1. Log in to the Azure portal and click on **+ Create a resource**.

2. Search for Virtual machine scale set:

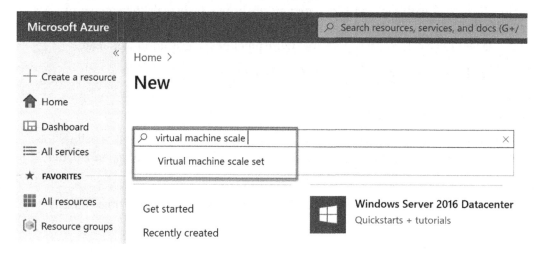

Figure 6.24 – A VM scale set in the Azure portal

3. Click **Create**.

4. Fill in the values as described here:

    --**Subscription**: Choose the subscription on which you wish to deploy this scale set.

    --**Resource group**: Choose an existing resource group or create a new one.

    --**Virtual machine scale set name**: Identifier of your choice.

    --**Region**: The Azure region of your choice; it is recommended to choose the one closest to you.

    --**Availability zone**: Recommended to choose all three for high availability.

    --**Image**: Choose a supported Windows or Linux image for the Azure Pipelines agent.

    --**Azure Spot instance**: Can help in minimizing cost. Refer to https://azure.microsoft.com/en-us/pricing/spot/ for details.

    --**Size**: The VM size for your agents.

--**Authentication**: Username/password or SSH key:

Home > New > Virtual machine scale set >

Create a virtual machine scale set

Project details

Select the subscription to manage deployed resources and costs. Use resource groups like folders to organize and manage all your resources.

Subscription *	▓▓▓▓▓▓▓▓▓▓▓▓▓▓ ⌄
└── Resource group *	(New) Scaleset-piplines ⌄
	Create new

Scale set details

Virtual machine scale set name *	AzurePipelines-ScaleSet ✓
Region *	(Asia Pacific) Southeast Asia ⌄
Availability zone ⓘ	None ⌄

Instance details

Image * ⓘ	Ubuntu Server 18.04 LTS ⌄
	Browse all public and private images
Azure Spot instance ⓘ	◯ Yes ⦿ No
Size * ⓘ	Standard_D2_v3 - 2 vcpus, 8 GiB memory ($91.25/month) ⌄
	Select size

Administrator account

Authentication type ⓘ	⦿ Password ◯ SSH public key
Username * ⓘ	AzureUser ✓
Password * ⓘ	•••••••••••• ✓
Confirm password * ⓘ	•••••••••••• ✓

Review + create	< Previous	Next : Disks >

Figure 6.25 – Creating a VM scale set

5. Click **Next: Disks >**.

6. You can customize the disk performance tier and encryption settings, and add additional disks if required. If you're unsure, accept the defaults and click **Next**.

7. On the networking page, you can choose to connect the scale set to an existing virtual network if your scale set needs to access any of your network resources securely. Please ensure that **Use a load balancer** is set to **No** for the Azure Pipelines scale set. Once configured, click **Next**:

Load balancing

You can place this virtual machine scale set in the backend pool of an existing Azure load balancing solution. Learn more

Use a load balancer   ○ Yes ⦿ No

Figure 6.26 – Azure VM scale set load balancing settings

8. On **Scaling**, provide an initial instance count and keep **Scaling policy** to **Manual**. Leave the other settings as the default and click **Next**:

Create a virtual machine scale set

Basics   Disks   Networking   **Scaling**   Management   Health   Advanced   Tags   Review + create

An Azure virtual machine scale set can automatically increase or decrease the number of VM instances that run your application. This automated and elastic behavior reduces the management overhead to monitor and optimize the performance of your application. Learn more about VMSS scaling

Instance

Initial instance count * ⓘ | 2 |

Scaling

Scaling policy ⓘ   ⦿ Manual ○ Custom

Scale-In policy

Configure the order in which virtual machines are selected for deletion during a scale-in operation.
 Learn more about scale-in policies.

Scale-in policy | Default - Balance across availability zones and fault domains, then delete V... ⌄ |

Figure 6.27 – Scale set settings

9. On **Management**, ensure that **Upgrade mode** is set to **Manual**. Leave the other settings as the default and click **Next**:

Upgrade policy

Upgrade mode * ⓘ | Manual - Existing instances must be manually upgraded   ⌄ |

Figure 6.28 – Scale set upgrade policy

10. On the **Health and Advanced Setting** page, optionally change any settings you want to customize for your environment. Click **Review and Create** once you're ready to start creating the scale set.

11. Once the validation is successful, click **Create** to start the deployment.

It may take a few minutes for the deployment to complete. Please wait while the deployment finishes. One the VM scale set is ready, we'll set it up to be used as an Azure Pipelines agent.

Setting up Azure pipeline agents with VM scale set

In the last section, we created a VM scale set. Now, we will set that up as an Azure pipeline agent:

1. Log in to your Azure DevOps organization and browse to **Project Settings** > **Agent Pools**.

2. Click on **Add Pool**.

3. Fill in the values as defined here:

   --**Pool Type**: Virtual machine scale set

   --**Project for Service Connections**: Choose your Azure DevOps project

   --**Azure Subscription**: Select the Azure subscription where you created the VM scale set:

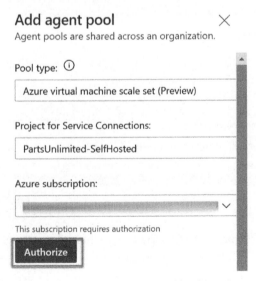

Figure 6.29 – Adding an agent pool for the scale set

4. Click **Authorize** to enable access to your Azure subscription. You may be asked to log in to your Azure account in this process.

5. Once authenticated, select an existing VM scale set and fill in the values as described here:

    --The name and description of your choice for this agent pool.

    --Optionally, configure the scale set to delete the VM after each execution.

    --The maximum number of VMs.

    --The number of agents to keep as standby. While this can help you in completing jobs quickly, it may increase your Azure cost.

6. Click **Create** once you have filled in all the values:

Figure 6.30 – Creating a scale set-based agent pool

7. Your agent pool creation will now start. Please note that it may take around 15 minutes before your agent pool is ready to take up the jobs. You should see the agents live in your agent pool upon completion:

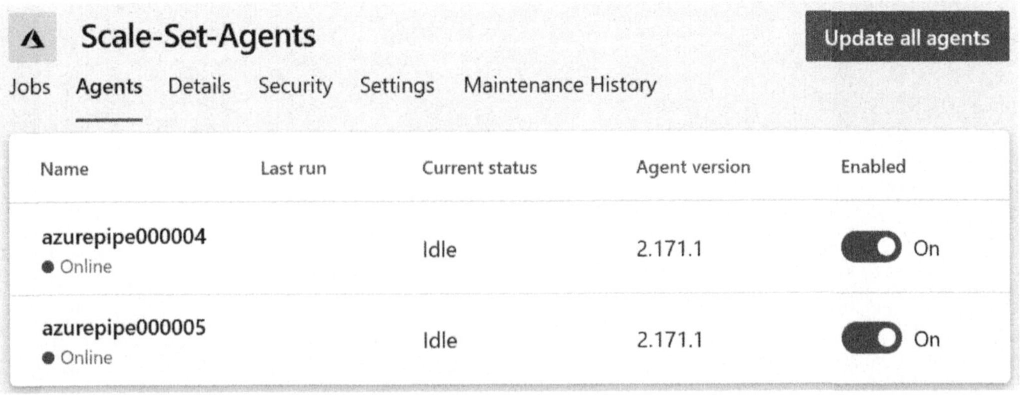

Scale-Set-Agents
Update all agents
Jobs
Agents
Details
Security
Settings
Maintenance History
Name
Last run
Current status
Agent version
Enabled
azurepipe000004
Online
Idle
2.171.1
On
azurepipe000005
Online
Idle
2.171.1
On

Figure 6.31 – Agents

Once your agent pool is ready, you can update your Azure pipeline to start using this pool for job execution.

Summary

In this chapter, we looked at using Microsoft-hosted agents and self-hosted agents to run your Azure pipeline jobs. We dug deep into the process of setting up a self-hosted agent and updated our pipelines to use the self-hosted agent.

We also looked at how you can use Docker containers, Azure container instances, and Azure VM scale sets as your Azure pipeline agents. With this chapter, you should be able to plan and implement the appropriate pipeline agent solution for your projects

In the next chapter, we'll learn about Artifacts in Azure DevOps.

Section 3: Artifacts and Deployments

In this section, we are going to cover how to use artifacts with Azure DevOps and how to deploy your applications using pipelines.

This section contains the following chapters:

- *Chapter 7, Using Artifacts with Azure DevOps*
- *Chapter 8, Deploying Applications with Azure DevOps*

7
Using Artifacts with Azure DevOps

In the previous chapter, we covered how to host build agents in Azure Pipelines. In this chapter, we are going to cover how to use artifacts with Azure DevOps. We will begin by explaining what artifacts are. Then, we will look at how to create them in Azure DevOps, as well as how to produce the artifact package from a built pipeline. Next, we are going to cover how to deploy the feed using a release pipeline. Then, we are going to cover how to set the feed permissions and how to consume the package in Visual Studio. Finally, we are going to cover how to scan for package vulnerabilities using WhiteSource Bolt.

The following topics will be covered in this chapter:

- Introducing Azure Artifacts
- Creating an artifact feed with Azure Artifacts
- Producing the package using a build pipeline
- Publishing the package to the feed from a build pipeline
- Configuring the feed permissions from the feed settings
- Consuming the package in Visual Studio from the Artifacts feed
- Scanning for package vulnerabilities using WhiteSource Bolt

Technical requirements

To follow this chapter, you need to have an active Azure DevOps organization. The organization we'll be using in this chapter is the **PartsUnlimited** organization, which we created in *Chapter 1, Azure DevOps Overview*. You also need to have Visual Studio 2019 installed, which can be downloaded from `https://visualstudio.microsoft.com/downloads/`.

The source code for our sample application can be downloaded from `https://github.com/PacktPublishing/Learning-Azure-DevOps---B16392/tree/master/Chapter%207`.

Introducing Azure Artifacts

It is likely that every developer has used a third-party or open source package in their code to add extra functionalities and speed up the development process of their application. Using popular, pre-built components that have been used and tested by the community will help you get things done more easily.

Functionalities, scripts, and code that have been built by various teams in your organization are often reused by other teams and in different software development projects. These different artifacts can be moved into a library or package so that others can benefit from this.

There are different ways to build and host these packages. For instance, you can use NuGet for hosting and managing packages for the Microsoft Development platform or npm for JavaScript packages, Maven for Java, and more. Azure Artifacts offers features so that you can share and reuse packages easily. In Azure Artifacts, packages are stored in feeds. A feed is a container that allows you to group packages and control who has access to them.

You can store packages in feeds that have been created by yourself or other teams, but it also has built-in support for **upstream sources**. With upstream sources, you can create a single feed to store both the packages that your organization produces and the packages that are consumed from remote feeds, such as NuGet, npm, Maven, Chocolatey, RubyGems, and more.

It is highly recommended to use Azure Artifacts as the main source for publishing internal packages and remote feeds. This is because it allows you to keep a comprehensive overview of all the packages being used by the organization and different teams. The feed knows the provenance of all the packages that are saved using upstream resources; the packages are saved into the feed even when the original source goes down or the package is deleted. Packages are versioned, and you typically reference a package by specifying the version of the package that you want to use in your application.

Many packages allow for unrestricted access, without the need for users to sign in. However, there are packages that require us to authenticate by using a username and password combination or access token. Regarding the latter, access tokens can be set to expire after a given time period.

In the next section, we are going to look at how to create an **Artifact Feed** in Azure DevOps.

Creating an artifact feed with Azure Artifacts

In this demo, we are going to create an artifact feed in Azure Artifacts. Packages are stored in feeds, which are basically organizational constructs that allow us to group packages and manage their permissions. Every package type (NuGet, npm, Maven, Python, and Universal) can be stored in a single feed.

For this demonstration, we are going to use our **PartsUnlimited** sample project again and add a new artifact feed to the project. To do this, perform the following steps:

1. Open a web browser and navigate to `https://dev.azure.com/`.

2. Log in with your Microsoft account and from the left menu, select **Artifacts**. Then, click the **+ Create Feed** button.

3. In the **Create new feed** dialog box, add the following values (make sure that **Upstream sources** is disabled; we are not going to use packages from remote feeds in this chapter):

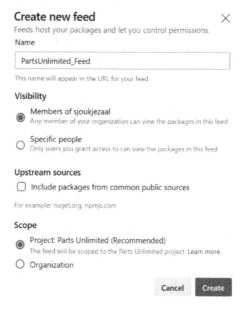

Figure 7.1 – Creating a new feed

4. Click the **Create** button.

With that, we have created a new feed so that we can store our packages. In the next section, we are going to produce a package using a build pipeline.

Producing the package using a build pipeline

Now that we have created our feed, we are going to create a build pipeline that automatically creates a package during the build of the project. For this example, you can use the sample project provided in this book's GitHub repository. This sample project consists of all the models from the **PartsUnlimited** project. We are going to add all the models to a package and distribute it from Artifacts. This way, you can easily share the data model across different projects.

The first step is to import the GitHub repository into the **PartsUnlimited** organization in Azure DevOps.

Adding the sample project to the PartsUnlimited repository

To add the sample models project to the PartsUnlimited repository, perform the following steps:

1. Navigate to the **PartsUnlimited** project in Azure DevOps and go to **Repos** > **Files**.

2. Select **Import repository** from the **PartsUnlimited** dropdown:

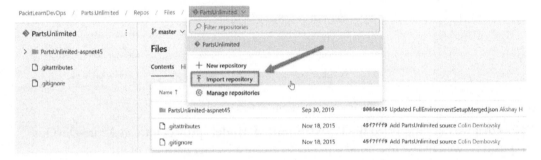

Figure 7.2 – Importing a repository

3. Enter the URL of the source repository into the **Clone URL** box and add a name for your new GitHub repository:

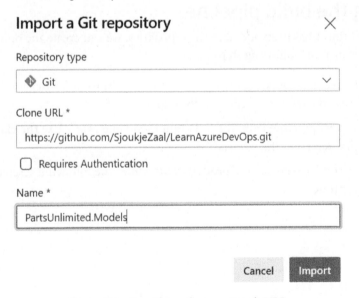

Figure 7.3 – Specifying the repository's URL

4. Click **Import**.

5. Once the project has been imported, the repository will look as follows:

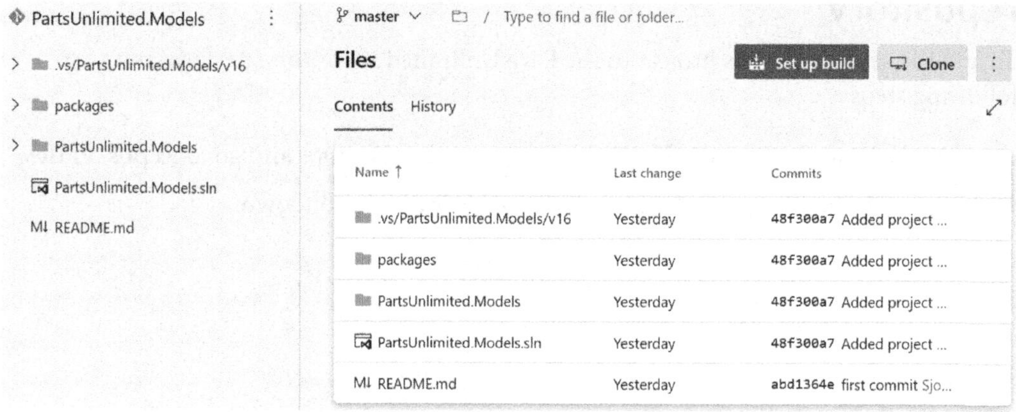

Figure 7.4 – Repository in Azure DevOps

Now that we have imported the **PartsUnlimited.Models** project into an Azure DevOps repository, we can use in a build pipeline to create a NuGet package of it.

In the next section, we are going to create a build pipeline that will automatically package our project into an Artifact package.

Creating the build pipeline

Now that the project has been added to the repository, we can create the build pipeline. To do this, perform the following steps:

1. Navigate to Azure DevOps and open the **PartsUnlimited.Models** project once more. From the left menu, click on **Pipelines**.

2. Click on **New pipeline** from the top-right menu and select **Use the classic editor** on the first screen of the wizard.

3. On the second screen, set the properties shown in the following screenshot and click **Continue**:

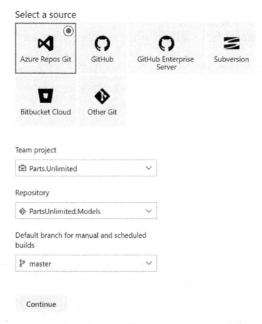

Figure 7.5 – Selecting a source

4. Select **ASP.NET** on the next screen of the wizard and click **Apply**. With that, the Build pipeline will be created. Click on the + sign on the right-hand side of **Agent job 1** and search for **NuGet**.

5. Add the NuGet task to the pipeline:

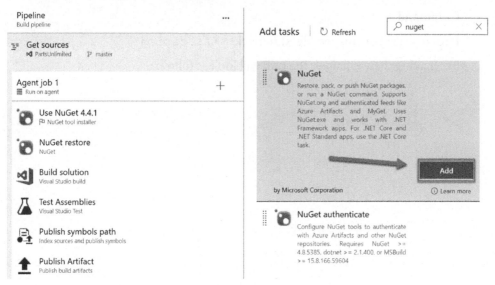

Figure 7.6 – Adding the NuGet task

6. Reorder the tasks and drag the NuGet task so that it's after the **Build Solution** task. Delete the **Test Assemblies** method since we don't have any tests in this project:

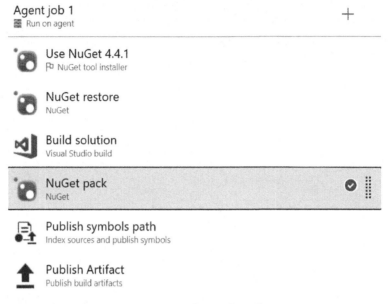

Fig. 7.7 – Reordering the tasks

7. Make the following changes to the settings of the newly added task:

    --**Display name**: NuGet pack

    --**Command**: pack

    --**Path to csproj or nuspec file(s) to pack**: **/*.csproj

8. After making these changes, the task will look as follows:

NuGet ⓘ   ⮌ Link settings   📋 View YAML   🗑

Task version 2.*   ⌄

Display name *

NuGet pack

Command *   ⓘ

pack   ⌄

Path to csproj or nuspec file(s) to pack *   ⓘ

**/*.csproj   ...

Configuration to package   ⓘ

$(BuildConfiguration)

Package folder   ⓘ

$(Build.ArtifactStagingDirectory)   ...

Pack options ⌄

Advanced ⌄

Control Options ⌄

Output Variables ⌄

Figure 7.8 – Configuring the task

9. Next, let's set the versioning of the package. A recommended approach to versioning packages is to use **Semantic Versioning**. Expand the **Pack Options** section and add the following values to set up versioning:

    --**Automatic package versioning**: Use the date and time

    --**Major**: 1

    --**Minor**: 0

    --**Patch**: 0

    --**Time zone: UTC**

10. From the top menu, select **Save & queue** and then **Save and run.**

The build pipeline will now run successfully. In the next section, we are going to publish the **PartsUnlimited.Models** NuGet package that we created in the first demo to our feed.

Publishing the package to the feed from a build pipeline

Now that we've built the application and the package from our build pipeline, we can publish the package to the feed that we created in our first demo.

For this, we need to set the required permissions on the feed. The identity that the build will run under needs to have **Contributor** permissions on the feed. Once these permissions have been set, we can extend our pipeline to push the package to the feed.

Setting the required permissions on the feed

To set the required permissions, we need to go to the settings of our feed:

1. Log in with your Microsoft account and from the left menu, select **Artifacts**.

2. Go to the settings of the feed by selecting the **Settings** button from the top-right menu:

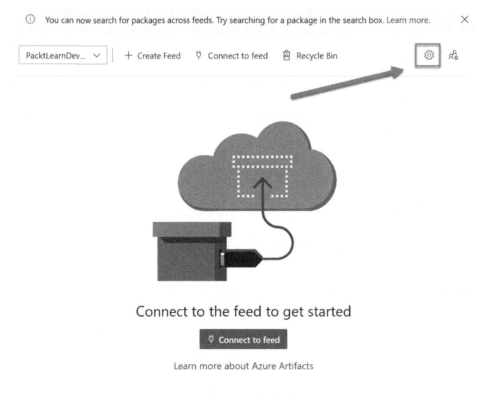

Figure 7.9 – Opening the feed's settings

3. Then, click on **Permissions** from the top menu and click on **+ Add users/groups**:

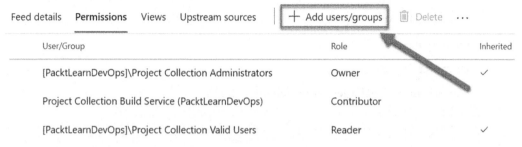

PacktLearnDevOps > Feed settings

| Feed details | **Permissions** | Views | Upstream sources | | + Add users/groups | 🗑 Delete | ... |

User/Group	Role	Inherited
[PacktLearnDevOps]\Project Collection Administrators	Owner	✓
Project Collection Build Service (PacktLearnDevOps)	Contributor	
[PacktLearnDevOps]\Project Collection Valid Users	Reader	✓

Figure 7.10 – Feed permission settings

4. Add the build that has the same name as the project, which in my case is the **Parts. Unlimited Build Service** identity:

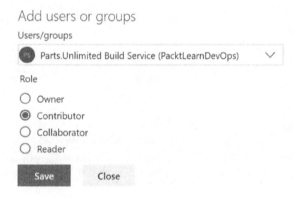

Figure 7.11 – Adding the build identity

5. Click **Save**.

Now that the identity of the build pipeline has the required permissions on the feed, we can push the package to it during while it's being built.

Publishing the package

We are now ready to extend our build pipeline and push the package from it to the feed. To do this, we need to perform the following steps:

1. Navigate to Azure DevOps and open the **PartsUnlimited.Models** project. Click on **Pipelines** in the left menu.

2. Select the build pipeline that we created in the previous step and click on the **Edit** button, which can be found in the top-right menu.

3. Click on the + button again next to **Agent job 1** and search for NuGet. Add the task to the pipeline.

4. Drag the newly added task below the NuGet task that we created in the previous step. Make the following changes to the settings of the task:

    --**Display name**: `NuGet push`

    --**Command**: **push**

    --Path to **NuGet package(s) to publish**: `$(Build.ArtifactStagingDirectory)/**/*.nupkg;!$(Build.ArtifactStagingDirectory)/**/*.symbols.nupkg`

    --**Target feed location**: **This organization/collection**

    --**Target feed**: **PacktLearnDevOps**

5. After making these changes, the task will look as follows:

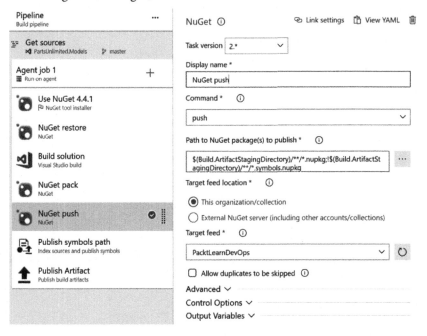

Figure 7.12 – Adding a NuGet push task

6. From the top menu, select **Save & queue** and then **Save and run.** Wait until the build pipeline has finished successfully.

7. Finally, let's check whether the package has been successfully published. Click on **Artifacts** from the left menu. You will see that the package has been pushed to the feed:

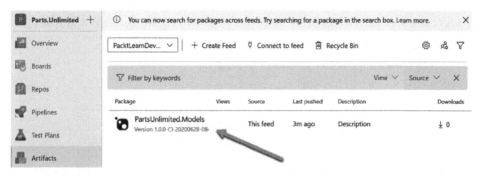

Figure 7.13 – Pushed package

Now that we have a package with models, we can use it in our Visual Projects. In the next section, we are going to create an application and consume the package from the feed in Azure DevOps.

Consuming the package in Visual Studio from the Artifacts feed

Now that our **PartsUnlimited.Models** package has been pushed to our feed in Artifacts, we can consume this package from Visual Studio. In this section, we are going to create a new console app in Visual Studio and connect to the feed from there.

Therefore, we need to perform the following steps:

1. Open Visual Studio 2019 and create a new .NET Core console application:

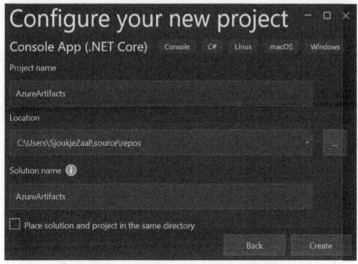

Figure 7.14 – Creating a new console package

2. Once the application has been created, navigate to Azure DevOps and from the left menu, select **Artifacts**.

3. From the top menu, select **Connect to feed**:

Figure 7.15 – Connect to feed

4. On the next screen, select **Visual Studio** from the list. We are going to use these settings to set up the machine in the next step:

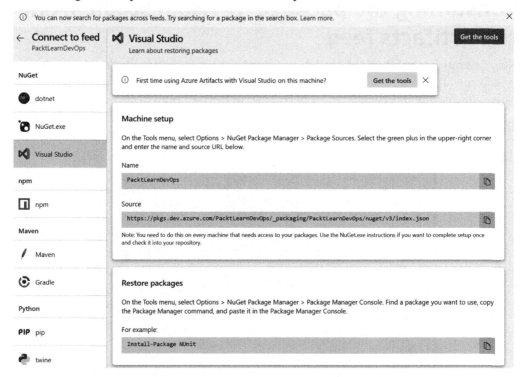

Figure 7.16 – Visual Studio machine setup

5. Navigate back to the console app in Visual Studio. Then, from the top menu, select **Tools** > **NuGet package manager** > **Manage NuGet Packages for Solution**:

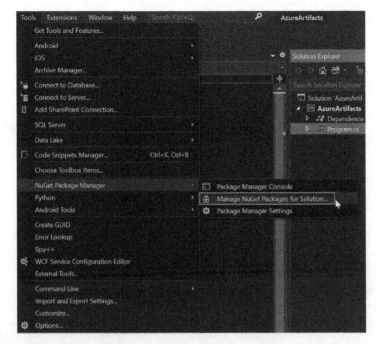

Figure 7.17 – NuGet package installer

6. To add the feed to the project, click on the settings icon:

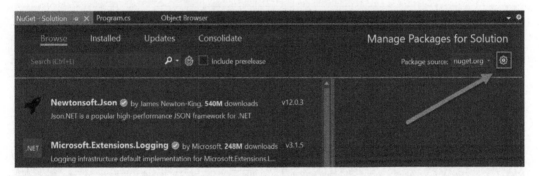

Figure 7.18 – NuGet settings

7. Click on the + sign in the top-right menu and specify the following values to add the feed:

    --**Name**: **LearnAzureDevOps**.

    --**Source**: Copy the feed URL from the machine's setup into Azure DevOps. In my case, this is `https://pkgs.dev.azure.com/PacktLearnDevOps/_packaging/PacktLearnDevOps/nuget/v3/index.json`.

The outcome of adding these values will look as follows:

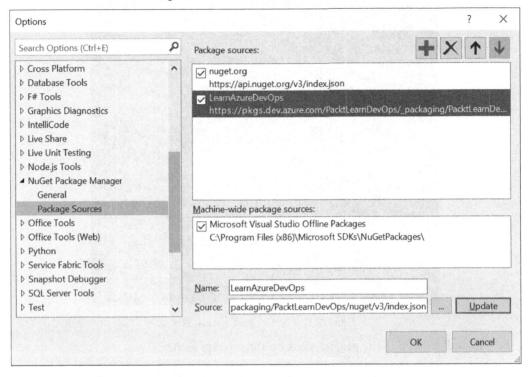

Figure 7.19 – Adding the feed's package source

8. Click **Update** and then **OK**.

9. Now, we can consume the feed in our application. In the NuGet package manager, select the package source that we just added. Make sure that **Include prelease** is selected since this package hasn't been released yet:

Figure 7.20 – Selecting the package source

10. Select the package and install it in the project.

11. Now, we can reference the package in our code and use the model classes. Add a using statement and create a new CarItem by replacing the code in the Program.cs file with the following:

```
using System;
using PartsUnlimited.Models;

namespace AzureArtifacts
{
    class Program
    {
        static void Main(string[] args)
        {
            Console.WriteLine("Hello World!");

            CartItem caritem = new CartItem()
            {
                CartId = "1",
                Count = 10,
                DateCreated = DateTime.Now,
                Product = new Product()
                {
                    Title = "Product1"
                },
                ProductId = 21
            };
        }
    }
}
```

In this demonstration, we consumed the package that is automatically built and released from the feed. In the next and last section of this chapter, we are going to look at how to scan a package for vulnerabilities using WhiteSource Bolt.

Scanning for package vulnerabilities using WhiteSource Bolt

WhiteSource Bolt can be used to scan packages for vulnerabilities directly from the build pipeline. It is a developer tool for scanning for security vulnerabilities in application code, as well as open source applications and packages. It offers extensions that can be installed through the Azure DevOps marketplace and through GitHub. WhiteSource Bolt can be downloaded free of charge, but this version is limited to five scans per day, per repository.

> **Important Note**
> For more information about WhiteSource Bolt, you can refer to the following website: `https://bolt.whitesourcesoftware.com/`.

In this section, we are going to install the extension in our Azure DevOps project and implement the tasks that come with it into our existing build pipeline. Let's get started:

1. Open a browser and navigate to `https://marketplace.visualstudio.com/`.

2. Search for WhiteSource Bolt in the search box and select the **WhiteSource Bolt** extension:

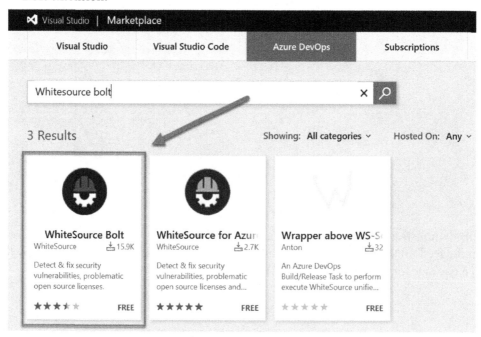

Figure 7.21 – Installing WhiteSource Bolt

3. Install the extension in your DevOps organization by selecting the organization and clicking the **Install** button:

Figure 7.22 – Installing the extension in your organization

4. Once you've installed the package, navigate back to **Azure DevOps** > **Pipelines**. You will see that **WhiteSource Bolt** has been added to the menu. Select it:

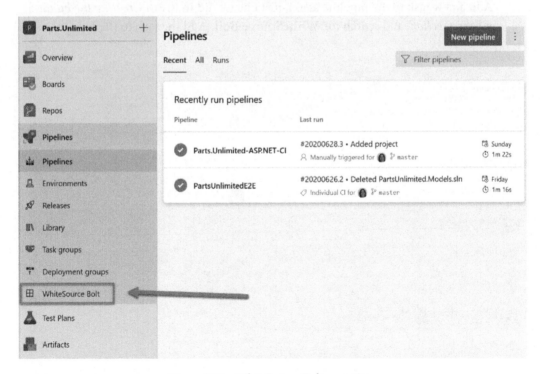

Figure 7.23 – WhiteSource Bolt menu item

5. On the **Settings** screen, specify a work email address, company name, and country. Then, click the **Get Started** button:

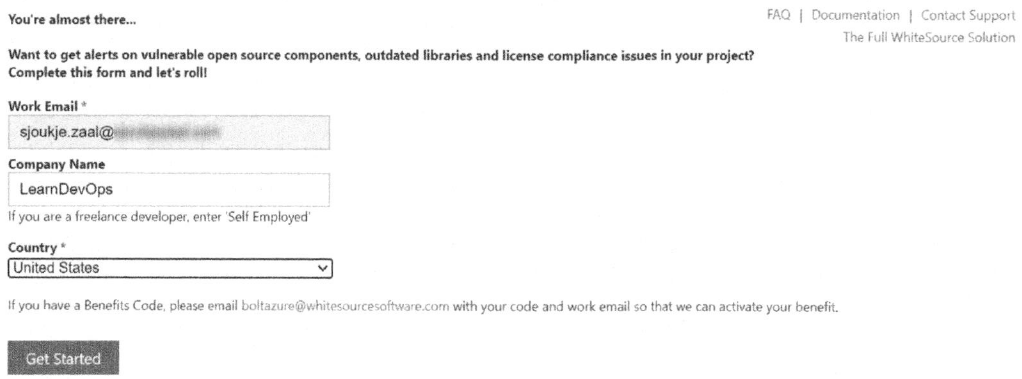

You're almost there...   FAQ | Documentation | Contact Support
                                                                          The Full WhiteSource Solution

Want to get alerts on vulnerable open source components, outdated libraries and license compliance issues in your project?
Complete this form and let's roll!

Work Email *

sjoukje.zaal@

Company Name

LearnDevOps

If you are a freelance developer, enter 'Self Employed'

Country *

United States

If you have a Benefits Code, please email boltazure@whitesourcesoftware.com with your code and work email so that we can activate your benefit.

Get Started

Figure 7.24 – WhiteSource Bolt settings

6. We can now use WhiteSource Bolt tasks in our pipeline. Select the build pipeline that we created in section *Creating the build pipeline*. Now, edit the pipeline.

7. Add a new task to the pipeline again, just like we did in the in *Creating the build pipeline section*, and search for **WhiteSource Bolt**. Add the task to the pipeline:

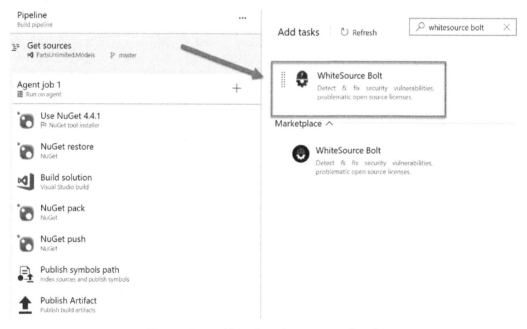

Figure 7.25 – Adding the WhiteSource Bolt task

8. Drag the task below the **Build solution** task since we want to scan the solution before the package is packed and pushed into the Artifact feed. This will look as follows:

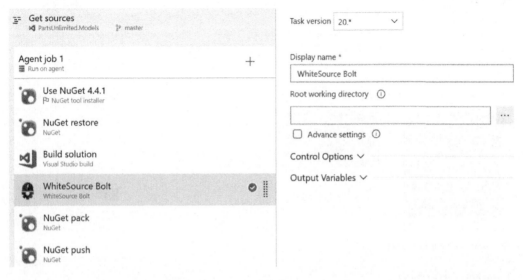

Figure 7.26 – Overview of the build pipeline

9. You don't have to specify any configuration values; this task will run without them.

10. From the top menu, select **Save & queue** and then **Save and run**. Wait until the build pipeline has finished successfully.

11. Go to the top menu once more and select **WhiteSource Bolt Build Support**. There, you will see an overview of the scan:

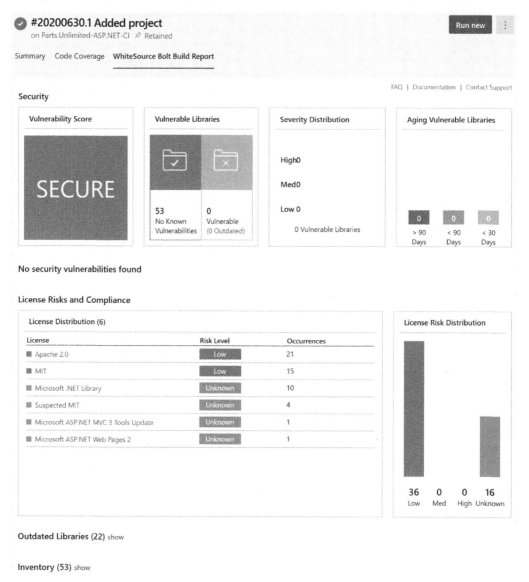

Figure 7.27 – WhiteSource Bolt vulnerability report

With that, we have installed the WhiteSource Bolt extension and scanned our solution for vulnerabilities before packaging and pushing the NuGet package to our feed in Azure Artifacts.

This concludes this chapter.

Summary

In this chapter, we looked at Azure Artifacts in more depth. First, we set up a feed and created a new NuGet package using the model classes in the **PartsUnlimited** project. Then, we created a build pipeline where we packed and pushed the package to the feed automatically during the build process. Finally, we used the WhiteSource Bolt extension from the Azure marketplace to scan the package for vulnerabilities.

In the next chapter, we are going to focus on how to deploy applications in Azure DevOps using release pipelines.

Further reading

Check out the following links for more information about the topics that were covered in this chapter:

- What is Azure Artifacts?: `https://docs.microsoft.com/en-us/azure/devops/artifacts/overview?view=azure-devops`

- Get started with NuGet packages in Azure DevOps Services and TFS: `https://docs.microsoft.com/en-us/azure/devops/artifacts/get-started-nuget?view=azure-devops`

8
Deploying Applications with Azure DevOps

In previous chapters, we saw how you can automate your development processes by using build pipelines for your code. But an important part of the software life cycle is also the release phase. In this chapter, we will cover an overview of release pipelines; we'll see how to create a release pipeline with Azure DevOps and how you can automate and improve the deployment of your solutions by using release approvals and multi-stage pipelines.

We will cover the following topics in this chapter:

- An overview of release pipelines
- Creating a release pipeline with Azure DevOps
- Configuring continuous deployment on a release pipeline
- Creating a multi-stage release pipeline
- Using approvals and gates for controlling your release process
- Using environments and deployment groups
- Using YAML-based pipelines for release

Technical requirements

To follow this chapter, you need to have an active Azure DevOps organization. The organization used in this chapter is the **PartsUnlimited** organization we created in *Chapter 1, Azure DevOps Overview*.

An overview of release pipelines

Release pipelines permit you to implement the continuous delivery phase of a software life cycle. With a release pipeline, you can automate the process of testing and deliver your solutions (committed code) to the final environments or directly to the customer's site (continuous delivery and continuous deployment).

With **continuous delivery**, you deliver code to a certain environment for testing or quality control, while **continuous deployment** is the phase where you release code to a final production environment.

A release pipeline can be triggered manually (you decide when you want to deploy your code) or it can be triggered according to events such as a code commit on the master branch, after the completion of a stage (for example, the production testing stage), or according to a schedule.

A release pipeline is normally connected to an **artifact store** (a deployable component for an application and output of a build). An artifact store contains a set of artifacts for a build (distinct artifact versions), and a release pipeline takes these artifacts and provisions the needed infrastructure and steps for deploying the artifacts.

A release pipeline (exactly as we saw in *Chapter 4, Understanding Azure DevOps Pipelines*, for the build pipeline definition) is composed of different stages (parts of the pipeline that can run independently), and each stage is composed of **jobs** and **tasks**.

A schema of a release pipeline is as follows:

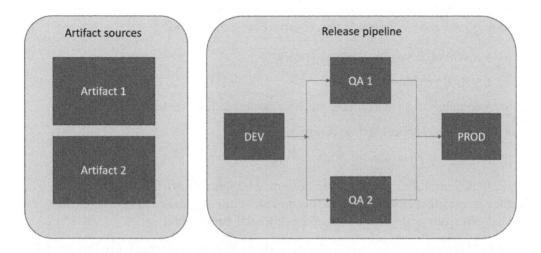

Figure 8.1 – Release pipeline schema

As you can see in the preceding diagram, a release pipeline starts from artifacts (the output of a successfully completed build) and then moves between stages, executing jobs and tasks.

In Azure DevOps, a release pipeline is executed according to the following steps:

1. When a deployment request is triggered, Azure Pipelines checks whether a pre-deployment approval phase is required and eventually sends approval notifications to the involved people in a team.

2. When approved, the deployment job is queued and waits for an agent.

3. An agent that is able to run this deployment job picks up the job.

4. The agent downloads the artifacts as specified in the release pipeline definition.

5. The agent runs the tasks defined in the deployment job and creates a log for each step.

6. When the deployment for a stage is completed, Azure Pipelines executes a post-deployment approval (if present).

7. The deployment then goes to the next stage.

In a release pipeline, an artifact is deployed to an **environment** (where your final application will run), and these environments can be the following:

- A machine on your corporate network

- A virtual machine in the cloud

- A containerized environment, such as Docker or Kubernetes

- A managed service, such as Azure App Service

- A serverless environment, such as Azure Functions

A way to define an Azure Pipelines environment is with a YAML file, where you can include an environment section that specifies the Azure Pipelines environment where you'll deploy your artifact, or by using the classic UI-based editor

In the next section, we'll see how to define a release pipeline with the Azure DevOps UI in detail.

Creating a release pipeline with Azure DevOps

The final goal for implementing a complete CI/CD process with DevOps is to automate the deployment of your software to a final environment (for example, the final customer), and to achieve this goal, you need to create a **release pipeline**.

A release pipeline takes the build artifacts (the result of your build process) and deploys those artifacts to one or more final environments.

To create our first release pipeline, we'll use the **PartsUnlimited** web application project previously deployed on Azure DevOps:

1. To create a release pipeline with Azure DevOps, click on **Pipelines** on the left menu, select **Releases**, and then click on **New release pipeline**:

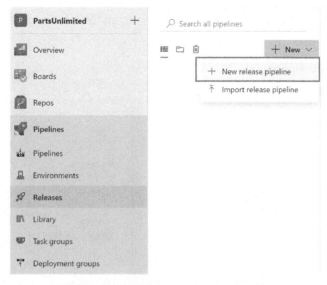

Figure 8.2 – Creating a new release pipeline

2. In the **Select a template** list that appears on the right, you have a set of available templates for creating releases for different types of applications and platforms. For our application, select **Azure App Service deployment** and click **Apply**:

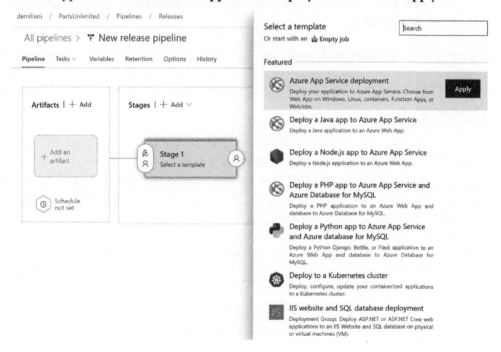

Figure 8.3 – Release pipeline template selection

3. Now, provide a name for the stage that will contain the release tasks. Here, I'm calling it `Deploy to cloud`:

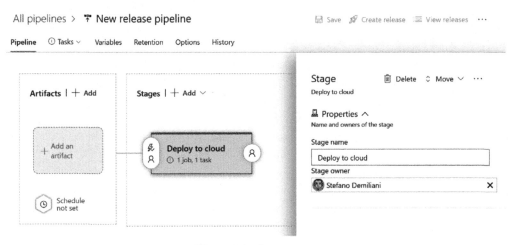

Figure 8.4 – Stage name

4. In the **Stages** section, click on the **1 job, 1 task** link. Here, you need to provide the settings of the Azure web app environment where your application will be deployed, such as your Azure subscription and the App Service instance (web app) where the code will be deployed:

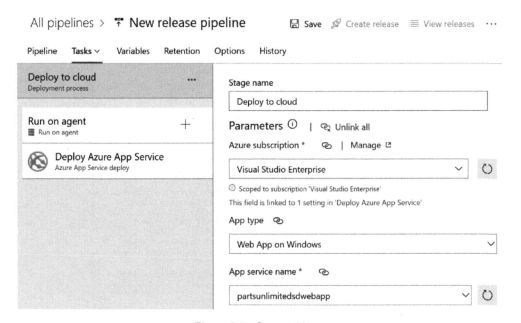

Figure 8.5 – Stage settings

You have now defined the stage of your release pipeline (single-stage). In the next section, we'll see how to specify the artifacts for your release pipeline.

Defining artifacts for a release pipeline

Artifacts are all the items (output of a build) that must be deployed in your final environment, and Azure Pipelines can deploy artifacts that come from different artifact sources:

1.   To select artifacts, on the main release pipeline screen, click on **Add an artifact**:

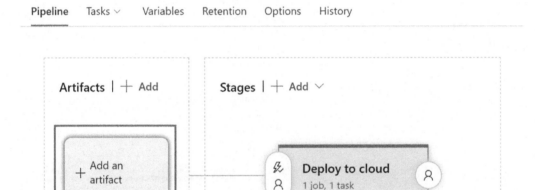

Figure 8.6 – Adding an artifact to a release pipeline

2. In the **Add an artifact** panel, you have **Source type** automatically set to **Build** (this means that you're deploying the output of a build pipeline). Here, you need to select the build pipeline that you want to use as the source (the name or ID of the build pipeline that publishes the artifact; here, I'm using the **PartsUnlimitedE2E** build pipeline) and the default version (the default version will be deployed when new releases are created. The version can be changed for manually created releases at the time of release creation):

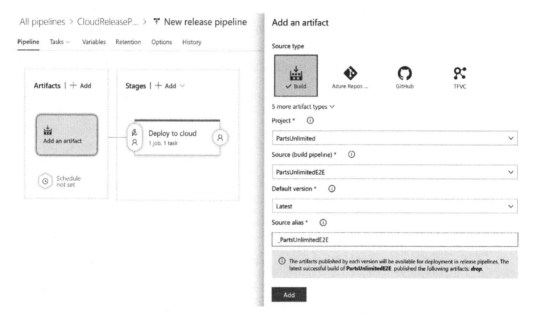

Figure 8.7 – Add an artifact

3. Click on the **Add** button to save the artifact configuration, and then click on the **Save** button in the top-right corner to save your release pipeline:

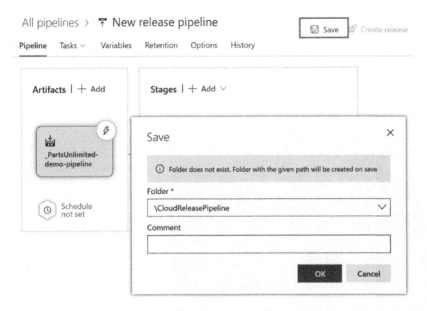

Figure 8.8 – Saving a release pipeline

Your release pipeline is now ready. In the next section, we'll see how to create the Azure DevOps release process.

Creating the Azure DevOps release

After defining our release pipeline (stages and artifacts), we need to create a **release**. A release is simply a run of your release pipeline:

1. To create a release, on the release pipeline definition page, click on the **Create release** button in the top-right corner:

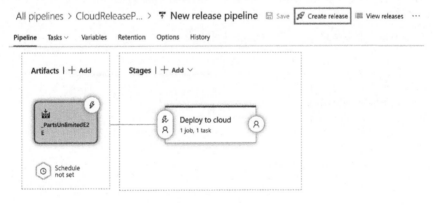

Figure 8.9 – Creating a release

2. On the **Create a new release** page, accept all the default values (you need to have a successfully completed build with artifacts created), and then click on **Create**:

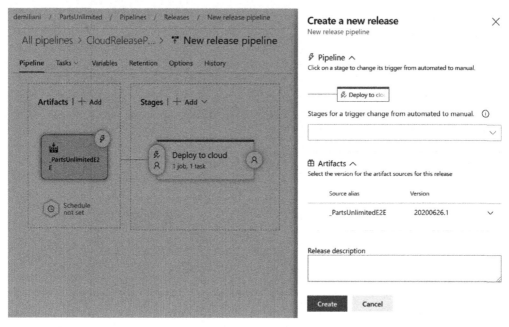

Figure 8.10 – Creating a release

3. A new release is now created, and you will see a green bar indicating that:

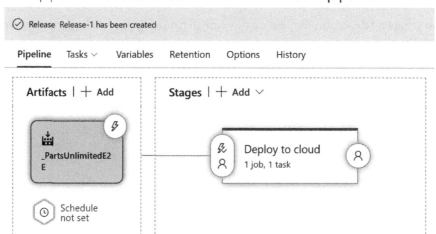

Figure 8.11 – Release created

4. Now, you can click on the release name (here, it is **Release-1**) and you will be redirected to the details of the release process:

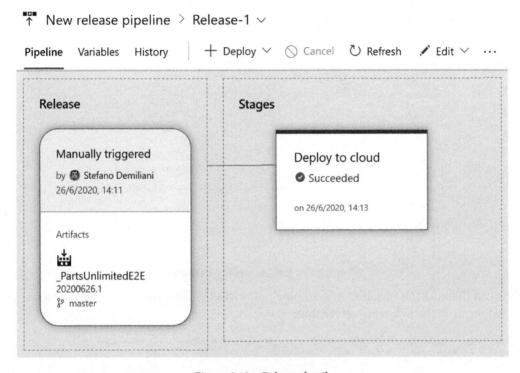

Figure 8.12 – Release details

5. If you click on the stage, you can see the details of each step:

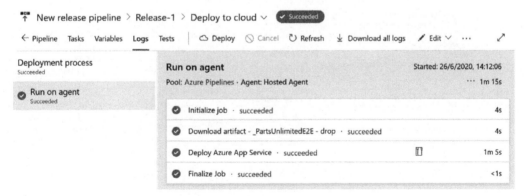

Figure 8.13 – Details of the stage

You have completed your first release pipeline. Here, we have triggered it manually. In the next section, we'll see how to use variables in your pipeline.

Using variables in a release pipeline

In a release pipeline, you can also use variables and variable groups to specify variable parameters that can be used in your pipeline tasks. To specify a variable for your release pipeline, select the **Variables** tab and specify the name and value of your variable:

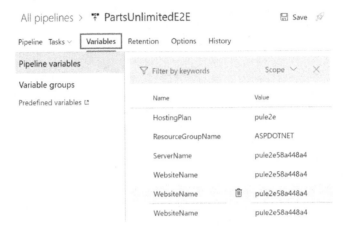

Figure 8.14 – Release pipeline variables

You can then use the variables in your pipeline's tasks by using the $(VariableName) notation, as in the following screenshot:

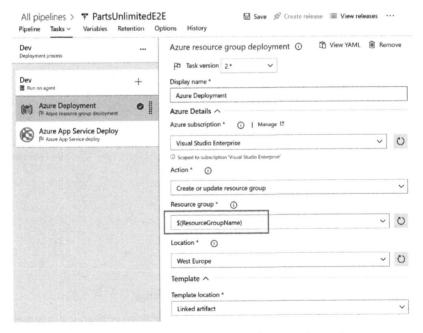

Figure 8.15 – Using a variable in a release pipeline task

Using variables is recommended if you have parameters that change on your pipeline. In the next section, we'll see how to configure triggers for continuous deployment.

Configuring the release pipeline triggers for continuous deployment

To automate the continuous deployment of your application, you need to configure triggers in your release pipeline definition:

1. To do that, click on the **Continuous deployment trigger** icon in the pipeline's **Artifacts** section:

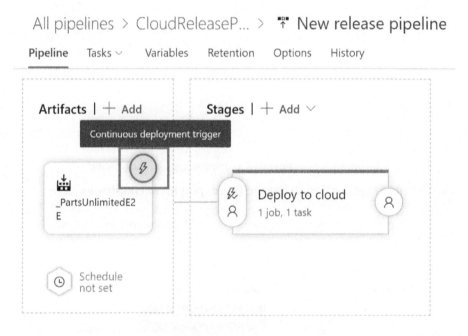

Figure 8.16 – Continuous deployment trigger

2. In the **Continuous deployment trigger** panel, enable it to automatically create a new release after every successfully completed build and select a branch filter (for example, the build pipeline's default branch):

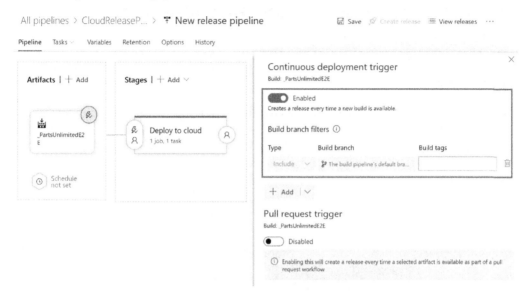

Figure 8.17 – Continuous deployment trigger configuration

3. Now, in the **Stages** section, select the **Pre-deployment conditions** icon:

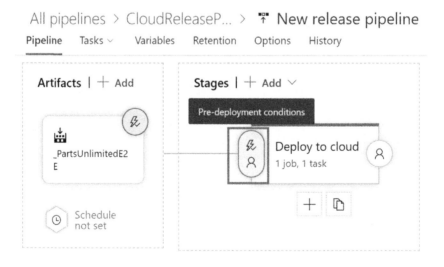

Figure 8.18 – Pre-deployment conditions

4. In the **Pre-deployment conditions** pane, check that the trigger for this stage is set to **After release** (this means that the deployment stage will start automatically when a new release is created from this pipeline):

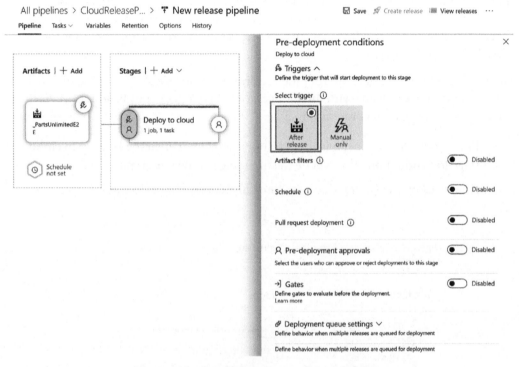

Figure 8.19 – Pre-deployment conditions definition

In this pane, you can also define other parameters, such as selecting artifact condition(s) to trigger a new deployment (a release will be deployed to this stage only if all the artifact conditions match), setting up a schedule for the deployment, allowing pull request-based releases to be deployed to this stage, selecting the users who can approve or reject deployments to this stage (pre-deployment approvals), defining gates to evaluate before deployment, and defining behavior when multiple releases are queued for deployment.

You have now created a release pipeline that takes your artifacts and deploys them to the cloud by using Azure DevOps and also by applying continuous deployment triggers and pre-deployment conditions checks.

In the next section, we'll see how to improve our release pipeline by using multiple stages.

Creating a multi-stage release pipeline

A multi-stage release pipeline is useful when you want to release your applications with multiple steps (staging), such as, for example, development, staging, and production. A quite common scenario in the real world is, for example, deploying an application initially to a testing environment. When tests are finished, the application is moved to a quality acceptance stage, and then, if the customer accepts the release, the application is moved to a production environment.

Here, we'll do the same: starting from the previously created single-stage pipeline, we'll create a new release pipeline with three stages, called **DEV**, **QA**, and **Production**. Each stage is a deployment target for our pipeline:

1. In the previously defined pipeline, as a first step, I renamed the **Deploy to cloud** stage to **Production**. This will be the final stage of the release pipeline.

2. Now, click on the **Clone** action to clone the defined stage into a new stage:

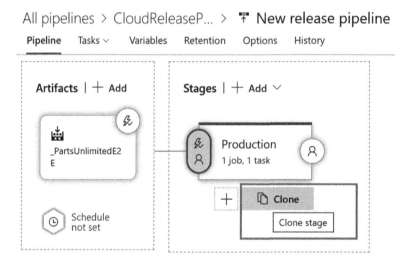

Figure 8.20 – Cloning a stage

3. A new cloned stage appears after the previously created stage. Change the name of this stage to QA:

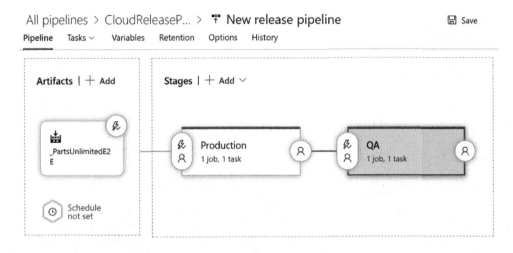

Figure 8.21 – Cloned stage (QA)

4. Now, we need to reorganize the stages because the **QA** stage must occur before the **Production** stage. To reorganize these stages, select the **QA** stage and choose the pre-deployment conditions. In the **Pre-deployment conditions** pane, select **After release** as the trigger (instead of **After stage**):

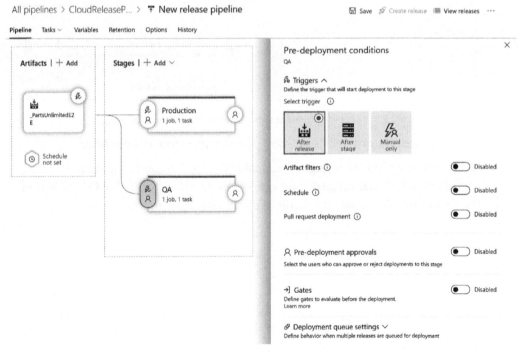

Figure 8.22 – Pre-deployment conditions for the QA stage

5. As you can see, the pipeline diagram has now changed (you have the **QA** and **Production** stages executed in parallel). Now, select the **Pre-deployment conditions** properties for the **Production** stage; set the trigger to **After stage** and select **QA** as the stage:

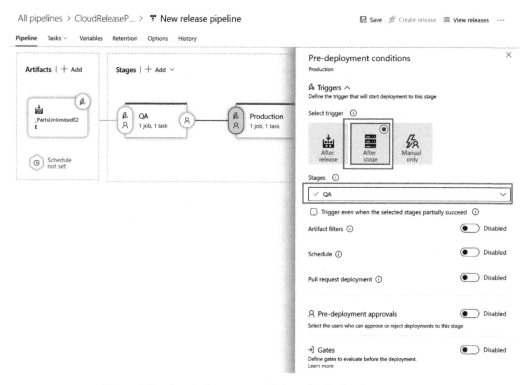

Figure 8.23 – Pre-deployment conditions for the Production stage

6. The stages are now ordered as we want (**QA** occurs before **Production**).

7. At this point, we have two stages that deploy the application to the same environment (**QA** was created as a clone of **Production**). Select the **QA** stage from the **Tasks** drop-down list and change **App service name** to a new instance:

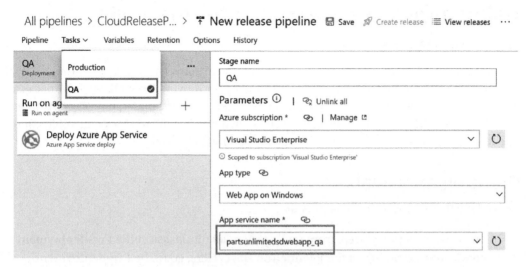

Figure 8.24 – QA stage details

8. Now, we need to repeat the same steps for creating the **DEV** stage. Clone it from **QA**, set its **Pre-deployment conditions** properties with the trigger set to **After Release**, and change the **QA** trigger to **After stage**, with **DEV** as the selected stage. Your pipeline will now look as follows:

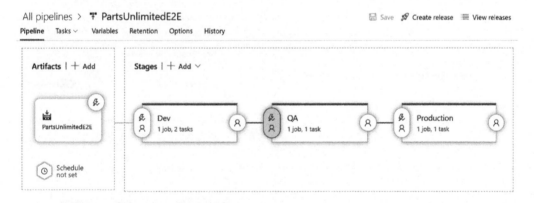

cYou have now created a release pipeline with different stages (**Dev**, **QA**, and **Production**) for controlling the deployment steps of your code.

In the next section, we'll see how to add approvals for moving between stages.

Using approvals and gates for managing deployments

As previously configured, our release pipeline will move between stages only if the previous stage is completed successfully. This is okay for moving from **DEV** to **QA** because on this transition, our application is deployed to a testing environment, but the transition from **QA** to **Production** should usually be controlled because the release of an application into a production environment normally occurs after an approval.

Creating approvals

Let's follow these steps to create approvals:

1. To create an approval step, from our pipeline definition, select the **Pre-deployment conditions** properties of the **Production** stage. Here, go to the **Pre-deployment approvals** section and enable it. Then, in the **Approvers** section, select the users that will be responsible for approving. Please also check that the **The user requesting a release or deployment should not approve it** option is not ticked:

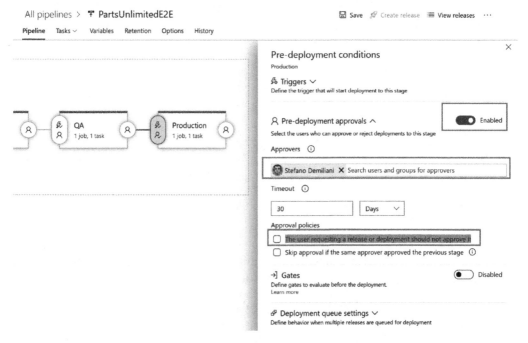

Figure 8.26 – Setting approvals

2. Click on **Save** to save your pipeline definition.

3. Now, create a new release to start our pipeline and click on the name of the created release (here, it is called **Release-2**):

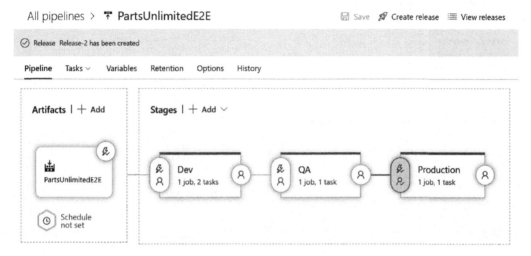

Figure 8.27 – Multi-stage release triggered

4. The release pipeline starts. The **DEV** and **QA** stages are completed, while on the **Production** stage, a **Pending approval** status appears:

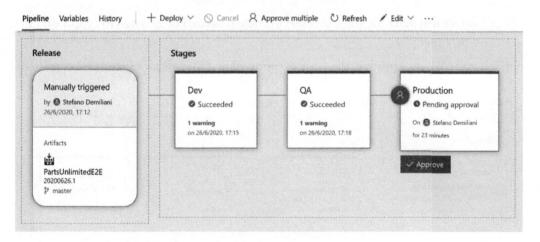

Figure 8.28 – Pending approval

5. The release pipeline is waiting for approval. You can click on the **Pending approval** icon and the approval dialog is opened. Here, you can insert a comment and then approve or reject the release:

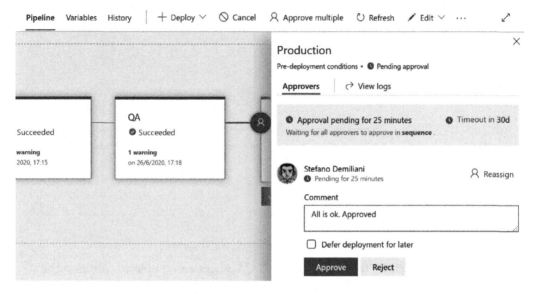

Figure 8.29 – Approving a stage

6. You can also defer the stage to a specific date if needed or reassign the approval to another user.

7. If you click on **Approve**, the stage is approved and the release pipeline is completed:

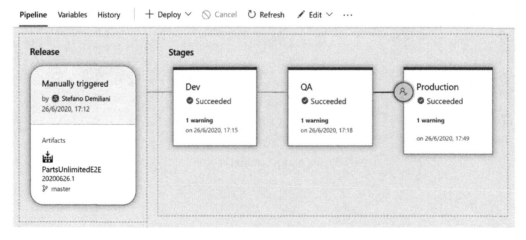

Figure 8.30 – Multi-stage pipeline completed

8. If you now click on the Azure App Service instance deployed by your pipeline, you can see that the final code (the **PartsUnlimited** website) is deployed in the cloud:

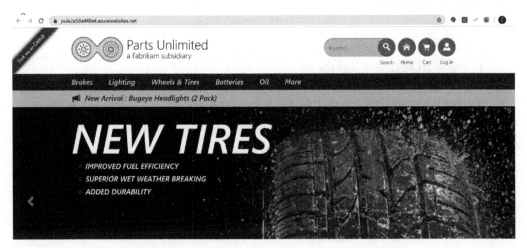

Figure 8.31 – Web app deployed from the release pipeline

Using gates to check conditions

In the previously explained scenario, we saw how to configure a manual approval process for a release pipeline. Sometimes, you need to avoid the manual process and instead have a policy in place that permits your pipeline to go ahead only if some checks are successfully performed. This is where **gates** come in action.

In Azure Pipelines, a gate allows you to automatically check for specific conditions from Azure DevOps from external services and then enable the release process only when the conditions are met. You can use gates to check the status of work items and issues of a project and enable the release only if you have no open bugs. You can also query test results, check whether security scans on artifacts are performed before releasing, monitor the infrastructure health before releasing, and so on.

As an example, here we want to configure a gate for our previously created release pipeline where we check for open bugs on Azure Boards. We will see how to do this with the help of the following steps:

> **Important note**
> If there are open bugs, the release pipeline cannot go ahead.

1. To check for open bugs in our project, we need to define a query for work items. From our Azure DevOps project, select **Boards**, click on **Queries**, and then select **New query**:

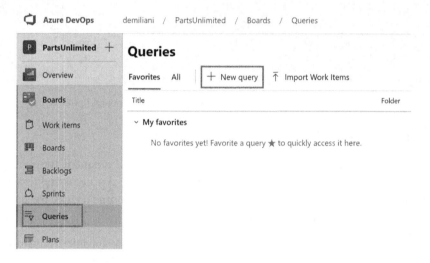

Figure 8.32 – Cresting a new query for the gate conditions

2. Here, I've defined a query as follows:

Figure 8.33 – Query definition

This query checks for active bugs in our project.

3. Save the query by giving it a name (for example, **ActiveBugs**) and specifying a folder (here, I've selected the **Shared Queries** folder):

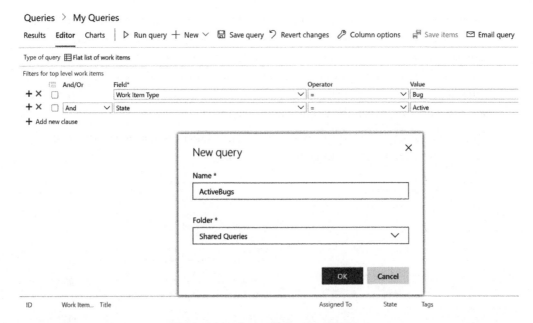

Figure 8.34 – Saving the query definition

4. Now we're ready to define our gate. From the multi-stage release pipeline we previously created, select the **Production** stage, click on the bolt icon, and then enable gates, as shown in the following screenshot:

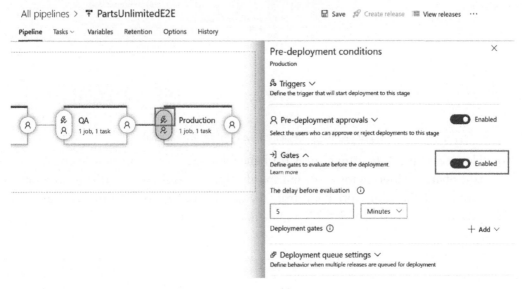

Figure 8.35 – Enabling gates

Here, you can also specify the delay before the evaluation of gates (the time before the added gates are evaluated for the first time. If no gates are added, then the deployment will wait for the specified duration before proceeding), and we can specify the deployment gates (adding gates that evaluate health parameters). These gates are periodically evaluated in parallel and if the gates succeed, the deployment will proceed; otherwise, the deployment is rejected.

5. To specify our gate, click on **Add** and then select **Query work items** (this will execute a work item query and check the results):

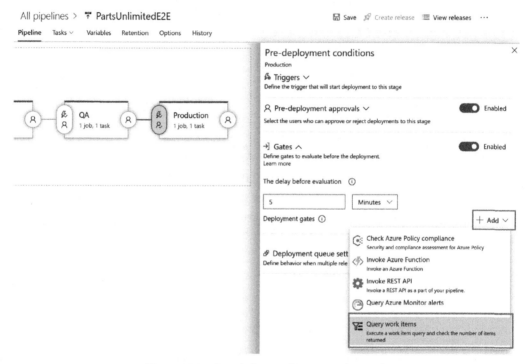

Figure 8.36 – Gate definition (Query work items)

6. Now, select the **ActiveBugs** query from the folder where you previously saved it (the **Shared folder**, in my case) and specify **Upper threshold** as 0 (the maximum number of matching work items from the query) because we want the release pipeline to only be completed if we have 0 active bugs:

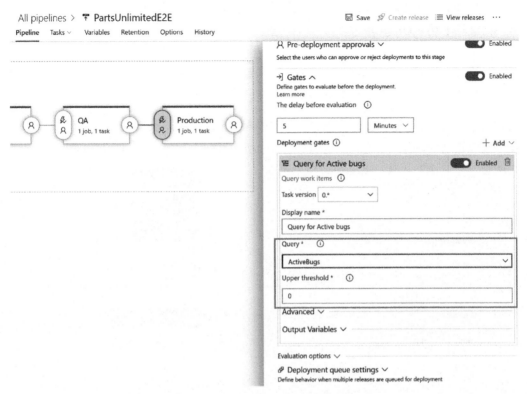

Figure 8.37 – Specifying conditions for the gate

Here, you can also define evaluations options such as **time between re-evaluation of gates** (the duration after which the gates are re-evaluated; this must be greater than the longest typical response time of the configured gates to allow all responses to be received in each evaluation), **Minimum duration for steady results after a successful gates evaluation** (all gates must continuously be successful for this duration; 0 means deployment will proceed when all gates succeed in the same evaluation cycle), **timeout after which gates fail** (the maximum evaluation period for gates; the deployment will be rejected if the timeout is reached before gates succeed).

Our gate is now defined and active. You can also define other types of gates and you can also have gates that call Azure Functions to evaluate a release condition (which is useful if you want to integrate your release check with specific conditions on an external system).

Using deployment groups

A **deployment group** is a set of machines with a deployment agent installed on each of them. Each deployment group represents a physical environment and it defines a logical group of target machines for parallel deployment.

You can define a deployment group in Azure DevOps by going to the **Pipeline** section and selecting **Deployment groups**:

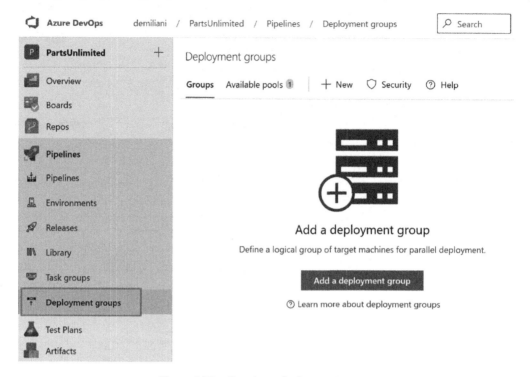

Figure 8.38 – Creating a deployment group

Here, you can add servers where the build and release agent is installed.

Each created deployment group is a member of a **deployment pool**, and this pool can also be shared across projects. Deployment groups can only be used on release pipelines.

You can add a deployment group job by going to the release pipeline editor, selecting the job, and clicking on the three-dots button. Here, you can see the **Add a deployment group job** option:

Figure 8.39 – Adding a deployment group job

At the time of writing, deployment group jobs are not yet supported on YAML pipelines.

YAML release pipelines with Azure DevOps

A recently added feature of Azure DevOps is the option to define release pipelines by using YAML (previously, this was possible only for the CI part). This is now possible by using multi-stage pipelines and with that, you can use a unified YAML experience for configuring Azure DevOps pipelines for CI, CD, and CI/CD.

Defining the release YAML pipeline can be done exactly as described in *Chapter 4, Understanding Azure DevOps Pipelines*. There are, however, some concepts to understand, such as **environments**.

Environments are a group of resources targeted by a pipeline – for example, Azure Web Apps, virtual machines, or Kubernetes clusters. You can use environments to group resources by scope – for example, you can create an environment called **development** with your development resources and an environment called **production** with the production resources. Environments can be created by going to the **Environments** section under **Pipelines**:

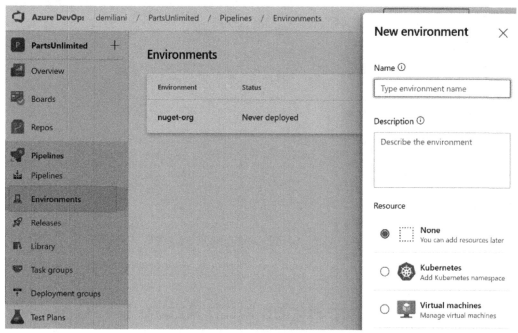

Figure 8.40 – Creating environments

The following is an example of a multi-stage release pipeline for deploying a .NET Core application on Azure Web Apps:

```
stages:
    - stage: Build_Source_# Build Source Code for Dotnet Core
Web App
     jobs:
     - job: Build
       pool: 'Hosted VS2017'
       variables:
         buildConfiguration: 'Release'
       continueOnError: false
       steps:
```

```yaml
      - task: DotNetCoreCLI@2
        inputs:
          command: build
          arguments: '--configuration $(buildConfiguration)'
      - task: DotNetCoreCLI@2
        inputs:
          command: publish
          arguments: '--configuration $(buildConfiguration)
--output $(Build.ArtifactStagingDirectory)'
          modifyOutputPath: true
          zipAfterPublish: true
      - task: PublishBuildArtifacts@1
        inputs:
          path: $(Build.ArtifactStagingDirectory)
          artifact: drop

  - stage: Deploy_In_Dev # Deploy artifacts to the dev
environment
    jobs:
    - deployment: azure_web_app_dev
      pool: 'Hosted VS2017'
      variables:
        WebAppName: 'PartsUnlimited-dev'
      environment: 'dev-environment'
      strategy:
        runOnce:
          deploy:
            steps:
            - task: AzureRMWebAppDeployment@4
              displayName: Azure App Service Deploy
              inputs:
                WebAppKind: webApp
                ConnectedServiceName: 'pay-as-you-go'
                WebAppName: $(WebAppName)
                Package: $(System.WorkFolder)/**/*.zip
  - stage: Deploy_In_QA # Deploy artifacts to the qa
environment
```

```
jobs:
- deployment: azure_web_app_qa
  pool: 'Hosted VS2017'
  variables:
    WebAppName: 'PartsUnlimited-qa'
  environment: 'qa-environment'
  strategy:
    runOnce:
      deploy:
        steps:
        - task: AzureRMWebAppDeployment@4
          displayName: Azure App Service Deploy
          inputs:
            WebAppKind: webApp
            ConnectedServiceName: 'pay-as-you-go'
            WebAppName: $(WebAppName)
            Package: $(System.WorkFolder)/**/*.zip
- stage: Deploy_In_Production # Deploy artifacts to the
production environment
  jobs:
  - deployment: azure_web_app_prod
    pool: 'Hosted VS2017'
    variables:
      WebAppName: 'PartsUnlimited'
    environment: 'prod-environment'
    strategy:
      runOnce:
        deploy:
          steps:
          - task: AzureRMWebAppDeployment@4
            displayName: Azure App Service Deploy
            inputs:
              WebAppKind: webApp
              ConnectedServiceName: 'pay-as-you-go'
              WebAppName: $(WebAppName)
              Package: $(System.WorkFolder)/**/*.zip
```

As you can see in the preceding YAML file, the pipeline defines four stages: **Build Source**, **Deploy in Dev**, **Deploy in QA**, and **Deploy in Production**. At each of these stages, the application is deployed on the specified environment.

Summary

In this chapter, we had a full overview of how to work with release pipelines in Azure DevOps.

We created a basic release pipeline for the **PartsUnlimited** project, defined artifacts, and created our first release by adding continuous deployment conditions.

Then, we improved our pipeline definition by using multiple stages (**DEV**, **QA**, and **Production**), and at the end of this chapter, we saw how to define approvals and gates for managing the release of our code in a more controlled way and the concepts around YAML-based release pipelines

In the next chapter, we'll see how to integrate Azure DevOps with GitHub.

Section 4: Advanced Features of Azure DevOps

In this part, we are going to integrate Azure DevOps with GitHub and we are going to cover some real-world examples.

This section contains the following chapters:

- *Chapter 9, Integrating Azure DevOps with GitHub*
- *Chapter 10, Using Test Plans with Azure DevOps*
- *Chapter 11, Real-World CI/CD Scenarios with Azure DevOps*

9
Integrating Azure DevOps with GitHub

GitHub is one of the most popular development platforms that's used by open source developers and businesses across the globe to store their code. In this chapter, you will learn how to leverage Azure DevOp's capabilities while you continue to use GitHub as your software development hub.

We'll be covering the following topics:

- An overview of Azure DevOps and GitHub integration
- Integrating Azure Pipelines with GitHub
- Integrating Azure Boards with GitHub
- Overview of GitHub Actions

Technical requirements

To follow this chapter, you need to have an active Azure DevOps organization and a GitHub account. You can sign up for a GitHub account here: `https://github.com/join`.

Let's get this chapter's prerequisites ready. This chapter requires that you have the **Parts Unlimited** GitHub repository cloned to your GitHub account. You will also need an Azure DevOps project to follow the examples in this chapter. Follow these steps before moving on to the next section:

1. Launch a browser instance and go to `https://github.com/microsoft/PartsUnlimitedE2E`.

2. Click **Fork**, as shown in the following screenshot:

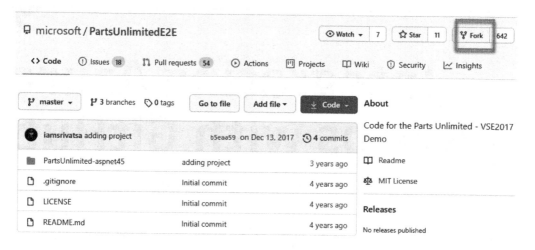

Figure 9.1 – GitHub repository for Parts Unlimited

3. GitHub should prompt you to log into your account if you're not logged in already. Select the account you wish to clone the repository to.

4. This will take a couple of minutes to complete. You should see the repository in your account upon completion.

5. We will be using this repository to test GitHub integration in this chapter.

6. Now, log into Azure DevOps (`https://dev.azure.com`) and create a new empty project:

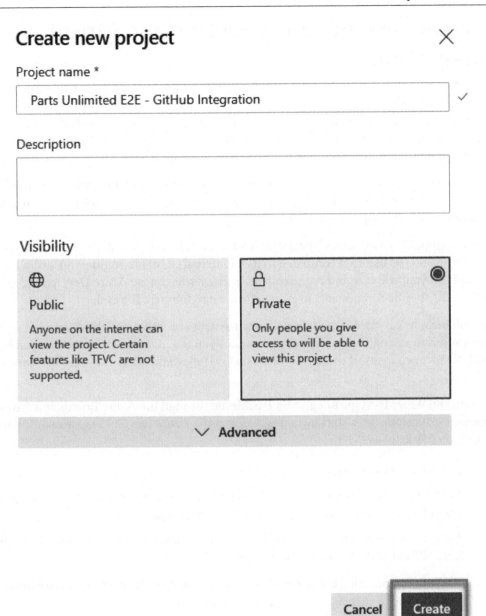

Figure 9.2 – Creating a new project

You're now ready to try out the examples described in this chapter.

An overview of Azure DevOps and GitHub integration

GitHub and Azure DevOps go hand in hand to provide a superior software development experience for teams, enabling them to ship and release software at a faster pace with minimal effort. In many scenarios, GitHub and Azure DevOps are competitors (for example, Azure Repos versus GitHub repositories), so it is typically up to you to choose the one that fits your needs and integrate them together for a wholesome platform setup.

Azure DevOps provides various RBAC levels, native enterprise identity integration, and so on, whereas GitHub enables simple collaboration across identities (while including AD integration in its Enterprise version).

When it comes to Continuous Integration/Continuous Development, Azure DevOps is way ahead and has matured compared to its counterpart, GitHub Actions. So, overall, it depends on your use case and requirements whether you choose Azure DevOps and/or GitHub for specific components in your software development life cycle.

GitHub includes an extension marketplace where you can find many third-party applications to extend GitHub to the applications you use. Azure DevOps integration is available through many of these extensions on GitHub Marketplace. Let's look at some of them.

GitHub and Azure DevOps integration is achieved through the Azure Boards and Azure Pipelines extensions. Let's start by taking a look at the Azure DevOps extensions available in GitHub Marketplace:

1. Launch a browser instance and go to `https://github.com/marketplace`.

2. Search for `Azure` in the extension marketplace. You'll find many extensions that can integrate Azure solutions with your GitHub repositories.

3. Here, we're interested in two specific extensions: Azure Boards and Azure Pipelines. Let's talk about them in a bit more detail:

    --**Azure Boards**: This extension allows you to link your Azure Boards work items to GitHub objects such as commits, pull requests, and issues:

Azure Boards ⊘
Connects Azure Boards with GitHub to plan, track, and discuss work across your teams

Figure 9.3 – Azure Boards extension

--**Azure Pipelines**: This extension allows you to build and release software using Azure Pipelines while your code is stored and maintained in your GitHub repository:

Figure 9.4 – Azure Pipelines extension

You can install these extensions from GitHub Marketplace and start configuration from GitHub itself, but in this chapter, we will be starting the integration process from Azure DevOps. GitHub and Azure DevOps integration is also supported for the on-premise variants of both products (GitHub on-premises and Azure DevOps Server).

Integrating Azure Pipelines with GitHub

Integrating Azure Pipelines with GitHub enables developers to continue using GitHub as their preferred source control management platform while leveraging Azure Pipelines' build and release capabilities. Azure Pipelines offers unlimited pipeline job minutes for open source projects.

We looked at Azure Pipelines in detail previously in this book, so in this section, we'll take a look at how to store our Azure Pipelines configuration and source code in GitHub and build a CI/CD process with GitHub and Azure DevOps.

Setting up Azure Pipelines and GitHub integration

In order to use Azure Pipelines with GitHub, you must authorize Azure Pipelines to access your GitHub repositories. Let's take a look at the steps for this:

1. Log into your Azure DevOps account and select the project we created in the *Technical requirements* section.

2. Click on **Pipelines** > **Create Pipeline**:

Figure 9.5 – Create Pipeline

3. Select **GitHub** as your code source location:

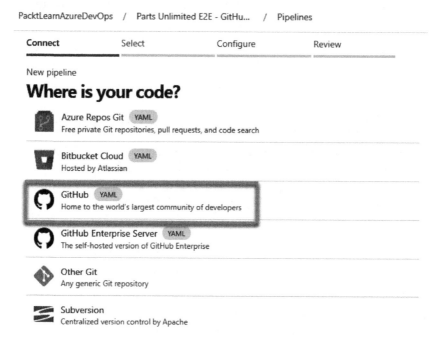

Figure 9.6 – GitHub source for Azure Pipelines

4. You will need to grant permission from Azure Pipelines to your GitHub account:

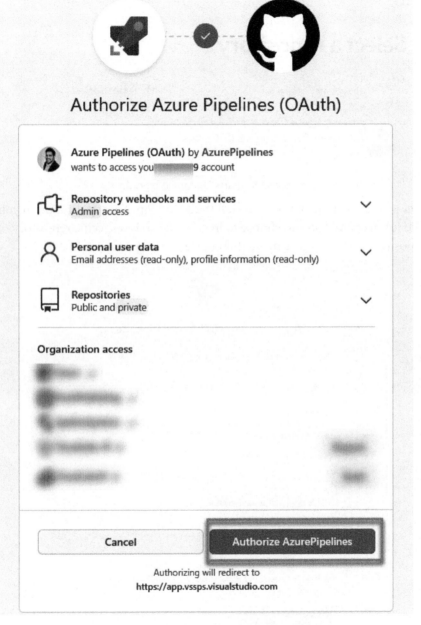

Figure 9.7 – Authorize Azure Pipelines (OAuth)

5. Upon successful completion, you will have your GitHub repositories listed in Azure DevOps. Select the newly created **PartsUnlimitedE2E** repository:

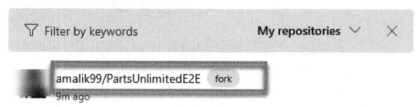

Figure 9.8 – Parts Unlimited repository

6. You will now get the option to install the Azure Pipelines application in your GitHub account. You can choose to install it for only a specific repository or for all repositories. Once you've made this choice, click **Approve & Install**:

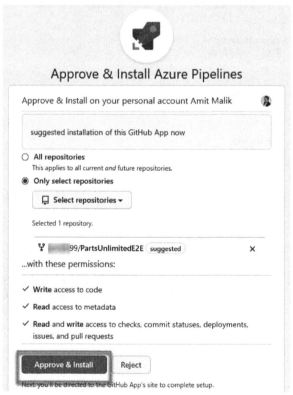

Figure 9.9 – Installing the Azure Pipelines extension

7. Since **Parts Unlimited** is a ASP.NET-based application, please choose **ASP.NET** as your pipeline configuration template:

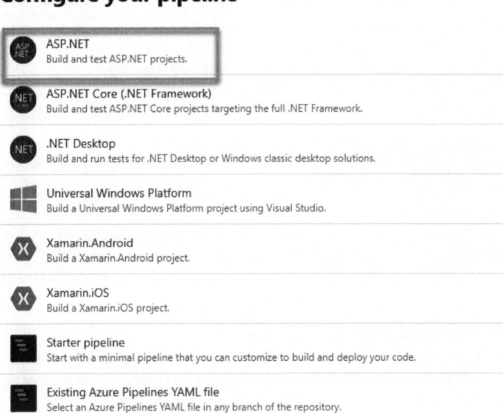

Figure 9.10 – Azure Pipelines task configuration

8. Azure DevOps will automatically generate a pipeline YAML file. You can review and modify it based on your requirements. **PartsUnlimited E2E** is designed to run build operations on Visual Studio 2017 on a Windows 2016 image. Please change the **vm-image** name to `vs2017-win2016` before continuing:

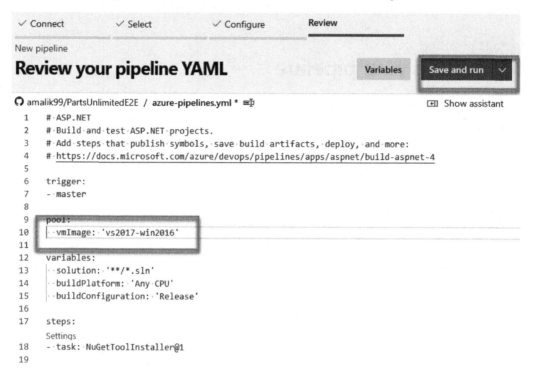

Figure 9.11 – Azure Pipelines task YAML

9. Click **Save and run** to save the pipeline.

10. You will need to make a commit to the repository to store the pipeline YAML file. You can commit the changes to the master branch or create a new branch to do so:

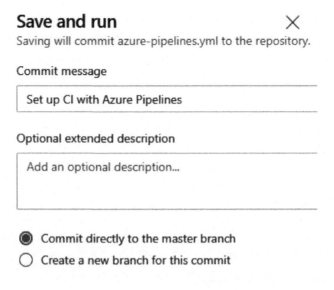

Figure 9.12 – Running an Azure pipeline

11. Clicking on **Save and run** will create the pipeline and start its execution. It may take a few minutes for the build job to complete:

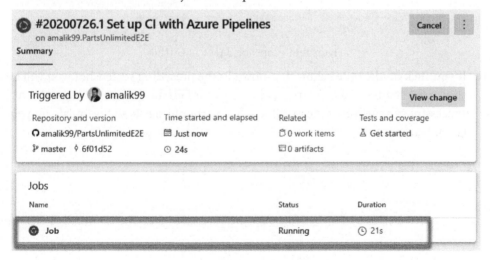

Figure 9.13 – Pipeline jobs

12. While this completes, let's look at the changes you made to your GitHub repository. Browse to your GitHub account and go to the **PartsUnlimitedE2E** repository.

13. You will see a commit and a newly added `azure-pipelines.yml` file, which stores the pipeline's configuration:

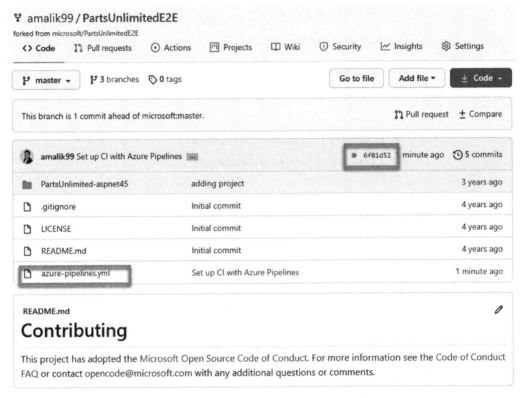

Figure 9.14 – Pipeline YAML in GitHub

14. If you click on the little yellow dot shown in the preceding screenshot, you will be shown the status of your Azure pipeline on your GitHub repository page. Upon successful completion of the pipeline job, you should see its status update on your GitHub account:

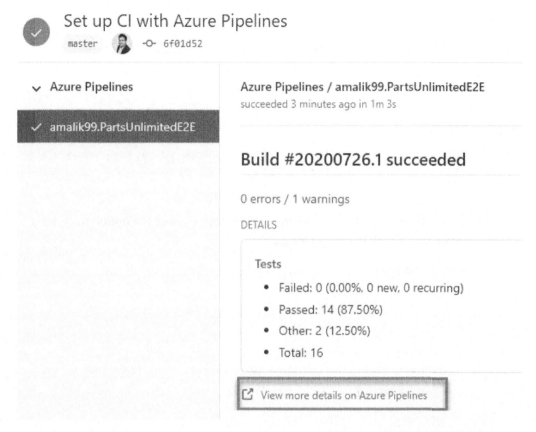

Figure 9.15 – Job logs in GitHub

With that, you have set up an Azure pipeline with GitHub.

Testing continuous integration

In this section, we will try out the CI capabilities of GitHub and Azure Pipelines. We'll make a code change in GitHub and raise a pull request that will trigger the Azure Pipelines job automatically.

Let's get started:

1. Browse to your GitHub account and open the **PartsUnlimited E2E** repository.

2. Click on `Readme.MD` and click **Edit**:

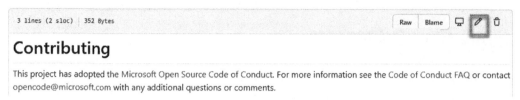

Figure 9.16 – Readme.MD

3. Update the file so that it includes some sample text. Choose the option to create a new branch and click **Propose changes**:

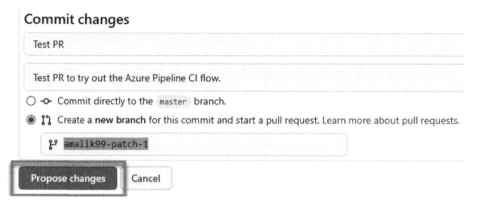

Figure 9.17 – Propose changes

4. Click Create pull request, as shown in the following screenshot:

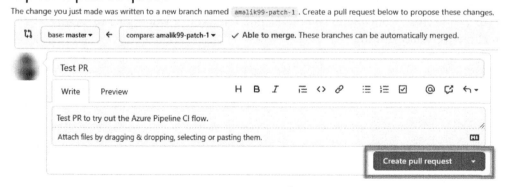

Figure 9.18 – Create pull request

5. This will open the **Pull request** page. It'll take a couple of minutes for the Azure
    Pipelines job to start. Once started, you can click on **Details** to see the status of the
    pipeline job:

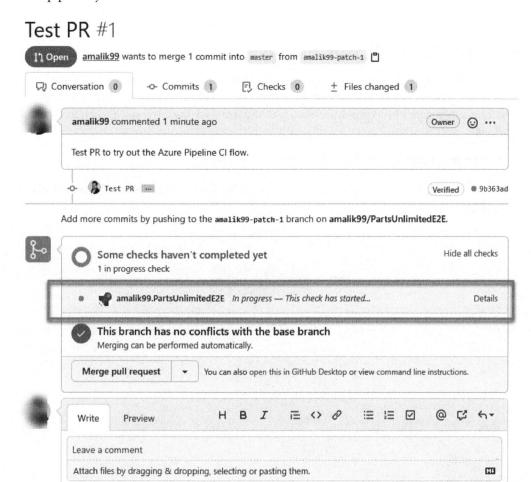

Figure 9.19 – Pull request automated checks

6. This concludes testing out the continuous integration capabilities of GitHub and Azure Pipelines. As we can see, Azure Pipelines and GitHub integrate very well and provide a whole new DevOps experience. You can merge the pull request to complete this process.

Adding a build Status badge

Azure Pipelines provides markup text that can be used in your GitHub repository documentation to provide the status of the pipelines job for the project. This can help developers be aware of the pipeline's status at any time, without the need to go to Azure DevOps.

Let's learn how to set up an Azure Pipelines Status badge:

1. Log into Azure DevOps and browse to **Your project** > **Pipelines** > **PartsUnlimited E2E**.

2. Click on the ellipses (**…**) and select **Status badge**:

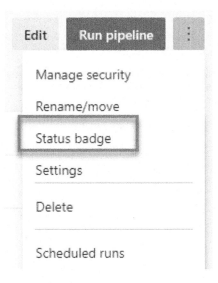

Figure 9.20 – Status badge

3. Copy the **Sample markdown** text box's value. Optionally, you can choose to get the markdown for a specific branch. Please save this markdown in a temporary location:

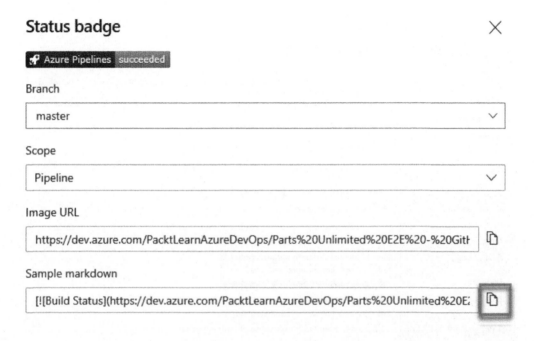

Figure 9.21 – Status badge URL

4. Now, before we can use this in GitHub, we must allow anonymous access to the project's badge.

5. Click on **Project Settings > Pipelines > Settings**.

6. Turn off the **Disable anonymous access to badges** setting. If you find this option grayed out, you must turn this off in the organization settings first:

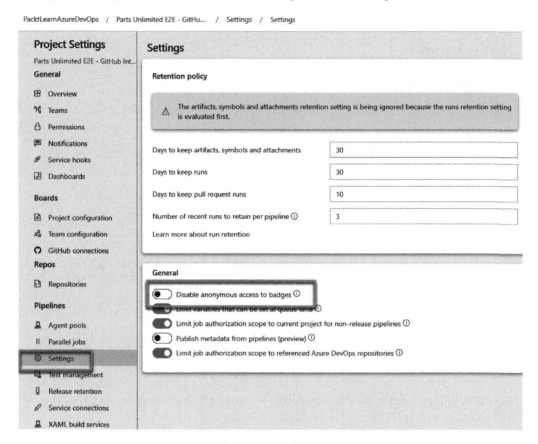

Figure 9.22 – Status badge access

7. Now, you can use this markdown in your GitHub documentation. It is recommended that you keep this in your repository's README file so that it's the first thing anyone will see:

Figure 9.23 – Status badge markdown

8. Upon committing your changes, you should see the Azure Pipelines badge:

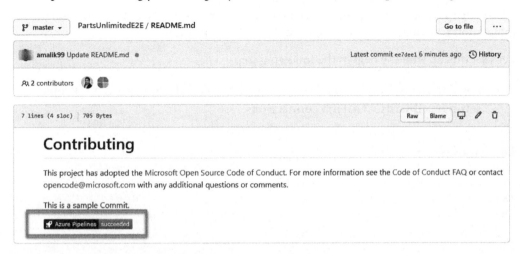

Figure 9.24 – Status badge showcase

With that, you've completed the Azure Pipelines integration with GitHub. In the next section, we'll take a look at integrating Azure Boards with GitHub.

Integrating Azure Boards with GitHub

Azure Boards is the best place to plan and track your work items. Integrating Azure Boards with GitHub allows you to keep using Azure Boards as your planning and managing platform while you continue using GitHub as your source control management platform.

By integrating Azure Boards with GitHub, you can link objects from Azure Boards to GitHub. A few examples are as follows:

- Work item and Git commit/issue/pull request linking means you can link your work items to the corresponding work being done in GitHub.

- You can update your work item's status from GitHub itself.

- Overall, integration allows us to track and link the deliverable across the two platforms easily.

Now, let's set up our Azure Boards integration.

Setting up Azure Boards and GitHub integration

Azure Boards is another extension available in GitHub Marketplace. You can configure the integration from both Azure DevOps and GitHub Marketplace.

Let's set this up with the help of the following steps:

1. Log into Azure DevOps and browse to your **Parts Unlimited** project > **Project settings** > **Boards** > **GitHub connections**:

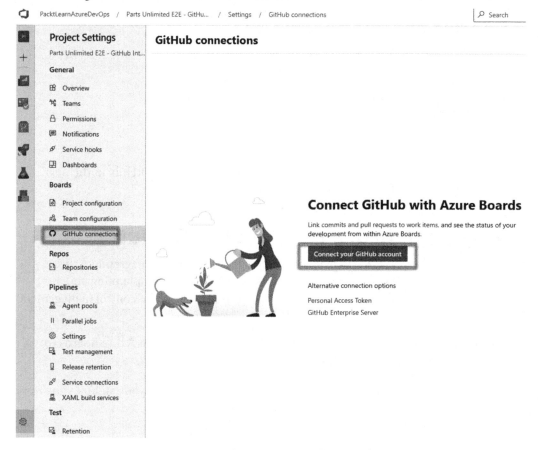

Figure 9.25 – Connecting GitHub to Boards

2. Click on **Connect your GitHub account**. You will need to authorize Azure Boards in order to access your GitHub account. Upon successfully linking them, you'll need to select the GitHub organization you want to connect to.

3. Azure DevOps will list your repositories. Please choose **PartsUnlimited E2E** for the purpose of this project and click **Save**:

← **Add GitHub repositories**   ✕

Add the GitHub repositories you want to use with your Azure Boards.

▽ parts   ✕

Viewing 2 of 49, 1 selected

○   fork

✓   9/PartsUnlimitedE2E   fork

Figure 9.26 – Selecting a GitHub repository

4. This will redirect you back to GitHub so that you can install the Azure Boards application. You can choose to install it for specific repositories or for all your repositories:

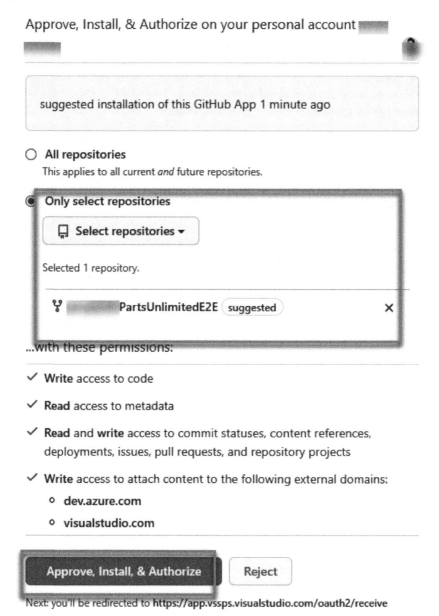

Figure 9.27 – Approving the Azure Boards extension

5. Upon installing Azure Boards, you should see your GitHub connection listed with a green checkmark, meaning it has been successful:

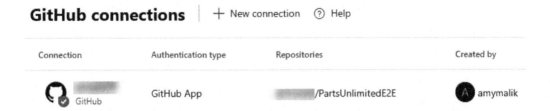

Figure 9.28 – GitHub connection status

With that, you have set up Azure Boards and GitHub integration.

Adding an Azure Boards Status badge

Like the Azure Pipelines status badge, Azure Boards also provides a status badge that can show stats about the work items inside your GitHub repository.

In this section, we'll add a status badge from Azure Boards to our GitHub repository with the help of the following steps:

1. Log into Azure DevOps, browse to **Boards**, and click on the settings gear icon:

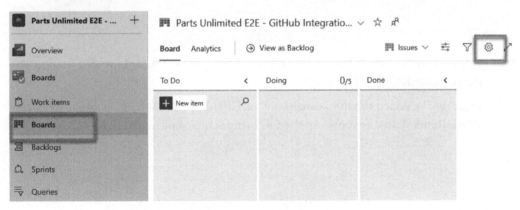

Figure 9.29 – Azure Boards work items

2. On the Settings page, browse to the status badge and set the following settings:

a) Check the **Allow anonymous users to access the status badge** box.

b) You can choose to show only the 'In Progress' columns or include all columns.

Your screen should look as follows:

Figure 9.30 – Azure Boards status access

3. Copy the sample markdown field and save the settings. You can use this markdown in your GitHub documentation.

4. Once you've added the markdown to your GitHub README file, it should show the **Work Items** status, as shown in the following screenshot:

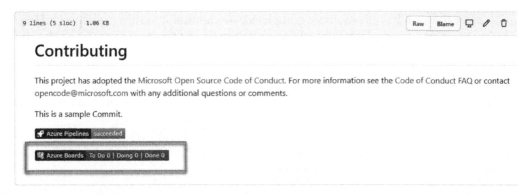

Figure 9.31 – Azure Boards status showcase

Next, we'll look at linking Azure Boards objects to GitHub objects.

Linking Azure Boards work items to GitHub objects

Now that we have Azure Boards integrated with GitHub, let's learn how to link and track items across the two platforms. Let's get started:

1. In Azure Boards, create a new work item. You can use the Azure board status badge task we completed earlier as an example here:

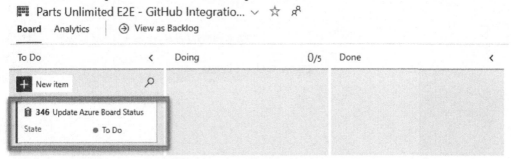

Figure 9.32 – Azure Boards work items

2. You will see that your status badge icon in GitHub gets updated immediately upon being refreshed, with one item in the **To Do** state.

3. Since this task has already been completed, we can link it to the respective GitHub commit. Open the newly created task and click on **Add link**:

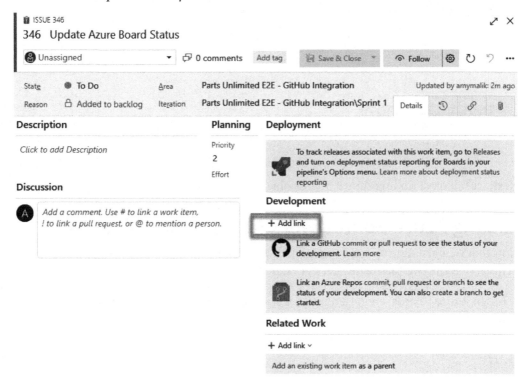

Figure 9.33 – Add link

4.   Click on the **Link type** drop-down and choose **GitHub Commit**. Provide your GitHub commit URL and click **OK**. Note that you also have the options to link to a GitHub issue or pull request:

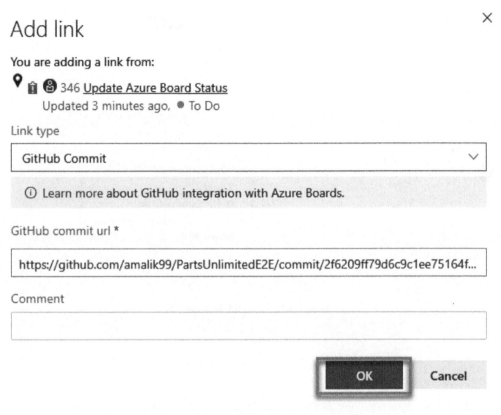

Figure 9.34 – The Add link window

5.   You will now see the GitHub commit linked to the work item. Change its **State** to **Done**:

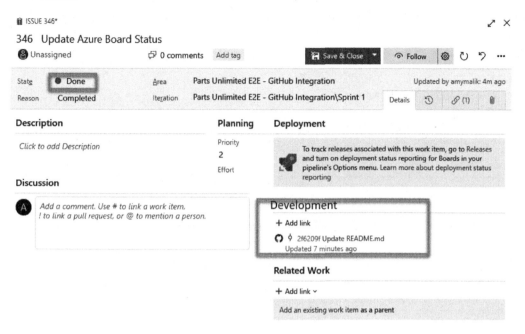

Figure 9.35 – GitHub link added

6. By doing this, you can view your GitHub objects in Azure Boards, which can be used to directly open the respective commit link in GitHub:

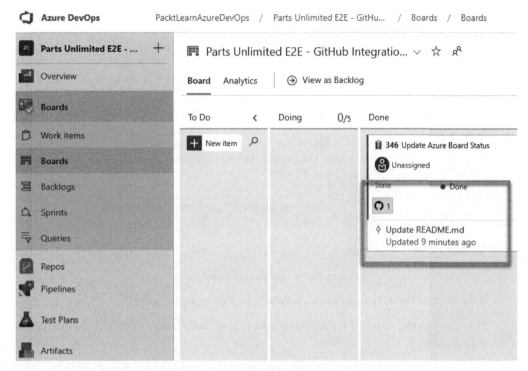

Figure 9.36 – GitHub link added to Azure Boards

Next, we'll learn how to update a work item's status from GitHub.

Updating work items from GitHub

In this section, we'll learn how to change the state of a work item in Azure Boards from GitHub itself. This will help you link your GitHub objects to an Azure Boards work item, enabling a two-way linking and tracking system.

Let's get started:

1. Go to **Azure Boards** > **Boards** > **New item**. Create a test work item with a name of your choice:

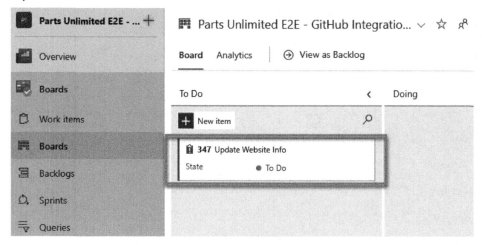

Figure 9.37 – Updating the work item

2. Take note of the ID of the work item (it's 347 in this example).

3. Now, go to your GitHub repository, make any minor change to any file, and create a pull request.

4. In the pull request information box, you can refer to the Azure Boards task by using AB#347, where 347 is your work item ID:

Figure 9.38 – Pull request information box

5. Once you've completed the pull request, you will see that the commit message is now hyperlinked to Azure Boards and that the status for this work item in Azure Boards is updated to **Done**:

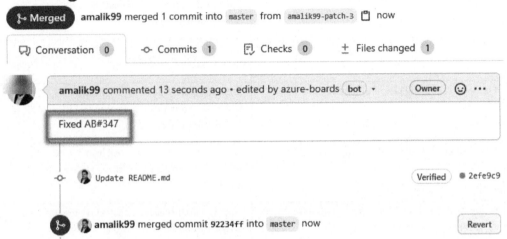

Figure 9.39 – Git comment on the pull request

This was a quick example of how to link GitHub objects by referring to Azure Boards work items by following some simple syntax; that is, AB#<Work Item ID >. As soon as you link the work item to GitHub, your Azure Board work item will also be updated with a link to the corresponding GitHub object.

6. Along with the link objective, in this demonstration, you also updated the state of the work item by using a simple instruction in the commit message. Let's take a look at some of the sample messages you can use:

Sample Commit Message	Action
Fixed AB#123	Links and transitions the work item to the "done" state.
Adds a new feature, fixes AB#123.	Links and transitions the work item to the "done" state.
Fixes AB#123, AB#124, and AB#126	Links to Azure Boards work items 123, 124, and 126. Transitions only the first item, 123, to the "done" state.
Fixes AB#123, Fixes AB#124, and Fixes AB#125	Links to Azure Boards work items 123, 124, and 126. Transitions all items to the "done" state.
Fixing multiple bugs: issue #123 and user story AB#234	Links to GitHub issue 123 and Azure Boards work item 234. No transitions.

Figure 9.40 – Sample messages

This concludes how to integrate with Azure Boards and GitHub. In this section, we looked at how to manage tasks better by using Azure Boards and GitHub together. In the next section, we'll take a look at GitHub Actions.

Overview of GitHub Actions

GitHub Actions is a CI/CD service from GitHub that's used to build and release applications being developed in GitHub repositories. Essentially, GitHub Actions is similar to Azure Pipelines, where you can set up your build and release pipelines to automate the entire software development life cycle.

GitHub Actions was launched in early 2019 to provide a simple DevOps experience built into GitHub itself. GitHub Actions includes enterprise-grade features, such as support for any language with built-in, self-hosted agents for various OSes and container images.

It includes various pre-built workflow templates built by the community, which can make it easier for you to build your DevOps pipeline.

It is outside the scope of this book to talk about GitHub Actions in detail, but you can refer to the GitHub Actions documentation at `https://github.com/features/actions` to get started.

Summary

In this chapter, we looked at how to use GitHub and Azure DevOps together to build an integrated software development platform for our software teams. To do this, we learned how to set up and manage Azure DevOps pipelines from GitHub, as well as build and integrate CI/CD solutions.

We also learned about how to plan and track our work better in Azure Boards while doing software development in GitHub. You should now be able to use GitHub and Azure DevOps together and improve your overall productivity and DevOps experience. You should also be able to set up integration between the two services and use it in your daily DevOps work.

In the next chapter, we'll look at several real-world CI/CD examples with the help of Azure DevOps.

10
Using Test Plans with Azure DevOps

In the previous chapter, we covered how you can integrate Azure DevOps with GitHub.

In this chapter, we are going to cover how to use test plans with Azure DevOps. Comprehensive testing should be added to each software development project, because it delivers quality and a great user experience for your applications. We will begin with a brief introduction to Azure Test Plans. Then we will look at how you can manage test plans, suites, and cases in Azure DevOps. We will run and analyze a test as well. After that, we will cover exploratory testing and we will install the Test & Feedback extension.

The following topics will be covered in this chapter:

- Introduction to Azure Test Plans
- Exploratory testing
- Installing and using the Test & Feedback extension
- Planned manual testing
- Test plans, test suites, and test cases
- Managing test plans, test suites, and test cases
- Running and analyzing a manual test plan

Technical requirements

To follow this chapter, you need to have an active Azure DevOps organization. The organization used in this chapter is the **Parts Unlimited** organization that we created in *Chapter 1, Azure DevOps Overview*. You also need to have Visual Studio 2019 installed, which can be downloaded from `https://visualstudio.microsoft.com/downloads/`.

The test plan that is used to run and analyze a manual test plan can be downloaded from `https://github.com/PacktPublishing/Learning-Azure-DevOps---B16392/tree/master/Chapter%2010`.

Introduction to Azure Test Plans

Manual and exploratory testing can be key testing techniques in delivering quality and a great user experience for your applications. In modern software development processes, quality is the responsibility of all the team members, including developers, managers, business analysts, and product owners.

To drive that quality, Azure DevOps Test Plans offers powerful tools that can be used by everyone in the team. And by embedding your test plans in Azure DevOps, testing can be done throughout the whole development life cycle as well.

Azure DevOps Test Plans offers support for planned manual testing, user acceptance testing, exploratory testing, and stakeholder feedback. This will be covered in more detail in the following sections.

Let's look at each of them in detail in the following sections. In the next section, we are going to cover exploratory testing.

Exploratory testing

With exploratory testing, testers are exploring the application to identify and document potential bugs. It focuses on discovery and relies on the guidance of the individual tester to discover defects that are not easily discovered using other types of tests. This type of testing is often referred to as *ad hoc* testing.

Most quality testing techniques use a structured approach by creating test cases up front (just like we did in our previous demo). Exploratory testing is the opposite of this and is mostly used in scenarios where someone needs to learn about a product or application. They can review the quality of the product from the user perspective and provide feedback quickly. This will also make sure that you don't miss cases that can lead to critical quality failures. The outcome of these ad hoc tests can later be converted into a test plan as well.

Microsoft has released a **Test & Feedback** extension for exploratory testing. This extension can be installed on the browser and used by all the stakeholders that are involved in the software development project, such as developers, product owners, managers, UX or UI engineers, marketing teams, and early adopters. The extension can be used to submit bugs or provide feedback to contribute to the quality of the software.

In the next demonstration, we are going to look at how we can install the **Test & Feedback** extension.

Installing and using the Test & Feedback extension

The **Test & Feedback** extension can be installed from the Visual Studio Marketplace and is currently available for Chrome and Firefox (version 50.0 and higher). Chrome extensions can also be installed in the Microsoft Edge browser. This browser is based on Chromium.

> **Important note**
>
> For a detailed overview of what browsers and features are supported, you can refer to the following article: `https://docs.microsoft.com/en-us/azure/devops/test/reference-qa?view=azure-devops#browser-support`.

To install the Test & Feedback extension, follow these steps:

1. Navigate to the Visual Studio Marketplace: `https://marketplace.visualstudio.com/`.

2. Select the **Azure DevOps** tab and search for `Test & Feedback`. Select the **Test & Feedback** extension for the list:

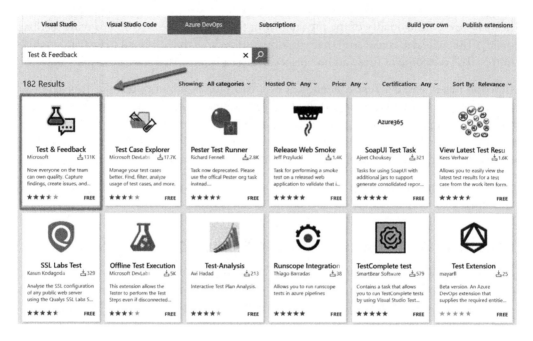

Figure 10.1 – Selecting the Test & Feedback extension

3. This will open the detail page for the extension. From here, you can install it. Click the **Install** button at the top of the screen:

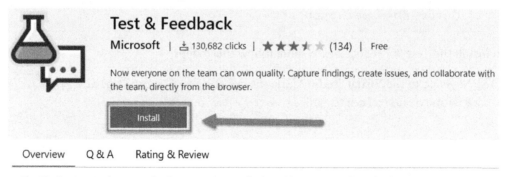

Figure 10.2 – Installing the Test & Feedback extension

4. Next, you will be redirected to the supported browsers where this extension can be installed. Click the **Install** button below the browser that you are currently using to install the extension. You will be redirected to the extension page of your current browser. There, you can install it.

5. Once the extension is installed, the icon will be added to the right of the address bar. Select the **Connections** button:

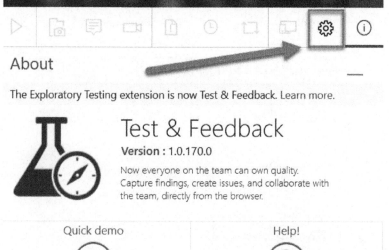

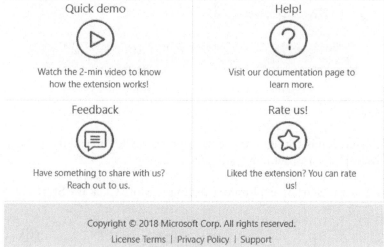

Figure 10.3 – Test & Feedback extension configuration

6. You need to specify the Azure DevOps server URL there to connect to your Azure DevOps instance. The URL begins with `https://dev.azure.com/` and ends with the project name. After providing the URL, click **Next**. After connecting to the project, you can select the team. Select **Parts.Unlimited Team**:

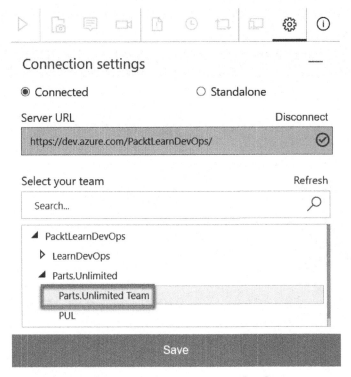

Figure 10.4 – Connecting to Azure DevOps

7. Click **Save**.

Now that the extension is configured, we can start using it. You can use the extension for exploratory testing or for providing feedback:

8. We are going to start an exploratory testing session. Click the **Start** button:

Figure 10.5 – Starting exploratory testing

9. This will activate the menus. Once you have a web application open for testing, you can find the area that has a bug, take screenshots, make notes, or record actions as a video:

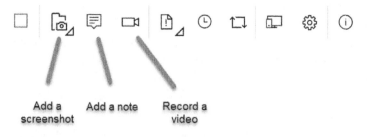

Figure 10.6 – Extension options

10. Once you are done with exploring and gathering and registering information, you can create a bug, task, or test case. Click **Create bug**:

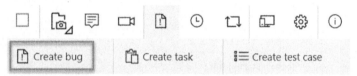

Figure 10.7 – Extension options

11. You can provide a title and include your discovered information in there as well:

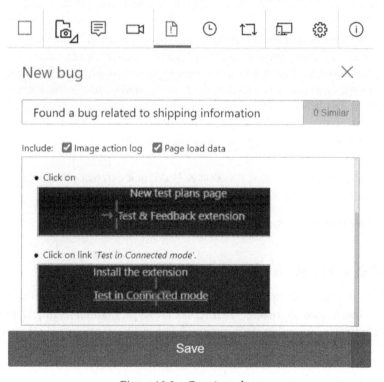

Figure 10.8 – Creating a bug

12. Click **Save**.

13. You can also view a list of all the activities from the extension. There you can also see the bug ID, so you can trace it in Azure DevOps as well:

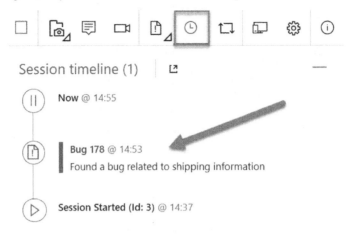

Figure 10.9 – Overview of actions

Important note

For more information about how to create feedback items in Azure DevOps, refer to the following website: `https://docs.microsoft.com/en-us/azure/devops/test/request-stakeholder-feedback?view=azure-devops`. To respond to this feedback items using the **Test & Feedback** extension, visit `https://docs.microsoft.com/en-us/azure/devops/test/provide-stakeholder-feedback?view=azure-devops#provide`.

In this demonstration, we installed the **Test & Feedback** extension from the Visual Studio Marketplace, which can be used for exploratory testing.

In the next section, we are going to look into planned manual testing.

Planned manual testing

Over the years, manual testing has evolved together with the software development process into a more agile approach. With Azure DevOps, manual testing is integrated into the different agile processes that are supported and can be configured in Azure DevOps.

> **Important note**
> The different agile processes that are supported and integrated in Azure DevOps are covered in more detail in *Chapter 2, Managing Projects with Azure DevOps Boards.*

Software development teams can begin manual testing right from the Kanban board from Azure Boards. From the board, you can monitor the status of the tests directly from the cards. This way, all team members can get an overview of what tests are connected to the work items and stories. From there the team can also see what the status is of the different tests.

In the following image, you can see the tests and statuses that are displayed on the board:

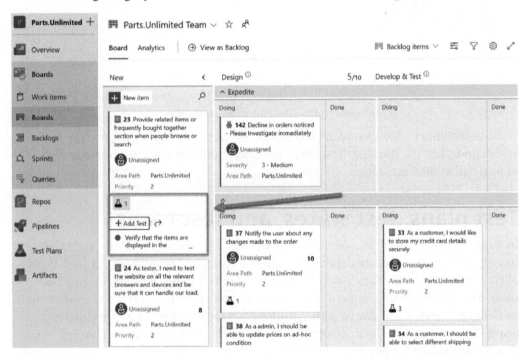

Figure 10.10 – Tests displayed in the work hub

If more advanced testing capabilities are needed, Azure Test Plans can also be used for all the test management needs. The **Test hub** can be accessed from the left menu, under **Test Plans**, and there it offers all the capabilities that are needed for a full testing life cycle.

In the following image, you see the how the Test Hub can be accessed from the left menu, together with the different menu options:

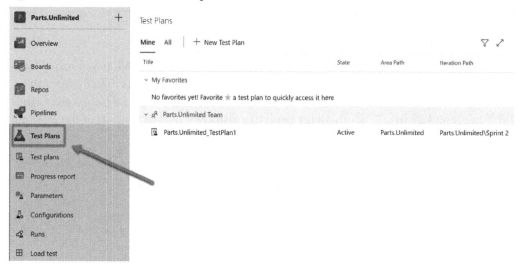

Figure 10.11 – Test Hub in Azure DevOps

These capabilities include test plans, test suites, test cases, test authoring, testing applications, and test tracking. Test plans, test suites, and test cases will be covered in more detail in the next section.

Test plans, test suites, and test cases

In Azure DevOps Test Plans, you can create and manage test plans and test suites for sprints or milestones that are defined for your software development project. Test Plans offers three main types of test management artifacts: **Test plans**, **Test suites**, and **Test cases**. These artifacts are all stored in the work repository as special types of work items and can be exported and shared with the different team members or across different teams. This also enables the integration of the test artifacts with all of the DevOps tasks that are defined for the project.

The three artifacts have the following capabilities:

- **Test plans**: A test plan groups different test suites, configurations, and individual test cases together. In general, every major milestone in a project should have its own test plan.

- **Test suites**: A test suite can group different test cases into separate testing scenarios within a single test plan. This makes it easier to see which scenarios are complete.

- **Test cases**: With test cases, you can validate individual parts of your code or app deployments. They can be added to both test plans and test suites. They can also be added to multiple test plans and suites if needed. This way, they can be reused effectively without the need to copy them. A test case is designed to validate a work item in Azure DevOps, such as a feature implementation or a bug fix.

In the next section, we are going to put this theory into practice and see how you can create and manage test plans in Azure DevOps.

Managing test plans, test suites, and test cases

For this demonstration, we are going to use the **Parts Unlimited** project again. It also has a test plan in Azure DevOps, so we are going to look at that first. Therefore, we have to follow these steps:

1. Open a web browser and navigate to `https://dev.azure.com/`.

2. Log in with your Microsoft account and select the **Parts.Unlimited** project. Then, in the left menu, select **Test Plans**. This will let you navigate to the test plan that has already been added to the project.

3. Select **Parts.Unlimited_TestPlan1** from the list to open it. The suites of tests are added to this plan. Select **As a customer, I would like to store my credit card details securely**. This will open the list of individual test cases that have been added to this suite:

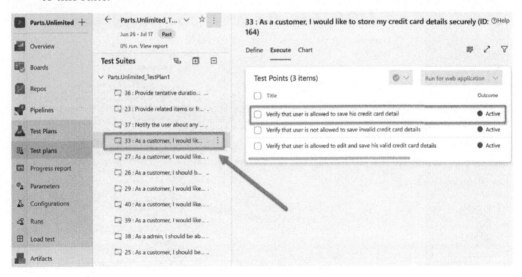

Figure 10.12 – Open the test suite item

4.   Then, right-click the first item in the list: **Verify that user is allowed to save his credit card detail**. In the menu, select **Edit test case**:

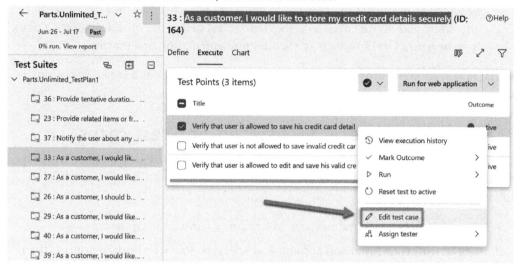

Figure 10.13 – Edit the test case

5.   On the edit screen of this test case, there are four steps. You can also link the test case to a commit, pull request, branch, or work item from here. We are going to add this test case to an existing work item. Under **Related Work**, select **+ Add link** and then click **Existing item**:

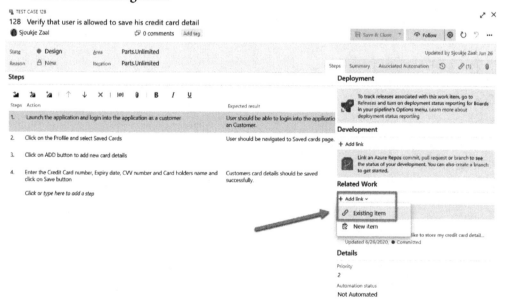

Figure 10.14 – Add a work item to the test case

6. In the **Add link** window, select **Parent** and then search for credit card. Select the **Credit Card Purchase** feature to link the test case to:

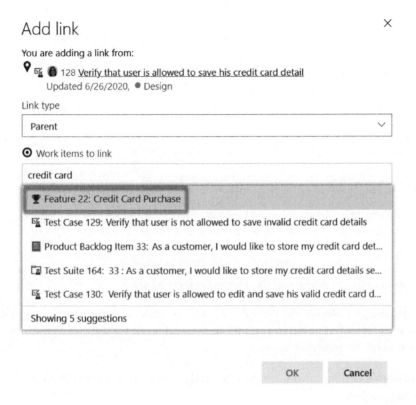

Figure 10.15 – Select the work item

7. Click **OK** to link the work item. The parent feature is now linked to the test case and test suite. Anyone can now navigate between them and view the relationship.

8. In the test case window, click **Save & Close**.

In some cases, test cases should be run in a specific order. To do this click **Define** in the top menu and select the **Verify that user is not allowed to save invalid credit card details** test case. Then drag the test case above the first test case in the list:

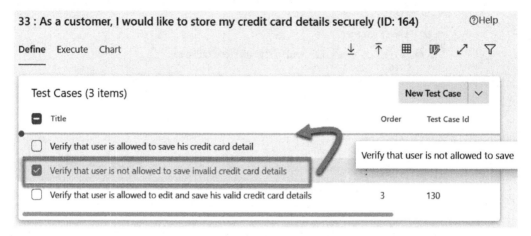

Figure 10.16 – Reordering test cases

You will now see that the order of the test cases has changed.

You can also assign different configurations to each test case. For example, you can assign configurations for different environments such as different versions of Windows or browsers, mobile devices, and so on:

1. To assign a configuration, right-click on the test case and select **Assign configuration**:

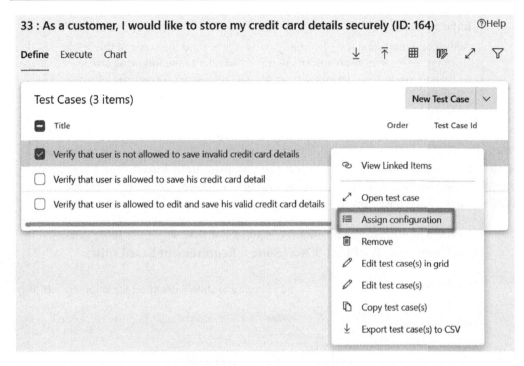

Figure 10.17 – Assign configuration

2. In the configurations overview list, you will see that there is already a configuration selected for this test case, which is Windows 10. If not, assign it and click **Save**. Close the list:

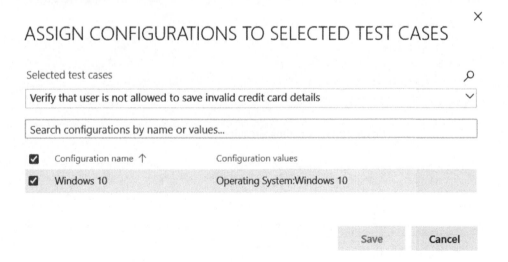

Figure 10.18 – Available and selected configurations

> **Important note**
> Adding and managing test plan configurations is beyond the scope of this book. However, if you want more information you can refer to the following article: `https://docs.microsoft.com/en-us/azure/devops/test/test-different-configurations?view=azure-devops`.

Next, we will create a new test suite. You can create three different types of test suites: **static**, where you manually assign the test cases; **requirement-based**, where you create the suite based on common requirements; and **query-based**, where test cases are automatically added based on the outcome of a query:

1. Let's add a new requirement-based test suite. For this, select the three dots next to **Parts.Unlimited_TestPlan1** > **New Suite** > **Requirement based suite**:

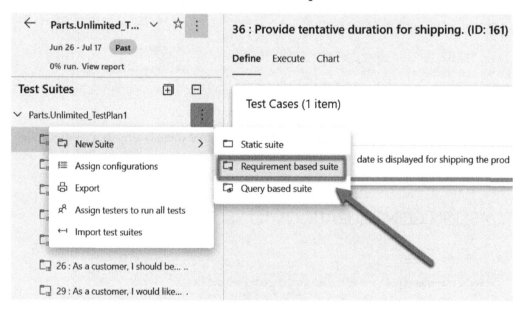

Figure 10.19 – Creating a requirement-based test suite

2. Here, you can create your own query for retrieving work items based on your requirements. For this demonstration, we will use the default settings. Click **Run query** and then select the three items that are related to shipping:

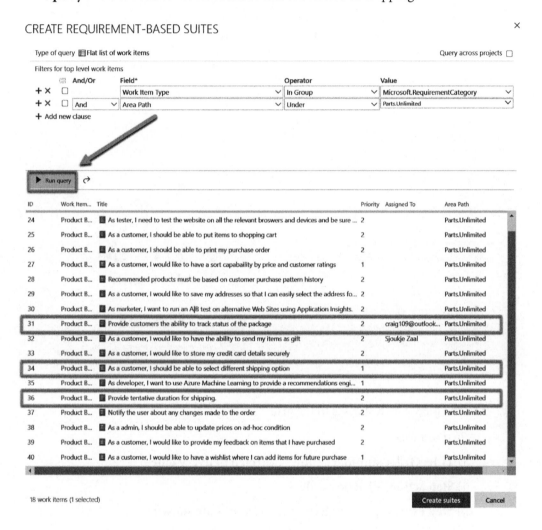

Figure 10.20 – Select the work items related to shipping

3. Click **Create suites** to create a test suite for each item.

4. We are going to add some test cases to this suite. You can add them one at a time or use a grid layout to quickly add many test cases. We are going to use the grid layout here. Select one of the added test suites, click the arrow new to the **New Test Case** button, and then click **Add test cases using grid**:

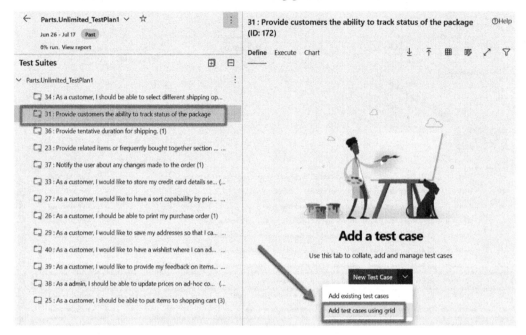

Figure 10.21 – Add test cases using grid

5. Add the following test cases to the grid:

    a) First test case:

        i) **Title: Order summary shows expected delivery date**

        ii) **Step action: Visit 'my orders'**

        iii) **Step expected result: Expected delivery date shown**

    b) Second test case:

        i) **Title: Delayed orders highlighted**

        ii) **Step action: Visit order page for delayed package**

        iii) **Step expected result: Delayed status is highlighted**

c) Third test case:

    i) **Title**: **Delivery steps for package**

    ii) **Step action**: **Visit order page for in-progress package**

    iii) **Step expected result**: **Delivery steps and status shown**

This will look like the following screenshot:

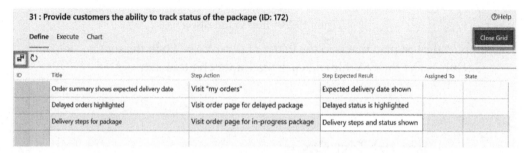

Figure 10.22 – Define the test cases

6. Click the **Save test cases** button on the left and then click **Close Grid** on the right of the screen.

In this demonstration, we have managed some test cases and created a new requirement-based test suite. In the next section, we are going to run and analyze a manual test plan.

Running and analyzing a manual test plan

In this demonstration, we are going to run and analyze a manual test plan. For this, we are going to use the test plan that is already added to the **Parts.Unlimited** project in Azure DevOps again and import a test suite. The test suite can be downloaded from the GitHub repository that belongs to this chapter. You can obtain the GitHub URL at the beginning of the chapter from the *Technical requirements* section:

1. Open the test plan of the **Parts.Unlimited** project again in Azure DevOps.

2. First, we need to add a new static test suite. For this, select the three dots next to **Parts.Unlimited_TestPlan1** > **New Suite** > **Static suite**. Name the suite `End-to-end tests`.

3. Select the newly created suite and in the top menu, select the import button to import test cases:

Figure 10.23 – Import test cases

4. Import the test plan that is in the folder of Chapter 10 in the source code on GitHub. Select the CSV file and click the **Import** button:

Figure 10.24 – Import the CSV file

5. After importing the file, double click on the test case and navigate to the parameters section. There add some parameters that can be used for testing, similar to the following screenshot:

Parameter values

Add a shared parameter set | Convert to shared parameters

Email	Password	Name	Phone	Address	City	State	PostalCode	Country	Promo
admin@packt.com	P@ssw0rd	Admin User	425-555-1234	One Packt Way	Redmond	NH	98052	USA	FREE
sjoukje@packt.com	P@ssw0rd	Sjoukje Zaal	555-555-5555	Amsterdam Square	Springfield	UT	11135	USA	FREE

Figure 10.25 – Parameter values

6. Click **Save & Close** in the top menu. Now that we have our test suite in place, we can start testing. Click on the **Execute** tab in the top menu and click on the **test case**, then **Run**, then **Run with options**:

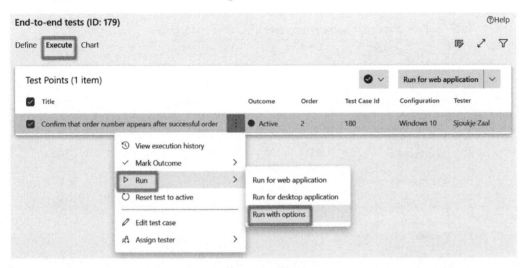

Figure 10.26 – Run the test

7. Keep the default settings in the **Run with options** window and click **Run**:

Run with options
Select test type and runner

Manual tests using Web Browser based runner   ⌄

Recommended for testing web applications. Capture screenshots, screen recordings and action logs with this option.

Select a build

Test results and defects filed are associated to the selected build.

Run

Figure 10.27 – Run with options

8. The test runner is now displayed with all the steps:

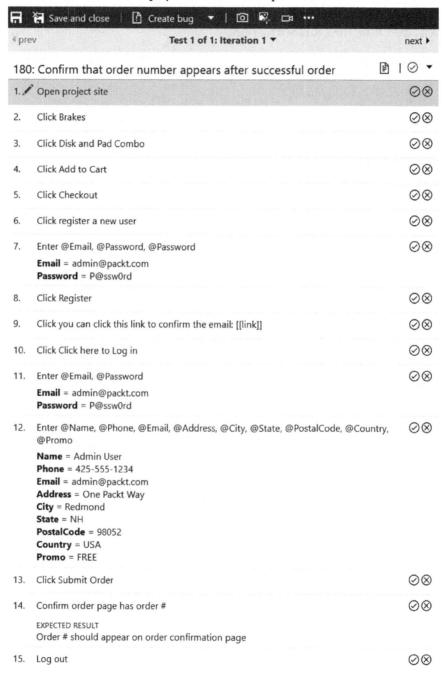

Figure 10.28 – Test runner window

Now we can start the actual testing:

1. Open the **Parts.Unlimited** project in Visual Studio. We already cloned the repository earlier in the book. If you need to clone the project again, refer to *Chapter 5, Running Quality Tests in a Build Pipeline*.

2. Run the application by pressing *F5* and wait until the **Parts Unlimited** website is running. Now add the browser next to the test runner window and start testing:

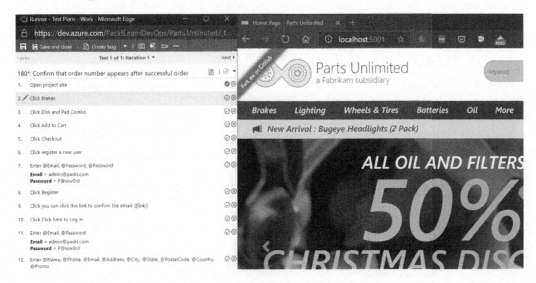

Figure 10.29 – Start testing the web application

3. Follow the instructions according to the test runner. Each time you finish a step, click on the pass test icon to the right of each step.

4. If you discover bugs or issues, you can add a comment to the step directly, or create a separate bug at the top:

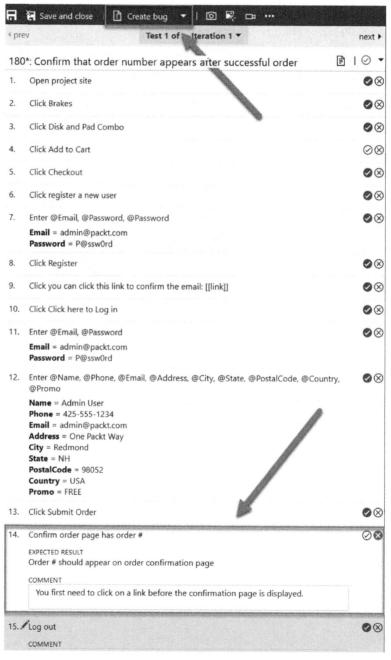

Figure 10.30 – Adding a comment or bug

5. To finish the test, click **Save and close** in the top menu of the test runner.

6. Now go back to Azure DevOps. In the left menu, click **Test Plans** > **Runs**.

7. In the list of recent runs, select the run that we just executed:

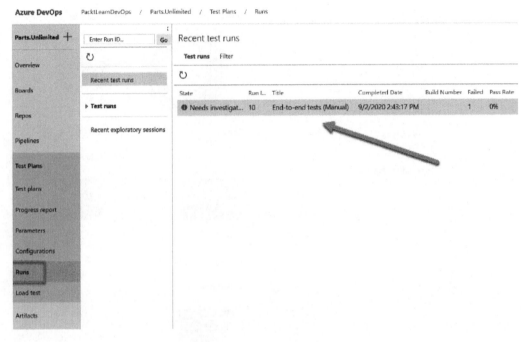

Figure 10.31 – Recent test runs

8.   There, you can see all the details of the test and the outcome:

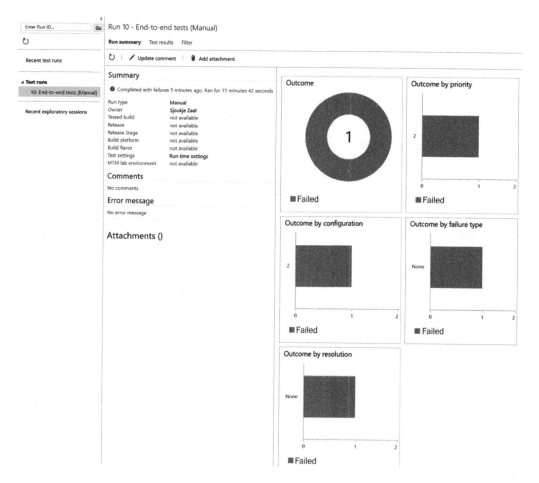

Figure 10.32 – Test results

In this demonstration, we have created a test suite and imported a test case. We then ran the test and tested the Parts Unlimited application, and we looked at the results in Azure DevOps.

This concludes this chapter.

Summary

In this chapter, we have covered Azure DevOps Test Plans. We looked at the different features and capabilities and managed test plans, test suites, and test cases. Then we imported a test case from a CSV file and tested the **Parts Unlimited** application. Then, we covered exploratory testing in detail, and we used the Test & Feedback extension to report a bug.

In the next chapter, we are going to focus on real-world CI/CD scenarios with Azure DevOps.

Further reading

Check out the following links for more information about the topics that were covered in this chapter:

- Exploratory and manual testing scenarios and capabilities: `https://docs.microsoft.com/en-us/azure/devops/test/overview?view=azure-devops`

- Creating manual test cases: `https://docs.microsoft.com/en-us/azure/devops/test/create-test-cases?view=azure-devops`

- Providing feedback using the Test & Feedback extension: `https://docs.microsoft.com/en-us/azure/devops/test/provide-stakeholder-feedback?view=azure-devops`

- Exploratory testing with the Test & Feedback extension in Connected mode: `https://docs.microsoft.com/en-us/azure/devops/test/connected-mode-exploratory-testing?view=azure-devops`

11
Real-World CI/CD Scenarios with Azure DevOps

In this chapter, we'll show you some sample projects where the **continuous integration and continuous delivery (CI/CD)** processes are handled by using Azure DevOps. We'll be taking sample applications and setting up a CI/CD pipeline using Azure DevOps for managing the software development, deployment, and upgrade life cycle.

We'll be covering the following topics in this chapter:

- Setting up a CI/CD pipeline for .NET-based applications
- Setting up a CI/CD pipeline for a container-based infrastructure
- Azure Architecture Center for DevOps

Technical requirements

To follow along with this chapter, you need to have an active Azure DevOps organization and an Azure subscription.

You can sign up for a test Azure DevOps organization at `https://dev.azure.com`. You can get a trial for an Azure subscription at `https://azure.microsoft.com/en-in/free/` if you do not have one already.

The code for this chapter is available at `https://github.com/PacktPublishing/Learning-Azure-DevOps---B16392/tree/master/Chapter11`.

Setting up a CI/CD pipeline for .NET-based applications

A typical .NET-based application includes applications developed using Microsoft's .NET Framework and uses a SQL database in the backend. You may have multiple layers of applications, such as a frontend, backend (also known as the middle tier or API tier), and data tier (SQL Server).

Azure Pipelines, which is part of Azure DevOps, provides a comprehensive solution to build, deploy, and manage your .NET-based infrastructure deployments. In this section, we'll look at the steps to configure CI/CD for a sample .NET-based application.

We will be creating two environments, named **staging** and **production**, for the application and setup of a CI/CD pipeline.

Introduction to the sample application

We'll be using a simple **ToDo** application for this walkthrough. It's a web-based application that uses a SQL database in the backend.

It is built using Microsoft ASP.NET, targeted for .NET Framework version 4.62. You can access the source code here: `https://github.com/Azure-Samples/dotnet-sqldb-tutorial/tree/master/DotNetAppSqlDb`.

It is recommended that you take a quick look at the application code to get familiar with it before we start building the CI/CD pipeline.

Preparing the pre-requisite Azure infrastructure

In this section, we'll create the required Azure infrastructure to host the application. We will be creating the following resources:

1. **Resource groups**: The following resource groups will be created for hosting the Azure resources for both environments:

    a) `Contoso-ToDo-Staging`

    b) `Contoso-ToDo-Production`

2. **Application components**: We'll be creating the following resources for both the staging and production environments:

    a) Azure App Service to host the web application

    b) Azure SQL Database to host the SQL database

Creating a resource group in Azure

A resource group is a container that holds resources in the Azure cloud. Typically, a resource group includes resources that you want to manage as a group or are maintained in a similar life cycle. We'll be creating two resource groups: one for production and one for staging. Let's create the resource groups in Azure:

1. Log in to the Azure portal, `https://portal.azure.com`, with your Azure credentials.

2. Click on + **Create a resource** and search for `resource group`:

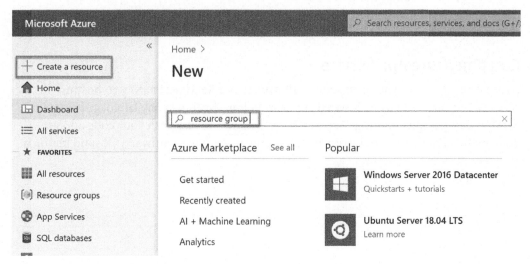

Figure 11.1 – Resource groups in the Azure portal

3. Click **Create** on the resource group page.

4. Select your subscription and enter the resource group name as Contoso-ToDo-Staging.

5. Choose a region close to your location:

Create a resource group

Basics   Tags   Review + create

Resource group - A container that holds related resources for an Azure solution. The resource group can include all the resources for the solution, or only those resources that you want to manage as a group. You decide how you want to allocate resources to resource groups based on what makes the most sense for your organization. Learn more ☑

Project details

Subscription * ⓘ

Resource group * ⓘ   Contoso-ToDo-Staging

Resource details

Region * ⓘ   (US) East US

Figure 11.2 – Resource group creation

6. Click on **Review + Create** and then **Create** to start the deployment.

7. Repeat the steps to create another resource group for the production environment named Contoso-ToDo-Prod.

You've now created resource groups to host Azure resources.

Creating Azure App Service

Azure App Service is Microsoft Azure's **Platform as a Service (PaaS)** web hosting service. You can host any web-based application built in almost any language using App Service. Being a PaaS offering, App Service allows you to just push your code and get your application live without worrying about the underlying hardware, OS, and platform components.

In this example, we'll be using Azure App Service to host the **ToDo** application:

1. In the Azure portal, click on **+ Create a resource** and click on **Web App**:

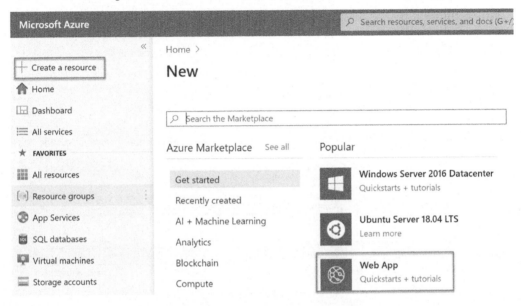

Figure 11.3 – Azure Web App in the portal

2. On the **Web App Creation** page, please enter the following values:

    a) **Subscription**: Choose your Azure subscription.

    b) **Resource Group**: Select the **staging** resource group created in the previous task.

    c) **Name**: Enter a unique name for your web application – for example, `contosotodostagingXX`, where XX is your initials.

    d) **Publish**: Choose **Code**.

    e) **Runtime stack**: Choose **ASP.NET V4.7**.

f) **Operating System**: Choose **Windows.**

g) **Region**: Choose a region close to your location:

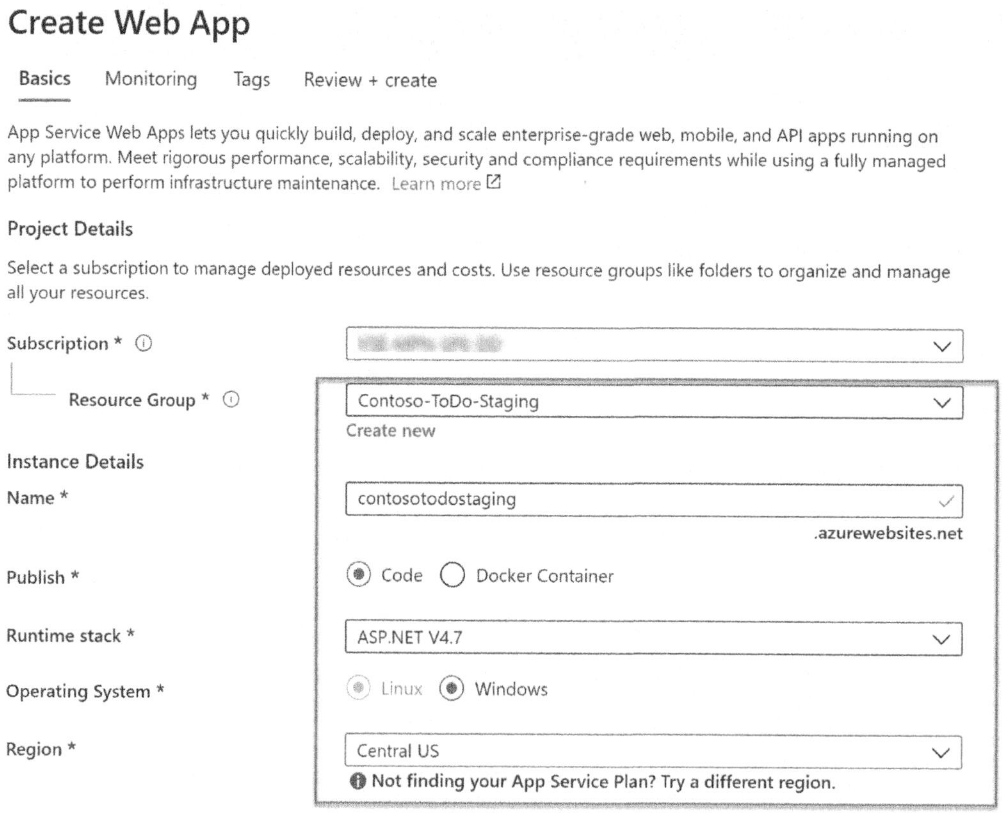

Create Web App

Basics   Monitoring   Tags   Review + create

App Service Web Apps lets you quickly build, deploy, and scale enterprise-grade web, mobile, and API apps running on any platform. Meet rigorous performance, scalability, security and compliance requirements while using a fully managed platform to perform infrastructure maintenance. Learn more ☐

Project Details

Select a subscription to manage deployed resources and costs. Use resource groups like folders to organize and manage all your resources.

Subscription * ⓘ

Resource Group * ⓘ   Contoso-ToDo-Staging   ⌄
                       Create new

Instance Details

Name *   contosotodostaging   ✓
                                      .azurewebsites.net

Publish *   ⦿ Code   ◯ Docker Container

Runtime stack *   ASP.NET V4.7   ⌄

Operating System *   ◯ Linux   ⦿ Windows

Region *   Central US   ⌄
            ❶ Not finding your App Service Plan? Try a different region.

Figure 11.4 – Azure App Service creation

3. Under **App Service Plan**, choose the following:

    a) **Windows Plan**: Enter a new App Service plan name

    b) **Sku and Size**: You can choose any SKU; it is recommended using **S0** or **Basic** to avoid any significant Azure costs since this is for testing. In production, you'd use a size that is suitable for your application resources demand:

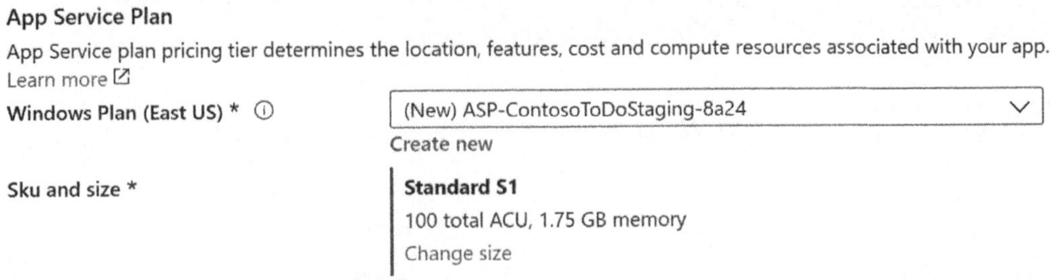

App Service Plan

App Service plan pricing tier determines the location, features, cost and compute resources associated with your app.
Learn more ☑

Windows Plan (East US) * ⓘ   (New) ASP-ContosoToDoStaging-8a24   ⌄
                                     Create new

Sku and size *   **Standard S1**
                                     100 total ACU, 1.75 GB memory
                                     Change size

Figure 11.5 – App Service SKU

4. Click **Review + Create** and then **Create** to start the deployment.

    Once completed, you'll receive a notification with the status displayed as completed.

5. Repeat the steps in this task to create another Azure app service for the production environment.

In this task, we created an Azure app service for hosting the **ToDo** web application.

Creating an Azure SQL database

Our sample **ToDo** app is using Microsoft SQL Server to store all its application data. In this task, we'll create a new Azure SQL database that will be used by the **ToDo** app to store all the persistent data:

1. In the Azure portal, click on **+ Create a resource** and select **SQL Database**:

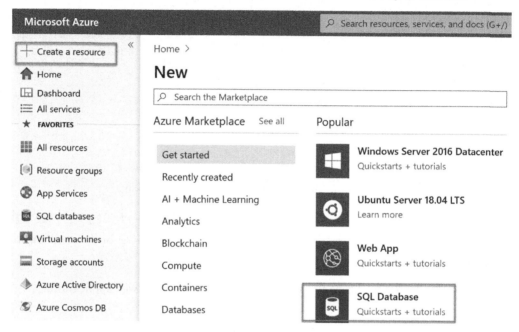

Figure 11.6 – SQL Database in Azure

2. On the SQL Server **Basics** details page, provide the following values:

    a) **Subscription**: Select your Azure subscription.

    b) **Resource group**: Select the staging resource group created earlier.

    c) **Database name**: `contosotodo-staging-db`.

    d) **Server**: **Create new**:

    　i) **Server Name**: Provide a unique **SQL Server name**, such as `contosotodo-staging-dbserver`.

    　ii) Provide a username and password of your choice.

    　iii) **Location**: The Azure region used for deploying the web application.

e) **Want to use SQL elastic pool?**: No.

f) **Compute + storage**: Change the SKU to **S0** or **Basic** to keep the Azure costs low during this test project. In reality, you'd need to choose the right compute and storage combination as per your application requirements:

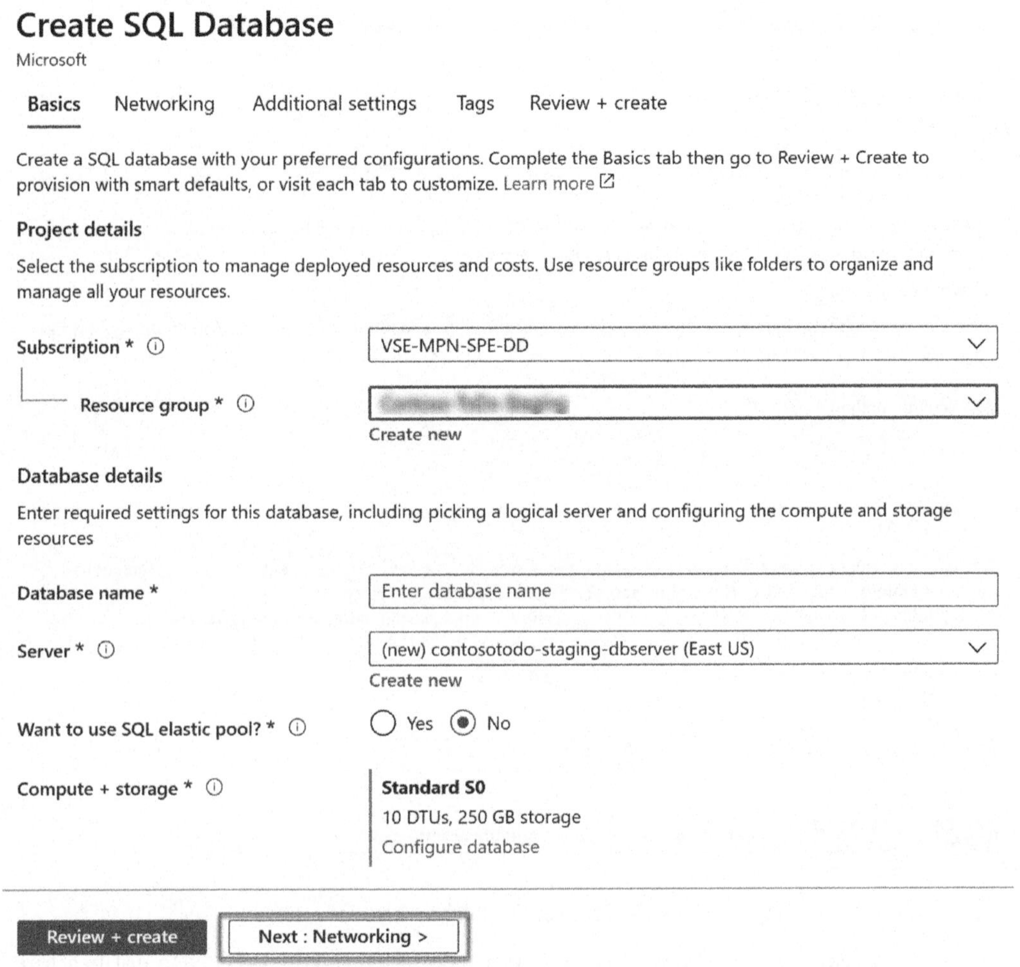

Create SQL Database

Microsoft

Basics   Networking   Additional settings   Tags   Review + create

Create a SQL database with your preferred configurations. Complete the Basics tab then go to Review + Create to provision with smart defaults, or visit each tab to customize. Learn more ☑

Project details

Select the subscription to manage deployed resources and costs. Use resource groups like folders to organize and manage all your resources.

Subscription * ⓘ	VSE-MPN-SPE-DD ⌄
└─ Resource group * ⓘ	⌄
	Create new

Database details

Enter required settings for this database, including picking a logical server and configuring the compute and storage resources

Database name *	Enter database name
Server * ⓘ	(new) contosotodo-staging-dbserver (East US) ⌄
	Create new
Want to use SQL elastic pool? * ⓘ	◯ Yes ⦿ No
Compute + storage * ⓘ	**Standard S0** 10 DTUs, 250 GB storage Configure database

[Review + create]   [Next : Networking >]

Figure 11.7 – Create SQL Database in Azure

3. Click on **Next: Networking >**.

4. For the **Networking** configuration, select **Public endpoint** for **Connectivity method** and choose **Yes** for **Allow Azure services and resources to access this server**. Please note that this is just for the purpose of this test project deployment; in production, it is advised to allow access to SQL Server from your specific application servers only. Once selected, click on **Review + create**:

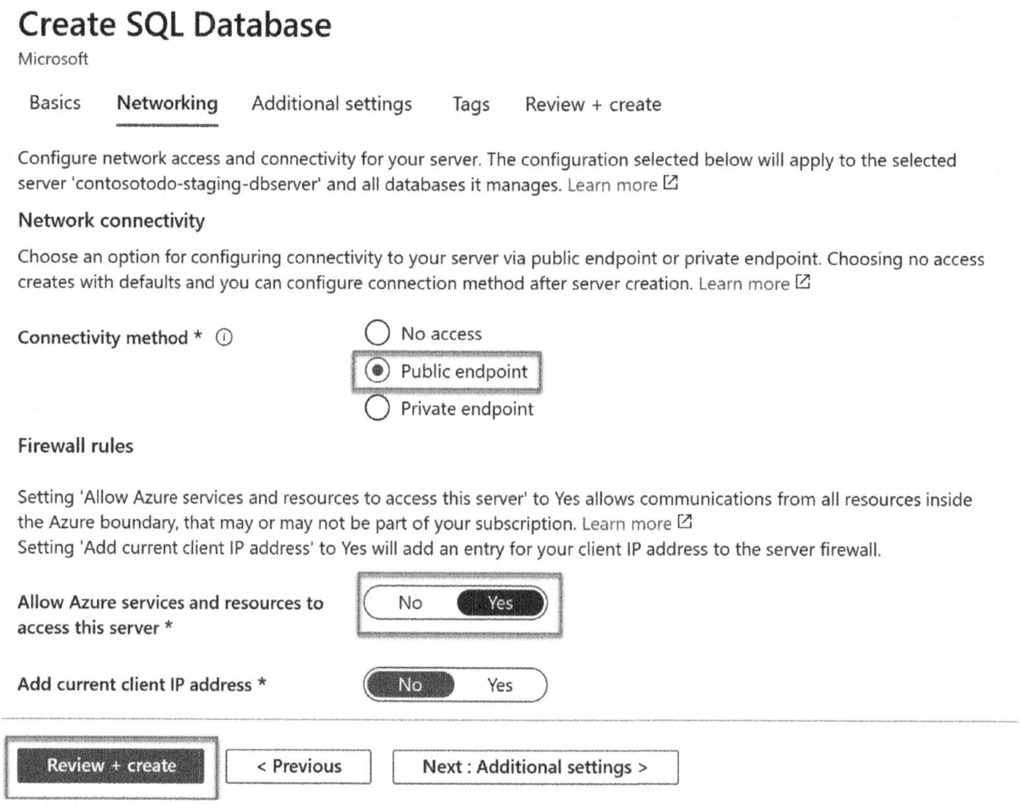

Create SQL Database

Microsoft

Basics   **Networking**   Additional settings   Tags   Review + create

Configure network access and connectivity for your server. The configuration selected below will apply to the selected server 'contosotodo-staging-dbserver' and all databases it manages. Learn more ☒

Network connectivity

Choose an option for configuring connectivity to your server via public endpoint or private endpoint. Choosing no access creates with defaults and you can configure connection method after server creation. Learn more ☒

Connectivity method * ⓘ   ◯ No access
                            ◉ Public endpoint
                            ◯ Private endpoint

Firewall rules

Setting 'Allow Azure services and resources to access this server' to Yes allows communications from all resources inside the Azure boundary, that may or may not be part of your subscription. Learn more ☒
Setting 'Add current client IP address' to Yes will add an entry for your client IP address to the server firewall.

Allow Azure services and resources to   No   **Yes**
access this server *

Add current client IP address *   **No**   Yes

Review + create   < Previous   Next : Additional settings >

Figure 11.8 – Reviewing SQL database creation in Azure

5. Click **Create** to start the deployment. Once completed, you'll receive a notification in the notification menu.

6. Navigate to the newly create Azure SQL database and copy the connection string. This will be used in the upcoming sections.

7. Repeat the steps to create another Azure SQL database for production.

In this task, we've created Azure SQL databases for our application.

Setting up an Azure DevOps project

Now that our Azure infrastructure is ready, we'll now set up an Azure DevOps organization to build the CI/CD pipeline. We will be using Azure Repos as our source control management system:

1. Log in to https://dev.azure.com using your Azure DevOps account.

2. Create a new project named Contoso ToDo in your DevOps tenant:

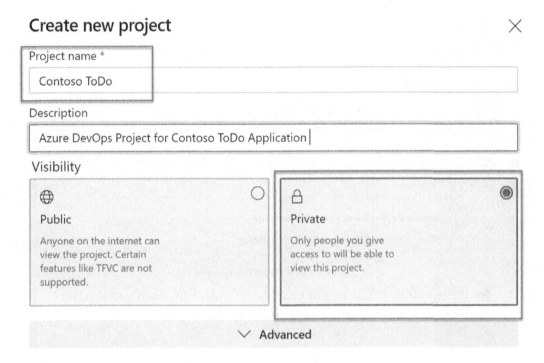

Figure 11.9 – Creating a DevOps project

3. We will start by importing the application code in Azure Repos. Click on **Repos**.

4.   Click on **Import** under **Import a repository**:

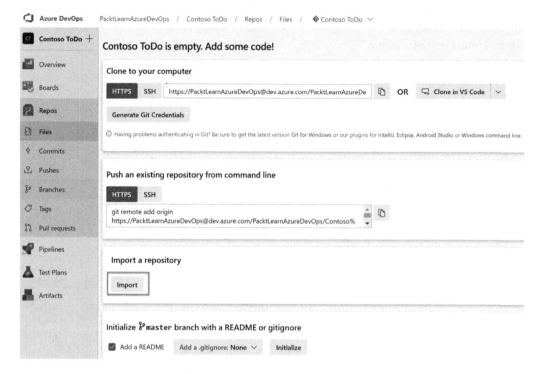

Figure 11.10 – Import a repository

5.   For the repository URL, enter `https://github.com/Azure-Samples/` `dotnet-sqldb-tutorial/` and click **Import**:

Import a Git repository   ✕

Repository type

◈ Git   ∨

Clone URL *

https://github.com/Azure-Samples/dotnet-sqldb-tutorial/|

☐ Requires Authentication

Figure 11.11 – Importing a repository from GitHub

Once the import is successful, we'll see that project files are now available in Azure Repos. You can explore the code files to look under the hood of the **ToDo** application. The folder named DotNetAppSQLDb contains the source file of the application:

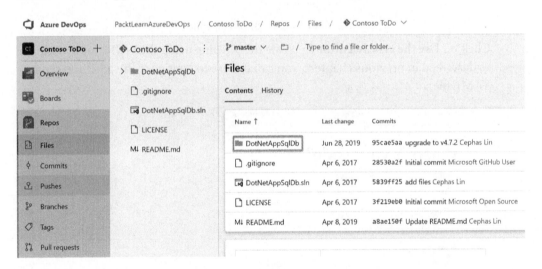

Figure 11.12 – Files in the Azure repo

We will now set up a build pipeline for the application.

Setting up CI for the application

Now that our application code is in Azure Repos, let's create a build pipeline that will build the application package to be deployed to Azure App Service:

1. In Azure DevOps, browse to **Pipelines** and click on **Create Pipeline**:

Create your first Pipeline

Automate your build and release processes using our wizard, and go from code to cloud-hosted within minutes.

Create Pipeline   :

Figure 11.13 – Creating a pipeline

2. Click on **Use the classic editor** to create the pipeline using the GUI (this is optional; as described in previous chapters, you can choose to configure the pipeline using a YAML file):

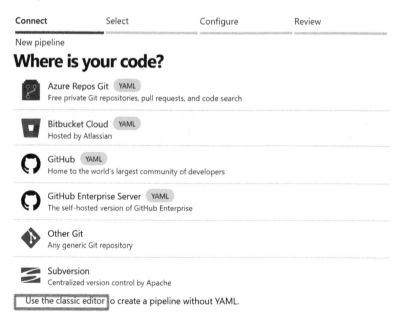

Connect	Select	Configure	Review

New pipeline

Where is your code?

Azure Repos Git   YAML
Free private Git repositories, pull requests, and code search

Bitbucket Cloud   YAML
Hosted by Atlassian

GitHub   YAML
Home to the world's largest community of developers

GitHub Enterprise Server   YAML
The self-hosted version of GitHub Enterprise

Other Git
Any generic Git repository

Subversion
Centralized version control by Apache

Use the classic editor o create a pipeline without YAML.

Figure 11.14 – Select the classic editor

3. Select your Azure repo and master branch, then click **Continue** to move to the next step:

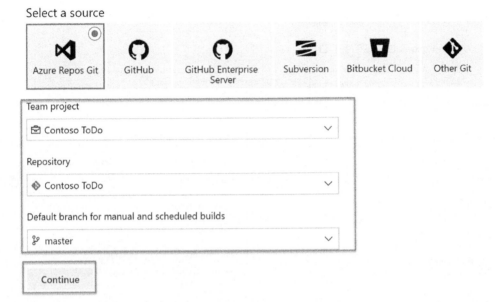

Figure 11.15 – Selecting the repo

4. Select **ASP.NET** as the pipeline template:

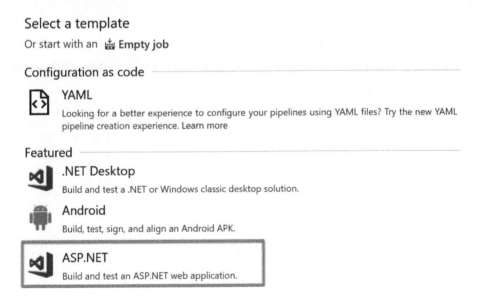

Figure 11.16 – Selecting the pipeline template

5. Review the pipeline configuration. For the purpose of this project, the default configuration does the job. Once it's reviewed, click on **Save & queue**:

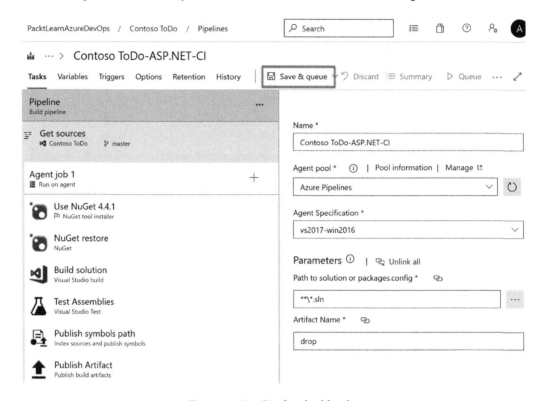

Figure 11.17 – Pipeline build tasks

6. In the **Run Pipeline** wizard, you can add a comment and click **Save and run to start execution**.

7. Once the job is in progress, you can review the status by click on the job name:

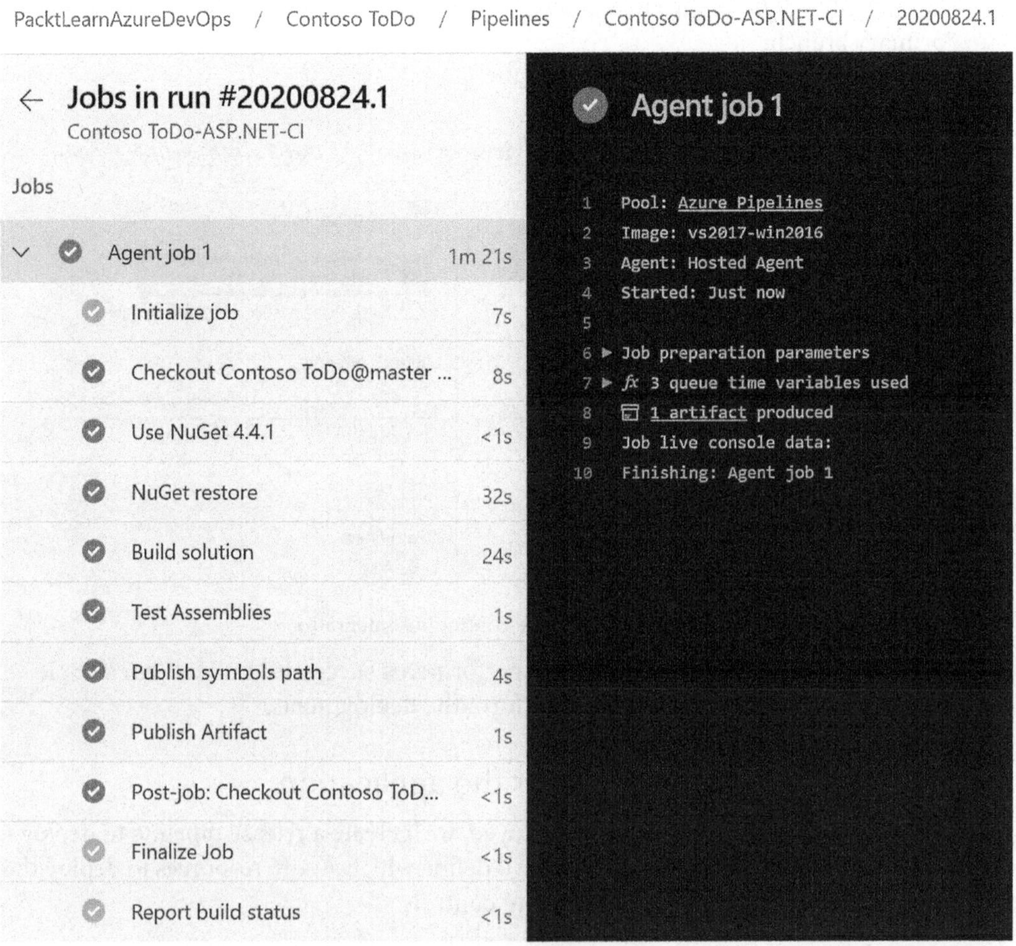

Figure 11.18 – Pipeline build status

8.   Now, let's enable CI on the pipeline to auto-start the build on commit to the **master** branch. Edit the pipeline and browse to **Triggers**, and enable CI. You can choose to filter by branch or change to a different branch if you are not using **master** as your primary branch:

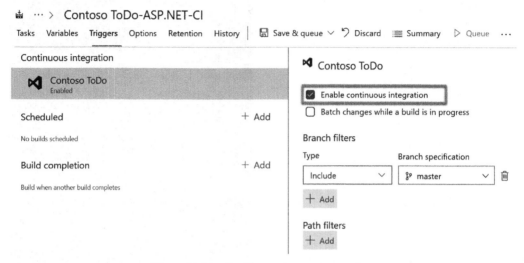

Figure 11.19 – Enable continuous integration

In this task, we created a build pipeline and performed a successful build of our sample **ToDo** application. In the next task, we'll perform the deployments.

Setting up continuous delivery for the application

Now that our application is ready to be deployed, we'll create a release pipeline to deploy the application in Azure. In this pipeline, we'll define which Azure resources to deploy the application to and add additional deployment controls.

Setting up the service connection

Azure DevOps requires access to an Azure subscription in order to be able to deploy and update Azure resources. Service connections in Azure DevOps allow you to connect your Azure DevOps project to external services. Let's create a service connection for Azure Pipelines:

1.   Log in to Azure DevOps and browse to **Project Settings | Service Connections**.

2.   Click on **Create service connection**.

3.   In the connections list, select **Azure Resource Manager**:

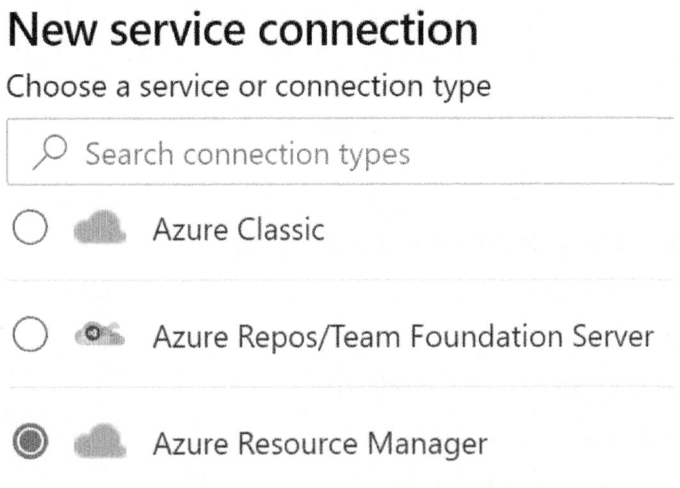

New service connection

Choose a service or connection type

🔍 Search connection types

○ ☁ Azure Classic

○ ☁ Azure Repos/Team Foundation Server

◉ ☁ Azure Resource Manager

Figure 11.20 – ARM service connections

4. For the service connection authentication method, choose **Service principal (automatic)**:

New Azure service connection   ✕

Azure Resource Manager

Authentication method

◉ ☁ Service principal (automatic)   Recommended

○ ☁ Service principal (manual)

○ ☁ Managed identity

○ ☁ Publish Profile

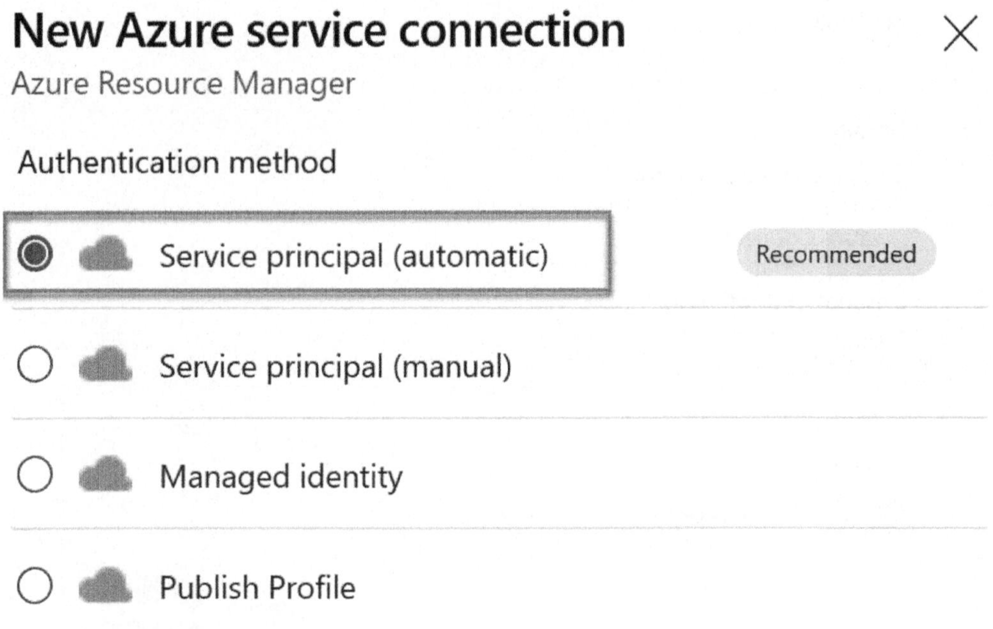

Figure 11.21 – ARM service connections service principal

5. Azure DevOps will now require you to authenticate to Azure. Please log in with an account with at least subscription owner rights and global admin rights in the Azure **Active Directory (AD)** tenant. You can choose to allow the service connection scope to be limited to a resource group or allow the entire subscription. Select your Azure subscription and give it a name:

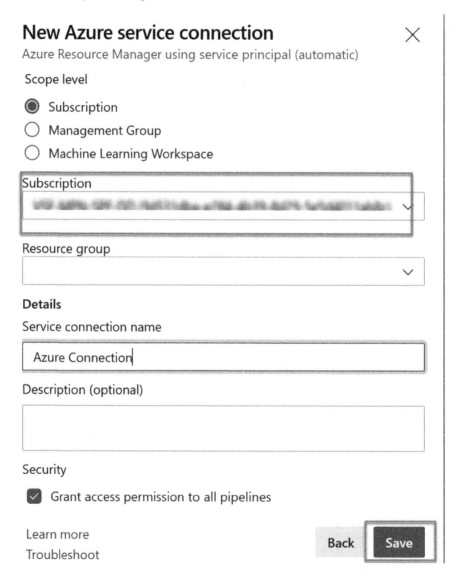

Figure 11.22 – Creating a service connections service principal

This service connection is now ready to be used in Azure Pipelines.

Creating a release pipeline

Release pipelines include all the steps and the workflow to deploy the application to various environments, such as development, staging, QA, and production. Let's start with creating a release pipeline for our **ToDo** app:

1. Log in to Azure DevOps and launch your `Contoso ToDo` project.

2. Browse to **Pipeline | Releases**.

3. Click on **New pipeline**:

No release pipelines found

Automate your release process in a few easy steps with a new pipeline

Figure 11.23 – New release pipeline

4. This will open a page to select a template. Since we're planning to deploy our **ToDo** app to App Service, select **Azure App Service deployment**:

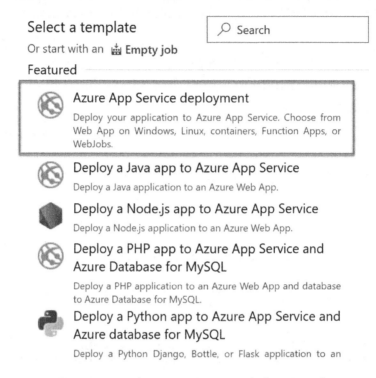

Figure 11.24 – The Azure App Service deployment task

5. Enter Staging Environment for **Stage name**. You can choose to give any other meaningful name that best depicts the scenario in your environment:

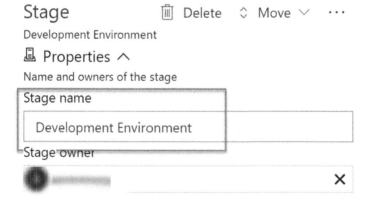

Figure 11.25 – Staging stage

6. You can now close the **Stage** blade. Your pipeline should look as follows:

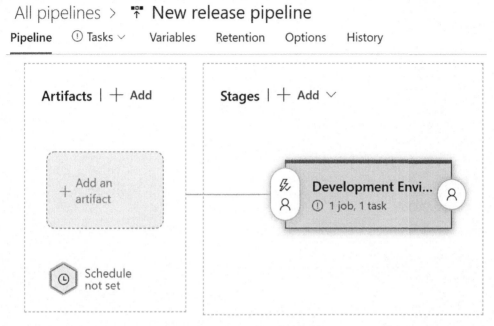

Figure 11.26 – Pipeline snapshot

7. In order to deploy the application, first we need to get the application package from the outputs of the build pipeline. Under **Artifacts**, click **+ Add**:

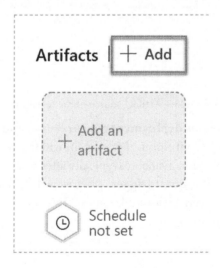

Figure 11.27 – Artifact in the release pipeline

8. Select **Build** as **Source type** and select the build pipeline created in the previous task. You can choose to configure which version is to be deployed by default:

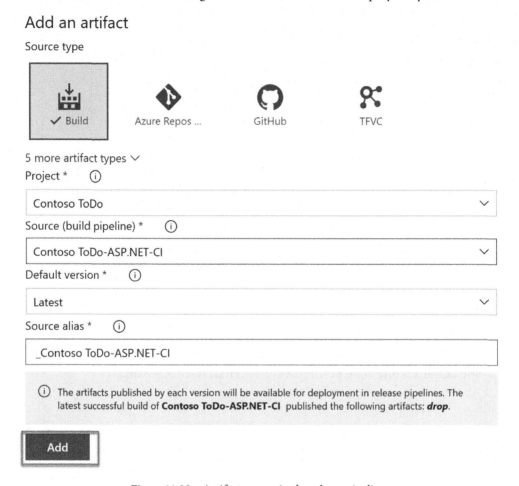

Add an artifact

Source type

5 more artifact types ∨

Project * ⓘ

Contoso ToDo ∨

Source (build pipeline) * ⓘ

Contoso ToDo-ASP.NET-CI ∨

Default version * ⓘ

Latest ∨

Source alias * ⓘ

_Contoso ToDo-ASP.NET-CI

ⓘ The artifacts published by each version will be available for deployment in release pipelines. The latest successful build of **Contoso ToDo-ASP.NET-CI** published the following artifacts: ***drop***.

Add

Figure 11.28 – Artifact source in the release pipeline

9. Click on the **Continuous deployment trigger** button and enable continuous deployment. Enabling continuous deployment will trigger a release every time there's a new build version available (typically after you run a build pipeline with CI). If you enable **Pull request trigger**, a release will be created every time we have a new build version, even with a pull request. This may be a useful scenario for pure development pipelines:

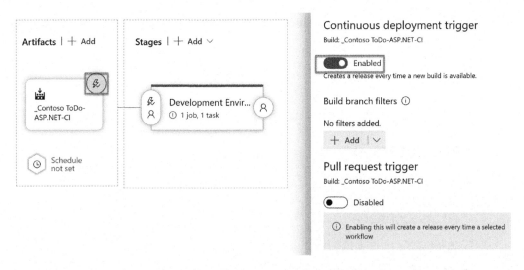

Figure 11.29 – Enabling continuous deployment

10. In **Stages**, click on **1 job, 1 task** in the development environment:

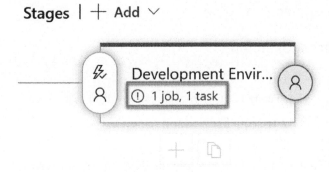

Figure 11.30 – Pipeline stage

11. Inside the tasks view, select your Azure subscription service connection and the app service that you deployed earlier:

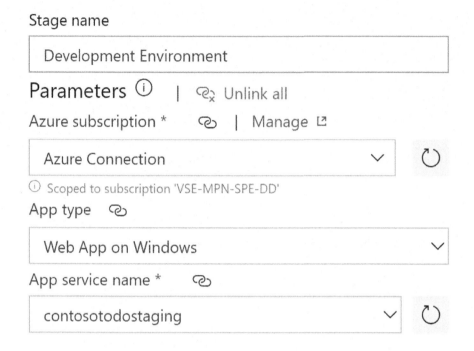

Stage name

Development Environment

Parameters ⓘ | ⧉ Unlink all

Azure subscription *   ⧉ | Manage ↗

Azure Connection   ⌄   ↺

ⓘ Scoped to subscription 'VSE-MPN-SPE-DD'

App type   ⧉

Web App on Windows   ⌄

App service name *   ⧉

contosotodostaging   ⌄   ↺

Figure 11.31 – App service deployment task

12. Click on **Deploy Azure App Service** and review the app service deployment information.

13. Click on + to add another task to apply the **SQL migration scripts** for getting the database ready. Search for SQL and select **Azure SQL Database deployment**.

14. In **Azure SQL Task**, change the following settings:

　　a) **Display Name**: Apply database migration script.

　　b) Select your Azure subscription and provide the database connection details captured while creating the Azure SQL database.

　　c) **Deploy Type**: Inline SQL script

d) **Inline SQL Script**: Provide the following script code. This will create the required tables in the SQL database. Please note that this is a sample SQL script to create the required schema (also available at `https://github.com/PacktPublishing/Learning-Azure-DevOps---B16392/tree/master/Chapter11`); in a production environment, you may choose to do so using the SQL Server Data Tools project in Azure Pipelines. Please refer to this documentation to learn more about doing Azure DevOps for SQL: `https://devblogs.microsoft.com/azure-sql/devops-for-azure-sql/`:

```sql
/****** Object:  Table [dbo].[__
MigrationHistory]    Script
Date: 8/24/2020 12:35:05 PM ******/
SET ANSI_NULLS ON


SET QUOTED_IDENTIFIER ON


IF NOT EXISTS
    ( SELECT [name]
      FROM sys.tables
      WHERE [name] = '__MigrationHistory'
    )
BEGIN
    CREATE TABLE [dbo].[__MigrationHistory](
        [MigrationId] [nvarchar](150) NOT NULL,
        [ContextKey] [nvarchar](300) NOT NULL,
        [Model] [varbinary](max) NOT NULL,
        [ProductVersion] [nvarchar](32) NOT NULL,
    CONSTRAINT [PK_dbo.__MigrationHistory]
PRIMARY KEY CLUSTERED
    (
        [MigrationId] ASC,
        [ContextKey] ASC
    )WITH (STATISTICS_NORECOMPUTE = OFF, IGNORE_DUP_
KEY = OFF) ON [PRIMARY]
    ) ON [PRIMARY] TEXTIMAGE_ON [PRIMARY]


END
/****** Object:  Table [dbo].[Todoes]    Script
```

```
Date: 8/24/2020 12:35:05 PM ******/
SET ANSI_NULLS ON


SET QUOTED_IDENTIFIER ON


IF NOT EXISTS
    (  SELECT [name]
       FROM sys.tables
       WHERE [name] = 'Todoes'
    )
BEGIN
    CREATE TABLE [dbo].[Todoes](
        [ID] [int] IDENTITY(1,1) NOT NULL,
        [Description] [nvarchar](max) NULL,
        [CreatedDate] [datetime] NOT NULL,
    CONSTRAINT [PK_dbo.Todoes] PRIMARY KEY CLUSTERED
    (
        [ID] ASC
    )WITH (STATISTICS_NORECOMPUTE = OFF, IGNORE_DUP_
KEY = OFF) ON [PRIMARY]
    ) ON [PRIMARY] TEXTIMAGE_ON [PRIMARY]



END
```

15. Click **Save** and + to add another task. We'll now need to add another task to update the connection string of the database in the connection settings of Azure App Service.

16. Search for **Azure App Service Settings** in the task's menu:

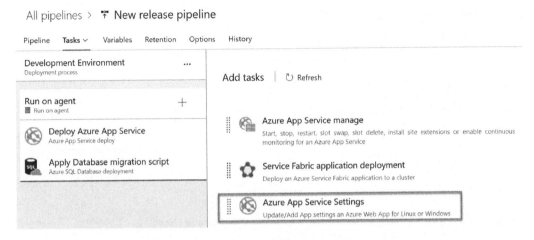

Figure 11.32 – The Azure App Service Settings task

17. In the **Azure App Service Settings** task, select the Azure subscription and app service connection details for the staging environment.

18. In **Connection Settings**, provide the database connection string in the following format. Please update your database connection details before saving. Since this is a test lab, we're storing the secure information directly in the pipeline task. However, in a production environment, please use variables and parameters to store any connection string or other information. Please refer to this documentation to learn more about securely using variables and parameters in an Azure pipeline: `https://docs.microsoft.com/bs-cyrl-ba/azure/devops/ pipelines/security/inputs?view=azure-devops`:

```
[
    {
        'name': 'MyDbConnection',
        'value': 'Server=tcp:contosotodostagingdb.database.
windows.NET,1433;Initial Catalog=ContoSoToDoStageDB;
Persist Security Info=False;User ID=azadmin;
Password=<YourPassword>;MultipleActiveResultSets=False;
Encrypt=True;TrustServerCertificate=False;
Connection Timeout=30;',
        'type': 'SQLAzure',
        'slotSetting': false
    }
]
```

19. Once all the tasks are updated, click on **Save**. You can save the pipeline in the root folder upon prompt. This should be the order of the tasks:

   a) **Apply Database migration script**

   b) **Apply Azure App Service Settings**

   c) **Deploy Azure App Service**:

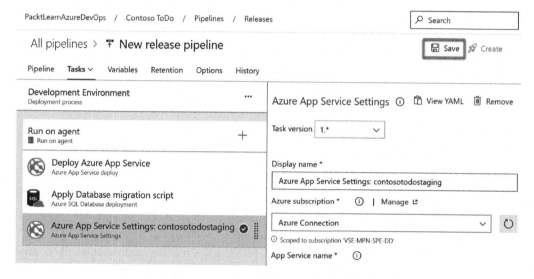

Figure 11.33 – Saving the release pipeline

20. In the pipeline, click on **+ Add** to add another stage for production. You can select the same Azure App Service deployment, or you can also clone your development environment stage. You can configure the production stage while targeting the production app service and SQL database instances. Your pipeline should now look as follows:

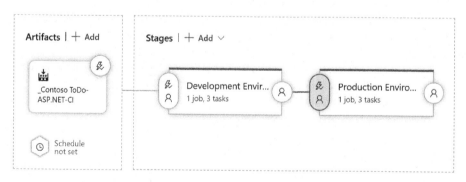

Figure 11.34 – Release pipeline

21. Typically, you wouldn't want to auto-deploy to production. Let's modify the flow to include a manual approval for production deployment. Click on **Pre-Deployment Conditions**:

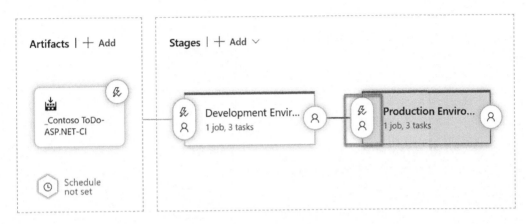

Figure 11.35 – Release pipeline trigger control

22. Enable the **pre-deployment approval** and select at least one user to approve before deployment to production happens.

23. You can add an additional stage, such as test cases, performance benchmarks, and so on, and prepare the overall flow. Click **Save** once you've completed reviewing the pipeline.

The Azure release pipeline to deploy the application is now ready. Let's create a release and see whether we can get our application up and running through CI/CD pipelines.

Creating a release

Let's test the release pipeline by creating a release manually:

1. In Azure DevOps, browse to **Releases** and click on **Create release**:

Figure 11.36 – Create release

2. Review the release details and click **Create**:

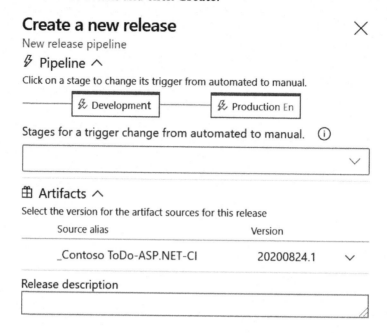

Figure 11.37 – Reviewing release creation

3. Clicking **Create** will start a release execution; you can review the progress by clicking on logs on the stage:

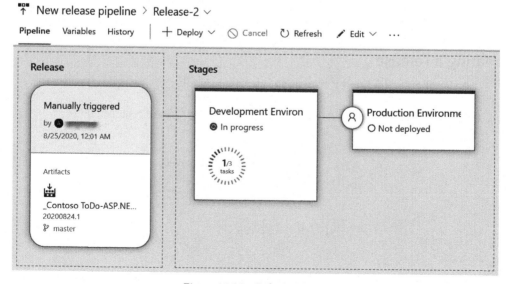

Figure 11.38 – Release status

Once the development environment deployment has completed, you should try to launch the app service and see whether the **ToDo** application is working well for you:

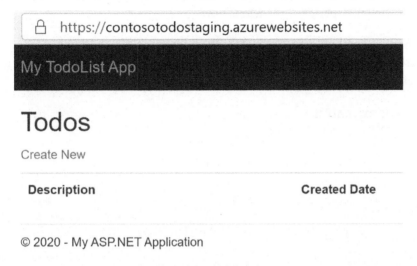

Figure 11.39 – The ToDo app

4. You can try to add **to-do** items and test the application. Once you're ready to approve this for production deployment, click **Approve** to start the production deployment:

Figure 11.40 – Approving the production deployment

You've now completed a release and your application is now ready to be used.

Trying out end-to-end CI/CD flow

Now that you've completed setting up an end-to-end CI/CD pipeline, go ahead and try out the following to experience the whole flow:

1. In Azure Repos, modify the view for the home page. Go to **Repos** | **DotNetAppSQLDB** | **Views** | **Todos** | **index.cshtml** and modify the label from **Create new** to **Create New ToDo Item**:

Index.cshtml

Contents   Highlight changes

```
 1  @model IEnumerable<DotNetAppSqlDb.Models.Todo>
 2
 3  @{
 4      ViewBag.Title = "Index";
 5  }
 6
 7  <h2>Todos</h2>
 8
 9  <p>
10      @Html.ActionLink("Create New ToDo Item", "Create")
11  </p>
12  <table class="table">
13      <tr>
14          <th>
15              @Html.DisplayNameFor(model => model.Description)
16          </th>
17          <th>
18              @Html.DisplayNameFor(model => model.CreatedDate)
19          </th>
20          <th></th>
21      </tr>
22
23  @foreach (var item in Model) {
24      <tr>
25          <td>
26              @Html.DisplayFor(modelItem => item.Description)
27          </td>
28          <td>
29              @Html.DisplayFor(modelItem => item.CreatedDate)
30          </td>
31          <td>
32              @Html.ActionLink("Edit", "Edit", new { id=item.ID }) |
33              @Html.ActionLink("Details", "Details", new { id=item.ID }) |
34              @Html.ActionLink("Delete", "Delete", new { id=item.ID })
35          </td>
36      </tr>
37  }
38
39  </table>
40  |
```

Figure 11.41 – Modifying the app code

2. Commit the change in a new branch and follow through the pull request. You should approve and complete the pull request.

   This should start an automated build pipeline execution followed through automated release execution.

   In the end, you should have your application updated with the change without having to do any manual steps except the approval task configured for production.

Congratulations, you've now completed the setup and testing of an end-to-end CI/CD pipeline! In the next section, we'll set up a similar pipeline for a Kubernetes-based application.

Setting up a CI/CD pipeline for a container-based application

In this example, we'll take a container-based application and build an end-to-end CI/CD pipeline. We'll take a Python and Redis-based sample application for the purpose of this demonstration.

In this example, we'll be using various Azure resources in the overall solution architecture. This includes the following:

- **Azure DevOps**: CI/CD pipeline
- **Azure Kubernetes Service (AKS)**: For hosting the containers
- **Azure Container Registry (ACR)**: Container image storage and management

Introduction to the sample app

In this section, we'll be using a sample application called **Azure Voting App**. It is a standard multi-container-based application that uses the following components:

- **The Azure Voting App backend**: This will be running on Redis.
- **The Azure Voting App frontend**: Web application built with Python.

You can review the application code here: `https://github.com/Azure-Samples/azure-voting-app-redis`.

Setting up the required infrastructure

In order to be able to build the pipeline, first we need to set up the required infrastructure, including the AKS cluster and Azure container registry. We will be creating separate resources for the staging and production environments as a standard best practice; however, it is possible to use a single environment for both the production and development environments by using a combination of tags and a Kubernetes namespace.

In this section, we'll be using the Azure **command-line interface** (**CLI**) for all infrastructure provisioning tasks.

Creating the Azure resource group

Let's start by creating an Azure resource group for organizing all the resources for your development and production environments:

1. Log in to Azure Cloud Shell (`https://shell.azure.com`) with your Azure credentials.

2. If this is your first time logging in to Azure Cloud Shell, it will prompt you to create an Azure storage account. Select your subscription and click **Create Storage**.

3. Select **Bash** on the shell type selection.

4. Run the following command to list all your subscriptions:

    ```
    az account list
    ```

5. If you need to select a specific subscription for provisioning resources, run the following command:

    ```
    az account set --subscription 'Your Subscription Name'
    ```

6. Create a resource named `Contoso-Voting-Stage` by running the following command. You can choose to upload the location with a region of your choice:

    ```
    az group create -l westus -n Contoso-Voting-Stage
    ```

7. Repeat the resource group creation command to create another resource group named `Contoso-Voting-Prod` for the production environment.

You have now completed the required resource groups. In the next step, you'll create an Azure Kubernetes cluster.

Creating an Azure Kubernetes service

AKS is a managed Kubernetes offering from Microsoft Azure. There are two types of hosts in Kubernetes clusters – master (aka the control plane) and nodes. In the world of AKS, there's no master for end users. Microsoft creates and manages master nodes and hides them away from end users. As a user, you only deploy AKS nodes (Kubernetes nodes) in your subscription, whereas the configuration of Kubernetes and the joining of Microsoft-managed Kubernetes masters happens in the background. With AKS, you only pay for the nodes' infrastructure costs; masters are provided for free by Microsoft.

We will be using AKS to host our containers.

Let's start by creating an AKS cluster:

1. Log in to Cloud Shell with your Azure credentials.

2. Run the following command to create an AKS cluster with the default configuration and latest version:

    ```
    az aks create --resource-group Contoso-Voting-Stage
    --name Contoso-Stage-AKS --node-count 1 --enable-addons
    monitoring --generate-ssh-keys
    ```

    Let's look at this command in detail:

    a) `az aks create`: The syntax for creating an AKS cluster.

    b) `--resource-group` & `--name`: The resource group's name and AKS cluster name.

    c) `--node-count`: The number of AKS nodes you're creating.

    d) `--enable-addons`: This specifies add-ons, such as monitoring and HTTP routing.

    e) `--generate-ssh-keys`: This is a flag that lets `az cli` create SSH keys to be used for agent nodes.

3. It may take up to 10 minutes for the AKS cluster to be ready. You can review the status by running the following command:

    ```
    az aks list
    ```

4. Once your cluster is ready, you can get the Kubernetes authentication configuration in your Cloud Shell session by running the following command:

    ```
    az aks get-credentials --resource-group Contoso-Voting-
    Stage --name Contoso-Stage-AKS
    ```

5. You can try running `kubectl` commands now to interact with Kubernetes. Run the following command to get a list of all the Kubernetes nodes:

```
kubectl get nodes
```

Your Azure Kubernetes cluster is now ready; please repeat the process to create another AKS cluster for the production environment.

Creating an Azure container registry

ACR is a private Docker container registry that's hosted and managed by Microsoft Azure. ACR is fully compatible with Docker and works in the same way, except that it's managed, hosted, and secured by Microsoft. We will be using ACR to store our container images.

Let's create a container registry for the project:

1. Log in to Azure Cloud Shell and run the following command to create a container registry:

```
az acr create --resource-group Contoso-Voting-Stage
--name ContosoStageACR --sku Basic
```

2. Once your container registry is ready, you can get the status and details of it by running the following command:

```
az acr list
```

Integrating ACR with AKS

AKS needs to have permissions to access the container images from ACR in order to run the application. Let's enable access for AKS to interact with our ACR.

Run the following command to integrate AKS with our ACR:

```
az aks update -n Contoso-Stage-AKS -g Contoso-Voting-Stage
--attach-acr ContosoStageACR
```

Now that our infrastructure is ready, we'll begin with setting up the code repository for the application.

Setting up Azure Repos for the voting application

In this section, we'll create a new Azure DevOps project and import the **voting app** source code in Azure Repos:

1. Log in to Azure DevOps and create a new project named `Contoso Voting App` or any other name of your choice.

2. Navigate to Azure Repos and click **Import a Git repository**. Please import the Azure voting app repository from: `https://github.com/Azure-Samples/ azure-voting-app-redis`:

Figure 11.42 – Importing the repository

Now that our repo is ready, let's start with a build pipeline.

Setting up the CI pipeline

The build pipeline will be responsible for building the container image and pushing them in ACR. Let's get started:

1. Log in to Azure DevOps and open **Contoso Voting App Project**.

2. Navigate to **Pipeline** and click **Create Pipeline**.

3. Click on **Use the Classic Editor** for creating the pipeline with the UI.

4. Select the source Azure repo that you created in the previous section as the source for the pipeline.

5.   For the template, select **Docker Container** as the template type:

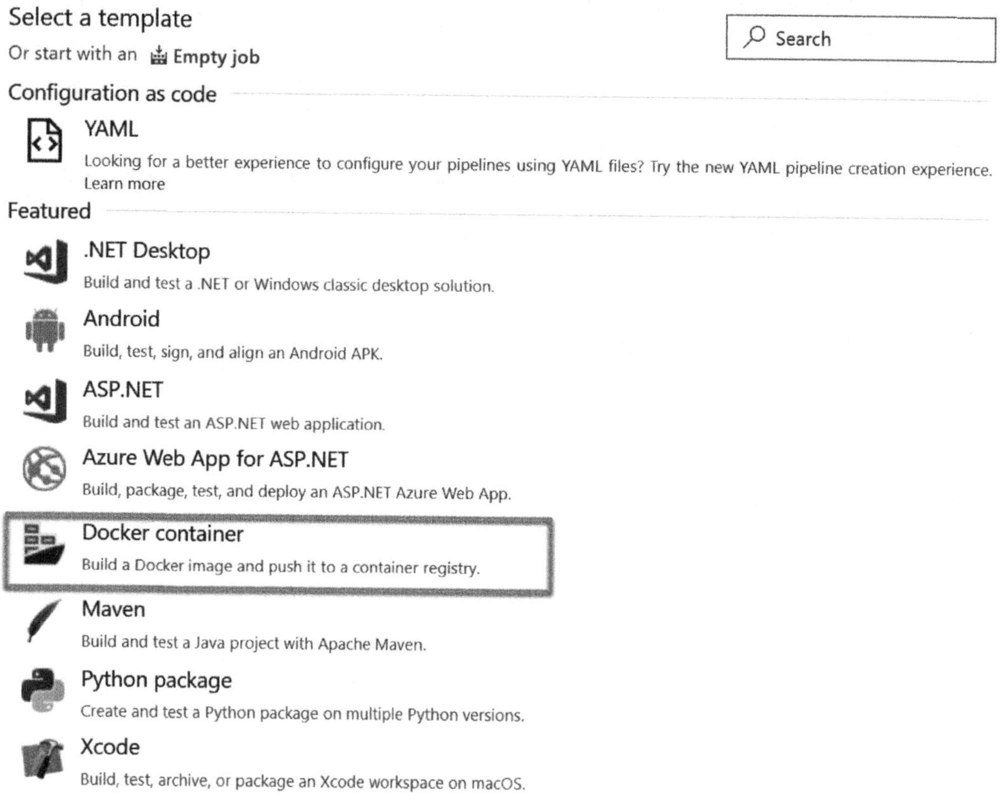

Select a template

Or start with an 🎛 Empty job

🔍 Search

Configuration as code

YAML

Looking for a better experience to configure your pipelines using YAML files? Try the new YAML pipeline creation experience. Learn more

Featured

.NET Desktop

Build and test a .NET or Windows classic desktop solution.

Android

Build, test, sign, and align an Android APK.

ASP.NET

Build and test an ASP.NET web application.

Azure Web App for ASP.NET

Build, package, test, and deploy an ASP.NET Azure Web App.

Docker container

Build a Docker image and push it to a container registry.

Maven

Build and test a Java project with Apache Maven.

Python package

Create and test a Python package on multiple Python versions.

Xcode

Build, test, archive, or package an Xcode workspace on macOS.

Figure 11.43 – Docker container pipeline template

6.   In the **Build an Image** task configuration, provide the following values:

a) **Container Registry Type**: **Azure Container Registry**.

b) Select your Azure subscription from the dropdown and authorize it.

c) Select **ACR** from the dropdown.

d) **Action**: **Build an image**.

e) **Docker File**: The `root/azure-vote/Dockerfile` repo.

f) Check **Include Latest Tag**:

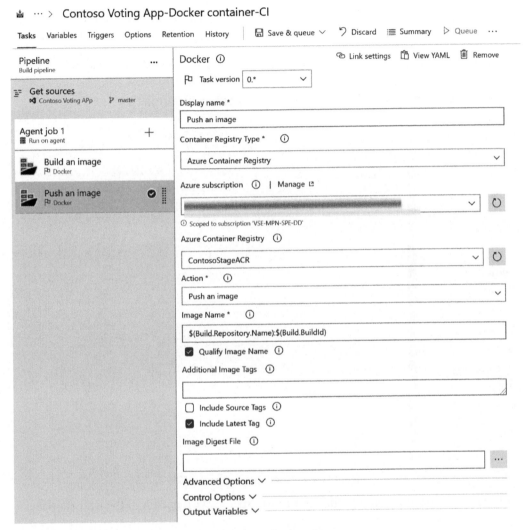

Figure 11.44 – Push an image

7. In the **Push an image** task, select the Azure subscription and ACR again, with the task being **Push an image**. Be sure to check **Include Latest Tag**.

8. Once you're done, review both tasks and click **Save and Run** to start the pipeline job execution.

9. Review the job logs to see the detailed information about image building and pushing to ACR.

10. Upon completion, navigate to the Azure portal and open the container registry you created earlier.

11. Navigate to **Repositories**; you should see a new image being created there. Let's look at the image and find out the image name to update in our application deployment configuration:

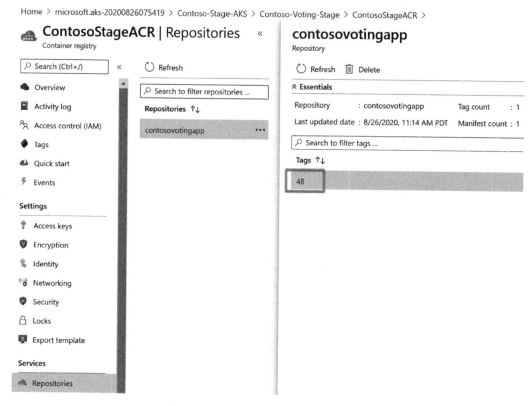

Figure 11.45 – Container image in ACR

12. Make a note of the image pull connection string. We'll need it in the next exercise:

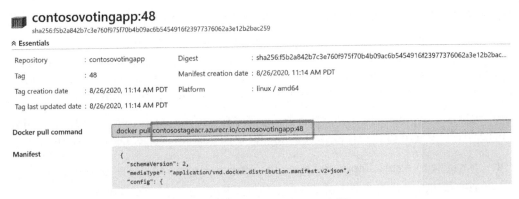

Figure 11.46 – Image syntax in ACR

13. Our pipeline is now ready and tested, so let's go back and enable CI in the pipeline trigger configuration:

Figure 11.47 – Enabling CI

Now that our CI pipeline is ready, let's start with the deployment pipeline.

Setting up the CD pipeline

In this section, we'll set up the deployment pipeline, which will deploy the application code to AKS and update when necessary. Azure Pipelines provides native integration with Kubernetes clusters hosted on-premises and in the cloud.

Updating the Kubernetes deployment manifest file

In the Kubernetes world, application deployment is managed through manifest files written in JSON or YAML. The deployment file for this sample application is already included in the Azure repo. You can review the deployment configuration by reviewing the `azure-vote-all-in-one-redis.yaml` file in the Azure Repos root.

By default, the deployment manifest is configured to use the Microsoft-provided container image. We'll need to update it to start using our own custom image. Let's get started:

1. Navigate to **Azure Repos** and open the `azure-vote-all-in-one-redis.yaml` file.

2. Click on **Edit** at the top-right corner of the file editor.

3. Look for the following part of the deployment manifest. This redirects the container engine to use a Microsoft-provided Docker image:

    ```
    image: microsoft/azure-vote-front:v1
    ```

4. Replace the value with your own container registry and image name. It should look like the one given as follows. You should specify the latest tag to ensure that the newest image is always used:

    ```
    image: contosostageacr.azurecr.io/
    contosovotingapp:latest
    ```

5. Commit the changes to save the deployment manifest file.

Your application manifest is now ready for deployment.

Setting up the release pipeline

The release pipeline will be applying the deployment manifest in the Kubernetes cluster and perform image update tasks. Let's build a pipeline to automate the deployment:

1. Log in to **Azure DevOps | Pipelines | Releases**.

2. Create a new release pipeline. Select the **Deploy to a Kubernetes cluster** template:

Figure 11.48 – The Deploy to a Kubernetes cluster template

3. Update the stage name to `Development Environment`.

4. Let's start with adding artifacts. Click on **Add** in **artifacts**.

5. In **Artifact**, select the Azure repo and choose the repository we imported. Click **Add**:

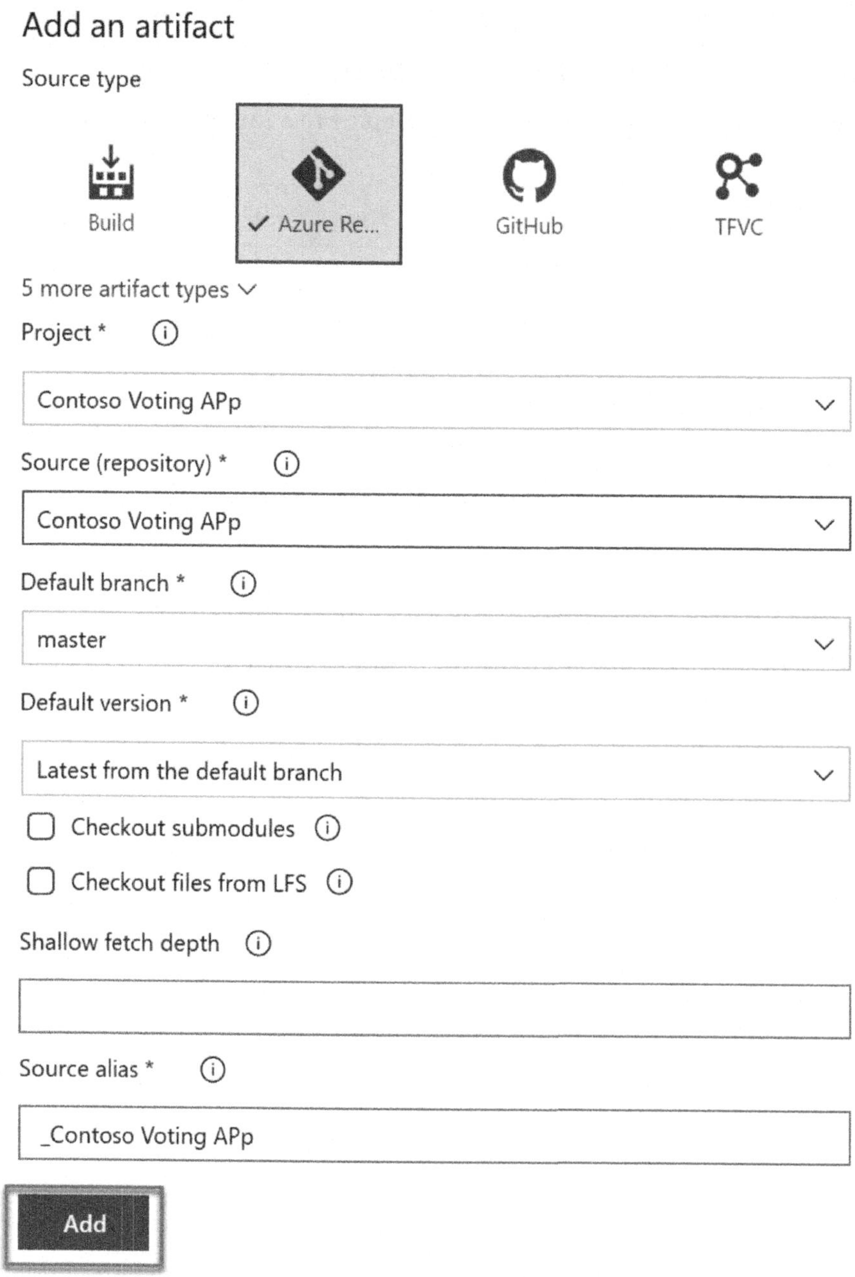

Figure 11.49 – Adding an artifact to a pipeline

6. In the **Tasks section,** let's configure a task to perform the application deployment. Configure the **kubectl** task as follows:

a) **Display Name**: Deploy to Kubernetes.

b) **Kubernetes Service Connection**: Create a new server connection and connect to your AKS cluster created earlier:

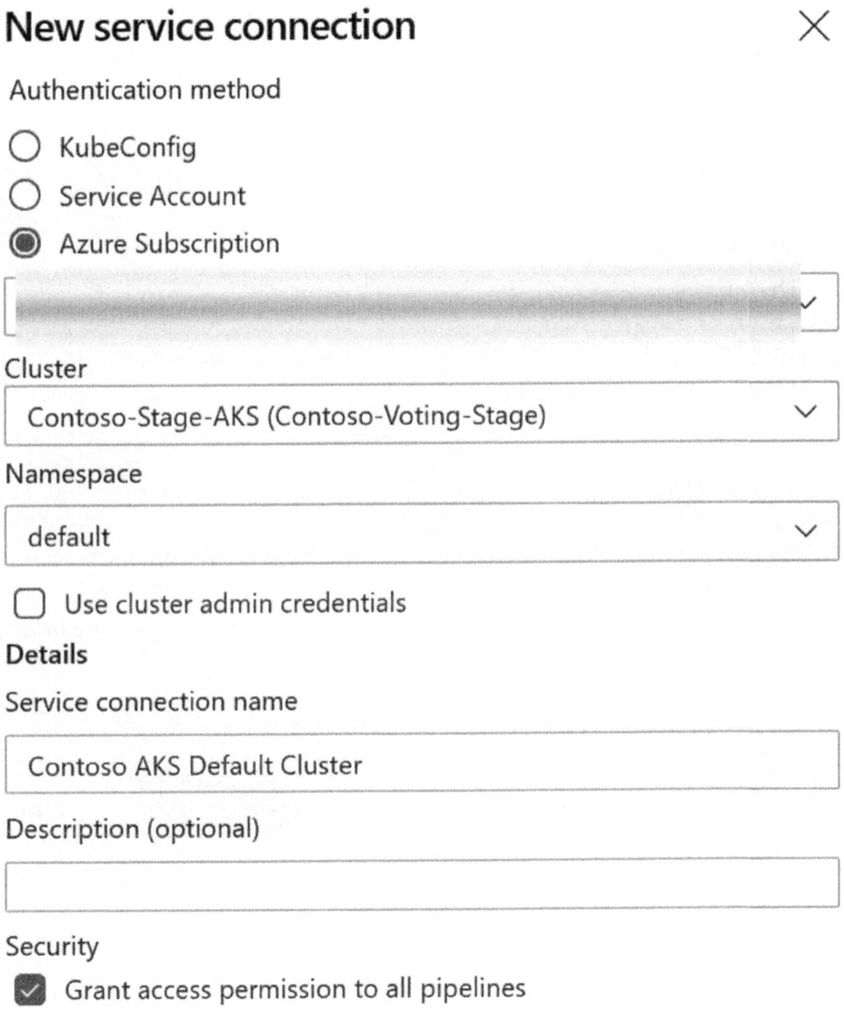

New service connection   ✕

Authentication method

○ KubeConfig

○ Service Account

◉ Azure Subscription

Cluster

Contoso-Stage-AKS (Contoso-Voting-Stage)   ⌄

Namespace

default   ⌄

☐ Use cluster admin credentials

Details

Service connection name

Contoso AKS Default Cluster

Description (optional)

Security

☑ Grant access permission to all pipelines

Figure 11.50 – Kubernetes service connection

c) **Command**: **Apply**.

d) Click on **Choose configuration file** to provide a path to your deployment YAML file (`azure-vote-all-in-one-redis.yaml`). Browse to your default directory and select the deployment YAML file. We can define additional options, such as Kubernetes secrets and config maps, if required. Click **Save** after verifying that all the configurations are valid:

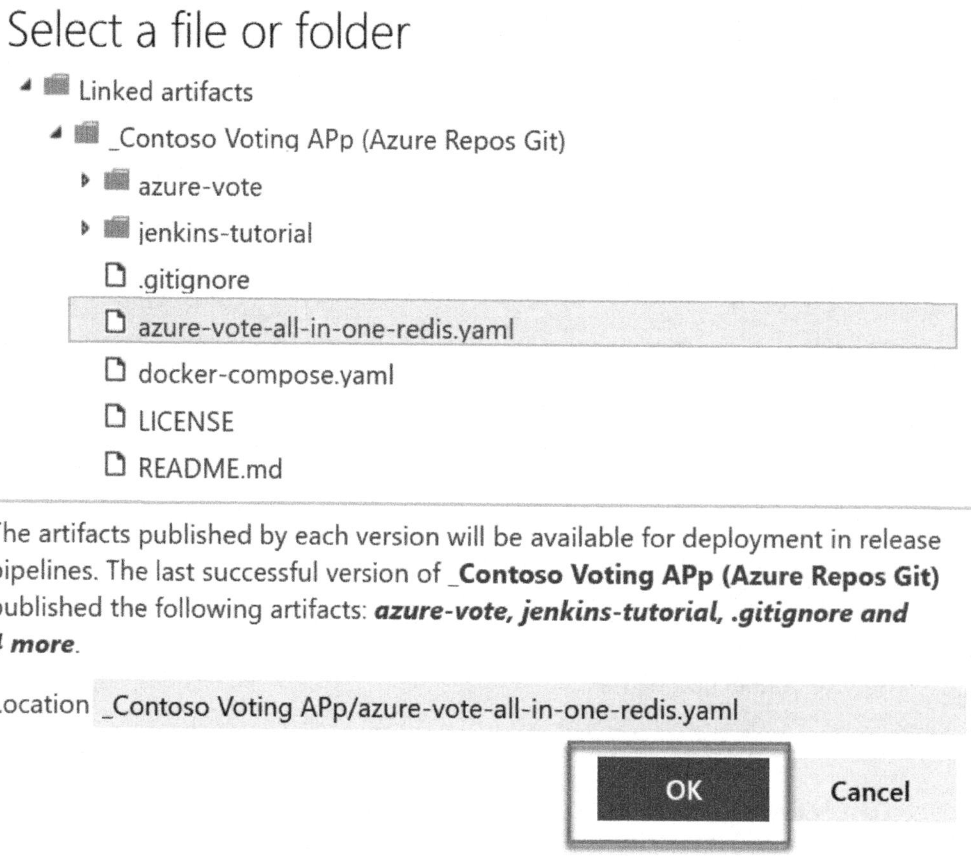

Select a file or folder

▲ 🖿 Linked artifacts

   ▲ 🖿 _Contoso Voting APp (Azure Repos Git)

      ▶ 🖿 azure-vote

      ▶ 🖿 jenkins-tutorial

      🗋 .gitignore

      🗋 azure-vote-all-in-one-redis.yaml

      🗋 docker-compose.yaml

      🗋 LICENSE

      🗋 README.md

The artifacts published by each version will be available for deployment in release pipelines. The last successful version of **_Contoso Voting APp (Azure Repos Git)** published the following artifacts: ***azure-vote, jenkins-tutorial, .gitignore and 4 more***.

Location   _Contoso Voting APp/azure-vote-all-in-one-redis.yaml

OK   Cancel

Figure 11.51 – Selecting the deployment YAML

e) Review the task configurations and click **Save** to save the progress so far:

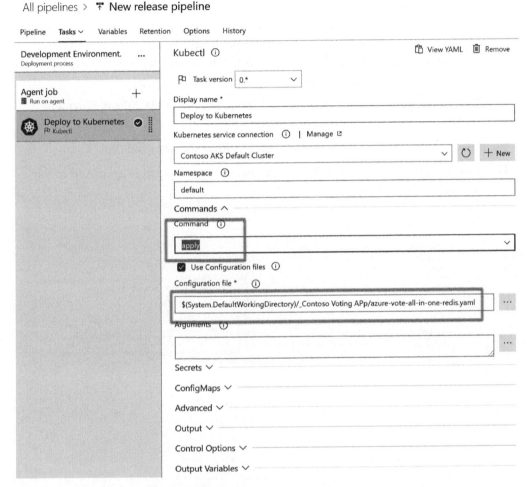

Figure 11.52 – Task configuration

7. Now, we'll add another step in the pipeline so that we can update the images in AKS after deployment. This will ensure that, at every release, Kubernetes is pulling the latest images. Click on the + sign to add another **kubectl** task to the pipeline.

8. Configure the task so that it uses the same Kubernetes connection. Under **Command**, keep **set** as the command and use `image deployments/azure-vote-front azure-vote-front=youracrname.azurecr.io/contosovotingapp:latest` as the argument. In a production deployment, you may not want to use the latest tag in your pipeline and rather refer to the version tag generated using the build pipeline. This will help you manage your deployments with specific versions and roll back easily if you wish to.

9. Once you're ready, save the pipeline and create a release to test the deployment pipeline.

10. Review the release logs to understand the deployment steps and flow.

11. Once it's completed successfully, go back to editing the pipeline again and enable continuous deployment:

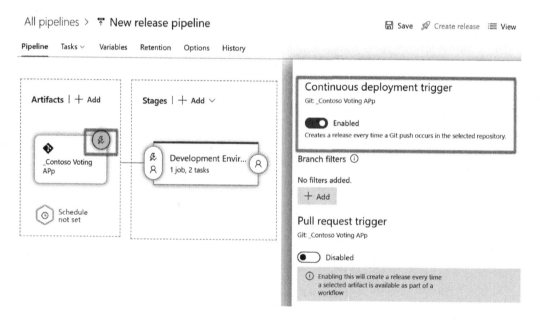

Figure 11.53 – Enabling continuous deployment

With that, our build and release configuration with full CI/CD automation is ready. Let's look at the AKS cluster to ensure that our application has been deployed properly and is accessible (with the release that we just did):

12. Connect to your AKS cluster using the Azure shell.

13. Run `kubectl get pods` and `kubectl get services`:

```
amit@Azure:~$ kubectl get pods
NAME                                   READY    STATUS     RESTARTS   AGE
azure-vote-back-f9cc849fb-dzw6j        1/1      Running    0          3m
azure-vote-front-fb8f5c676-9cz21       1/1      Running    0          3m
azure-vote-front-fb8f5c676-bdnp5       1/1      Running    0          3m
azure-vote-front-fb8f5c676-kdpn4       1/1      Running    0          3m
azure-vote-front-fb8f5c676-sr2ff       1/1      Running    0          3m
amit@Azure:~$ kubectl get services
NAME                TYPE           CLUSTER-IP     EXTERNAL-IP      PORT(S)         AGE
azure-vote-back     ClusterIP      10.0.59.133    <none>          6379/TCP        3m
azure-vote-front    LoadBalancer   10.0.207.40    13.76.128.239   80:30559/TCP    3m
kubernetes          ClusterIP      10.0.0.1       <none>          443/TCP         15d
amit@Azure:~$ ▊
```

Figure 11.54 – The kubectl results

14. Make a note of the public IP of the `azure-vote-front` application. You can try launching the public IP to check that the application is working as expected:

Figure 11.55 – Voting app launched

Next, we will be simulating an end-to-end CI/CD experience for this application.

Simulating an end-to-end CI/CD experience

In the previous sections, we set up a CI/CD pipeline. Let's try to play around with it and experience the overall flow. Let's start by updating the title of the application from **Azure Voting App** to **Contoso Voting App**:

1. Browse to **Azure Repos | Files | azure-vote | azure-vote | config_file.cfg** and click **Edit**.

2. Change the value of **Title** from **Azure Voting App** to **Contoso Voting App**:

Figure 11.56 – Updating the app name

3. Commit the changes through a pull request process.

4. Once the pull request is completed, a build pipeline will trigger that will build the Docker images and push to ACR.

5. Once the build pipeline is completed, it'll trigger the release pipeline to start another release. In the end, you should see that your web application is updated with the title.

This concludes setting up a CI/CD pipeline for container-based infrastructure hosted on AKS.

Azure Architecture Center for DevOps

Azure Architecture Center is a centralized place to take guidance for architecting solutions on Azure using established patterns and practices. There are several sample architectures available around DevOps.

You can access Azure Architecture Center here: `https://docs.microsoft.com/en-us/azure/architecture/`.

Refer to the following links to learn more about planning the right architecture for DevOps across various infrastructure and application scenarios:

- Azure DevOps: `https://docs.microsoft.com/en-us/azure/architecture/example-scenario/apps/devops-dotnet-webapp`

- DevOps with containers: `https://docs.microsoft.com/en-us/azure/architecture/example-scenario/apps/devops-with-aks`

- Microservices with AKS and Azure DevOps: `https://docs.microsoft.com/en-us/azure/architecture/solution-ideas/articles/microservices-with-aks`

- Secure DevOps for AKS: `https://docs.microsoft.com/en-us/azure/architecture/solution-ideas/articles/secure-devops-for-kubernetes`

- Azure DevOps CI/CD pipelines for chatbots: `https://docs.microsoft.com/en-us/azure/architecture/example-scenario/apps/devops-cicd-chatbot`

- CI/CD for Azure VMs: `https://docs.microsoft.com/en-us/azure/architecture/solution-ideas/articles/cicd-for-azure-vms`

- CI/CD for Azure web apps: `https://docs.microsoft.com/en-us/azure/architecture/solution-ideas/articles/azure-devops-continuous-integration-and-continuous-deployment-for-azure-web-apps`

- CI/CD for containers: `https://docs.microsoft.com/en-us/azure/architecture/solution-ideas/articles/cicd-for-containers`

- Container CI/CD using Jenkins and Kubernetes on AKS: `https://docs.microsoft.com/en-us/azure/architecture/solution-ideas/articles/container-cicd-using-jenkins-and-kubernetes-on-azure-container-service`

- DevSecOps in Azure: `https://docs.microsoft.com/en-us/azure/architecture/solution-ideas/articles/devsecops-in-azure`

- DevTest deployment for testing IaaS solutions: `https://docs.microsoft.com/en-us/azure/architecture/solution-ideas/articles/dev-test-iaas`

- DevTest deployment for testing PaaS solutions: `https://docs.microsoft.com/en-us/azure/architecture/solution-ideas/articles/dev-test-paas`

- DevTest deployment for testing microservice solutions: `https://docs.microsoft.com/en-us/azure/architecture/solution-ideas/articles/dev-test-microservice`

- DevTest Image Factory: `https://docs.microsoft.com/en-us/azure/architecture/solution-ideas/articles/dev-test-image-factory`

- Immutable infrastructure CI/CD using Jenkins and Terraform on Azure virtual architecture overview: `https://docs.microsoft.com/en-us/azure/architecture/solution-ideas/articles/immutable-infrastructure-cicd-using-jenkins-and-terraform-on-azure-virtual-architecture-overview`

- DevOps in a hybrid environment: `https://docs.microsoft.com/en-us/azure/architecture/solution-ideas/articles/java-cicd-using-jenkins-and-azure-web-apps`

- Java CI/CD using Jenkins and Azure web apps: `https://docs.microsoft.com/en-us/azure/architecture/solution-ideas/articles/java-cicd-using-jenkins-and-azure-web-apps`

- Run a Jenkins server on Azure: `https://docs.microsoft.com/en-us/azure/architecture/example-scenario/apps/jenkins`

- SharePoint Farm for development testing: `https://docs.microsoft.com/en-us/azure/architecture/solution-ideas/articles/sharepoint-farm-devtest`

- Sharing location in real time using low-cost serverless Azure services: `https://docs.microsoft.com/en-us/azure/architecture/example-scenario/signalr/`

Summary

In this chapter, we looked at a .NET and SQL-based application and set up a CI/CD pipeline for it using Azure DevOps. We looked at how you manage your production and staging environments through approval workflows.

Similarly, we also looked at a container-based application and did a walkthrough of setting up an end-to-end CI/CD pipeline for the application using ACR and AKS.

In the end, we talked about Azure Architecture Center, which can be referred to while planning your DevOps architecture.

This was the final chapter, and we hope you have enjoyed reading this book!

Other Books You May Enjoy

If you enjoyed this book, you may be interested in these other books by Packt:

Learn Azure Administration

Kamil Mrzygłód

ISBN: 978-1-83855-145-2

- Explore different Azure services and understand the correlation between them
- Secure and integrate different Azure components
- Work with a variety of identity and access management (IAM) models
- Find out how to set up monitoring and logging solutions
- Build a complete skill set of Azure administration activities with Azure DevOps
- Discover efficient scaling patterns for small and large workloads

Learn Azure Sentinel

Richard Diver, Gary Bushey

ISBN: 978-1-83898-092-4

- Understand how to design and build a security operations center
- Discover the key components of a cloud security architecture
- Manage and investigate Azure Sentinel incidents
- Use playbooks to automate incident responses
- Understand how to set up Azure Monitor Log Analytics and Azure Sentinel
- Ingest data into Azure Sentinel from the cloud and on-premises devices
- Perform threat hunting in Azure Sentinel

Leave a review - let other readers know what you think

Please share your thoughts on this book with others by leaving a review on the site that you bought it from. If you purchased the book from Amazon, please leave us an honest review on this book's Amazon page. This is vital so that other potential readers can see and use your unbiased opinion to make purchasing decisions, we can understand what our customers think about our products, and our authors can see your feedback on the title that they have worked with Packt to create. It will only take a few minutes of your time, but is valuable to other potential customers, our authors, and Packt. Thank you!

Index

B

C

Made in the USA
Monee, IL
13 February 2021